Great Houses of America

Great Houses of America

by Henry Lionel Williams
and Ottalie K. Williams

G. P. Putnam's Sons   New York

First Edition 1966
All rights reserved. This book, or parts thereof, must not be reproduced in
any form without permission.
Published simultaneously in the Dominion of Canada by Longmans Canada
Limited, Toronto.
Printed in Italy by Arnoldo Mondadori Editore Officine Grafiche, Verona.
Library of Congress Catalog Card Number: 66-19625.

Contents

Contents

Preface

The following pages picture and describe thirty American houses built between the last years of the seventeenth century and the late 1920's, each representative of its type, its period, its geographic location, and its style, with furniture and decoration to match.

In making this selection we have occasionally found it necessary to omit some particular example of architectural excellence because its interior décor and furnishing did not possess equal merit. In other instances the mansion was considerably less interesting than its furnishings. Compromise has therefore been the rule, with stress laid upon the interiors rather than the architecture.

In compiling the list of houses it has not been possible to include every state. In several states no worthwhile example of a period mansion still exists as such; elsewhere the houses have been converted to other uses. Normally there would be little difference between the style of house or quality of interior among the mansions of adjoining states, their location having little bearing on either. Period usually would be the deciding factor.

These periods divide naturally into a sequence of five historic phases each heralding social developments out of which arose changes in architectural fashion and furnishing style — the Late Colonial and the Revolutionary phases, the westward expansion, the Civil War period, and the great industrial era of Victorian times and later. From these we have gleaned examples of Early American, Georgian, Federal, Neoclassic, and Victorian mansions, culminating in the great houses of 1895-1920, most of which were adapted from the designs (usually on a reduced scale) of European châteaux, palazzos, and castles, replete with furniture, furnishings, and art treasures gathered from the four corners of the earth.

Compared with the monumental mansions of the late nineteenth and early twentieth centuries, some of the older "great" houses pictured here may seem relatively small and simple, but they do represent the best of their kind and day. Taken altogether, the thirty mansions present a vivid picture of one aspect of historical development in this country over a period of two hundred years, reflecting the evolution of American society from the days of plantation and manor to those of the magnates and tycoons whose great personal fortunes permitted them to erect palatial mansions which remain as monuments to them and their times.

H.L.W. and O.K.W.

Introduction

The eighteenth century ushered in one of the most interesting periods in American history—the time when the country's first great houses, all in the new and handsomely sophisticated Georgian style, were being erected in such far-flung localities as Tidewater Virginia, Philadelphia, Boston, and Portsmouth, New Hampshire.

From Pennsylvania the new fashion in architecture quickly spread to New Jersey, Delaware, and Maryland, modified here and there to suit local conditions and individual tastes. This was the beginning of a bright new era in which—despite a brief interlude occasioned by the Revolution half a century later—general prosperity brought wealth to many who celebrated their rising fortunes by building great houses and furnishing them in keeping with their new importance.

Here, of course, we are dealing not with mere everyday mansions but great houses, a distinction with a very important difference, for "great" suggests the best and the finest by any scale of measurement. But even these are terms that mean different things to different men, and the largest diamond may not be the most exquisite gem. The key is fitness—the fineness of the house and the high quality of its interiors which combine to make, as near as humanly possible, a comfortable and flawless home.

Within the next two centuries many such houses were to dot the landscape from coast to coast, some of them magnificent in concept and splendid in execution; others less ambitious as to size and splendor yet wholly representative of the best that their owner's means and taste afforded. All of these great houses in a progression of styles—Georgian, Federal, Classic Revival, and Victorian—with some eyebrow-raising variations, were finally eclipsed as to size and magnificence in the late nineteenth and early twentieth centuries by the ultimate in formal architecture and lavish décor derived from such exotic sources as the Italy of the Borghese and the France of *Le Roi Soleil.*

The Governor's Palace, Williamsburg, Va. (1706-1720), burned 1781, rebuilt 1930-1934

9

Hunter House, Newport,
R. I. (1748-1754)

The Lindens, built in
Danvers, Mass., 1754,
moved to Washington,
D. C., 1928

The story of these great houses, then, is the story of the nation—its vicissitudes and triumphs, its growth and westward expansion, its social, political, and industrial development from 1720 to the end of the first great war which heralded the passing of an era the like of which we shall never see again. And that record is filled with vastly intriguing contrasts—comparisons that illuminate and set apart the great periods into which its history can conveniently be divided—colonial, revolutionary, post-Civil War, and modern.

Today there still exist great houses dating from all these periods that may serve as reminders of our eventful history and the fantastic changes that have taken place in our society and our way of life. And, because of what they are and what they represent, these splendid survivals from our country's past are well worthy of preservation and study as examples of the best that two hundred years of American domestic architecture and interior decoration has had to offer.

Any study of old houses, whether mansion or cottage, is bound to have both intellectual and emotional aspects, for houses, to those who fully appreciate what they represent, are living things that can grow and flourish or wither and die. And where such a house of fair size and some importance is decorated and furnished in a manner consistent with its character, whatever its age, style, or period, it can become a work of art and therefore attain a certain greatness regardless of its architectural integrity or the quality of its interiors.

Today the most interesting of these great houses are those that remain substantially as they were when first carefully planned, erected, decorated, and furnished—the product of competent craftsmen who put so much of themselves into everything they did. Once completed, these dwellings became a part of people's lives, undergoing change and modification to meet the needs, the whims, and fancies of those who occupied them over the decades and centuries. That is why so very few of even the greatest surviving mansions have ended as they began, and why changes made in comparatively recent years have, with time, become a natural part of their history and growth that should no more be denied, or nullified, by restoration to some former condition—unless their beauty and authenticity have been wantonly destroyed—than changes made a century or more ago.

In spite of such well-intentioned vandalism, in spite of fire, floods, hurricanes, and wars, we are fortunate that there are still so many houses of distinction left for us to enjoy and to learn from. These houses represent all periods since the turn of the eighteenth century, by which time the colonies were expanding in a more or less stable fashion. It was then that the first massive fortunes were being accumulated by men of actual or potential importance in the future of the country. Some of them had arrived on these shores already possessed of inherited wealth; others were destined through their own efforts to become the founders of American dynasties; men who in so short a time were to own vast rice or tobacco plantations or fleets of ships engaged in whaling or plying the oceans in pursuit of trade.

Since a large proportion of these gentlemen of means were students of the arts, including architecture—in a century noted for universally high standards of culture and learning—they were, for the most part, familiar with the many books becoming available on exterior and interior design, from Vitruvius on. And they had one advantage over the professionals in that they were not handicapped by any rigid rules or architectural dogma. They picked and chose, eliminated and combined various ideas and details, often with little regard for the basic tenets of good architecture and purity of design. Nevertheless, they seem to have been either skillful enough, or sufficiently fortunate, to achieve workable plans that are agreeable enough to command our respect today.

Of course it is quite possible that, in some instances, architects in England were consulted, or some English-trained architect whose name history does not record actually worked in Virginia in the early 1700's. Be that as it may, it is an indisputable fact that some of the early mansions possessed features identifiable with those of specific buildings in England and, occasionally, Italy or France, or even traceable back to ancient Greece.

In the earlier American structures most of the classical designs were closely followed as to scale and proportion though they were, of necessity, reduced in overall size. In spite of this scaling down there was rarely any loss of impressiveness or dignity.

What these American adaptations lost in massiveness they gained in attractive appearance. And therein lay the genius of the architects and builders of America's first mansions—and so it has been ever since. These adaptations have in many ways made these architectural styles distinctively American, in the North and West as well as in the South. Actually, some of the most beautiful of these larger dwellings have been made even more appealing by the very fact that a local material has been substituted for the original; buildings designed for construction in stone have been duplicated in wood or brick or stucco, and actually gained in appearance in the process. Today these houses appeal to us as much for their design, proportions, texture, and decoration as they do for their mystery, and the sense of a romantic past that they evoke.

The earliest American Georgian houses were put up in Virginia by the great planters and landowners who had few imposing examples of domestic architecture to turn to for inspiration before 1720. If historians do not err, it was the college of William and Mary and the Governor's Palace at Williamsburg (in which Sir Christopher Wren may have had a finger) that gave the prosperous landowners their first taste of the fabulous and beautiful in architecture—in a style superseding the medieval Gothic that served as seventeenth-

Ford Mansion, Morristown, N. J. (1774), Washington's Headquarters 1779-1780

Longfellow House, Cambridge, Mass. (1759), Washington's Headquarters 1774

John Brown House,
Providence, R. I. (1786)

The Carrington House,
Providence, R. I. (1810-1811)

Pingree House, Salem,
Mass. (1804).
Designed by Samuel
McIntire

century Colonial. For this new Early Georgian, the masters of vast plantations such as Thomas Lee who was to build the fabulous Stratford Hall and Robert "King" Carter of Carter's Grove fame, could have all the brick they needed made on their own land, supplemented by various timbers from their own forests.

At this period, mansions with dependencies built onto the main structure were rare. Far more often we find the earliest Georgian types with separate "flankers" in line with the central house block as at Westover. In this house the one-and-a-half-story dependencies were joined to the house in recent times. This idea of connecting passages apparently originated with the young Thomas Jefferson, who is said to have suggested it to Nathaniel Harrison during the building of Harrison's house, Brandon, in 1765. This joining together of three units not only improves the appearance of the complete building, giving it added balance and importance, but provides useful extra space for modern living. The connecting units are usually lower and shallower than the "flankers," for which reason they have earned the appellation of "hyphens."

By the third quarter of the eighteenth century a number of Virginia mansions, such as Mount Airy, Mount Vernon, and Tryon Palace, had their dependencies placed forward of the house, being connected to it by quadrant-shaped passages or arcades. This plan follows closely the typical Palladian villa style adopted for certain English houses of the previous century such as Hackwood Park, Hampshire (1695), and Hardwick Hall, Shropshire. Still later houses of this magnitude, such as the aforementioned Brandon, were built to an entirely different plan having a central block one room deep (and three wide), and a pair of end units two rooms deep, all two stories high. These were joined by single-story rooms, forming an attenuated H-plan.

Brandon was the first of the later Georgian houses built on the extended plan in the manner of Palladio's Roman Country House. This so-called "five-part" plan, which provided about as much accommodation in the wings as in the central block, allowed of complete living quarters on the main floor. Later, it was adopted with enthusiasm by architect William Buckland for several houses in Annapolis. Similar mansions consisting of a central block and wings (without the "hyphens") such as the Semple House at Williamsburg—of which Monticello is a modification—were popularized by Jefferson just prior to the Revolution.

In Maryland, Delaware and Pennsylvania, progress was, in some areas, keyed to a slower pace, and here can be found somewhat smaller but equally well-designed mansions of stone and brick, less pretentious residences in both town and country that yet combine comfort with elegance.

By this time some few native architects were available to help in translating English house designs into elaborately detailed mansions of brick and of wood masquerading as stone.

In New England, where wood was far more readily available than masonry, the wooden houses reached the peak of perfection—highly decorative but still basically Georgian in a lighthearted manner distinctively American.

The major characteristics of these New England mansions therefore were frame construction, with clapboards, or rusticated wood siding simulating masonry, under a gabled, gambrel, or hipped roof. Applied pilasters, roof decks, twin end chimneys, and cupolas were common. Corners could be finished with two-story pilasters or rusticated quoins; giant pilasters and pediments set off central pavilions. Interiors often were lavishly decorated with carving or stucco ornamentation. This is not to say that some fine New England Georgians were not built of masonry; indeed, one of the first of such mansions was of granite blocks with sandstone trim.

All of this presaged the drift, vastly accelerated by the Revolution, toward the classical Federal style of 1780-1820. Federal houses have the reputation of being both the most sophisticated and most nearly perfect architectural style developed in the United States. It represents the Roman classicism so beloved of Jefferson, combined with the French architectural style of Louis XVI, imposed upon the American Georgian, together with a touch of Adam.

By 1820 this Federal style was being rapidly overtaken by the Greek Revival style which quickly became the rage as being most expressive of the American republican ideal. White, classical porticoes were stuck on all sorts of buildings. Some of the finest homes took the form of classical temples—if temples with three-foot doors, guillotine or French windows, and chimneys can be visualized. But the Gothic was not dead. That, too, underwent a revival, and joined other romantic styles—Romanesque, Tudor, Egyptian, Italian, and half a dozen others—to form a series of Victorian experiments in eclecticism derived from the use of the machine in building.

Even in this period, when the great Midwest was being populated at a fantastic rate, some remarkable mansions were erected there by men of comparatively great wealth—the new pioneers. The fact that many of them failed to achieve fame extending beyond their own states does not diminish the interest and importance of their houses.

In the years between the Revolution and the so-called mid-Victorian days, the territory comprising Mississippi and Louisiana enjoyed a romantic period in architecture unequaled elsewhere in the United States before or since. Along the flatlands bordering the Mississippi River and the many bayous, where frequent flooding was inevitable, the houses were built on foundations six or more feet high. Above this foundation the house might be one, one and a half, or two stories tall, with high-ceilinged rooms and wide porches protected from the hot suns by an overhanging roof which might, or might not, have dormers. The porch was usually supported by square pillars, with slender columns above to uphold the eaves.

Hampton Plantation,
McClellanville, S. C. (1735),
featuring early
Greek Revival portico

Fairfax, White Pine,
Tenn. (1832),
attributed to Benjamin
Latrobe

Terrace Hill, Des Moines,
Iowa (1868),
Italianate Victorian

Carson Mansion, Eureka,
Calif. (1884),
a gingerbread fashion plate

Access to the house was by an exterior stairway leading to the balcony.

In most of these houses the balconies or loggias were extended around all four sides, in which case the roof would be hipped in order to cover the end sections, and the peak lowered for better profile. This type of house was so admirably suited to the climatic conditions that it was adopted, with modifications, for areas in which flooding was unknown. One of these changes consisted of making the ground floor a full story high so that it could be used for kitchen, storage, and living quarters for the domestic help. This also made it possible to replace the square pillars with round ones extending from ground to eaves. Painted white, with handsome wood or iron balcony rails, and fancy cornices, these houses were, and are, among the most beautiful ever devised.

With the coming of the Greek Revival style between 1820 and 1830 all that then had to be done to bring them into fashion was to substitute classical columns. At the same time roofs were flattened and parapets added. Often the outside stairs were done away with and an impressive main entrance centered under the front balcony at garden level.

Beween 1830 and 1860 some of these plantation houses were built to the Victorian taste—the earlier ones in the so-called Steamboat Gothic style, later ones known simply as Victorian Gothic, both capable of being attractive in an amusing sort of way. But their pillars were gone and, too often, their balconies as well, their roofs a riot and their façades a jigsaw medley so that the romantic appeal of the classic plantation house is lost.

In the late nineteeth and early twentieth centuries a few stupendous mansions were built which had nothing in common with anything that had been attempted before. Financed by tremendous fortunes, these spectacular residences are never likely to be duplicated anywhere. Inspired by some of the greatest European architecture of the fifteenth and sixteenth centuries, or simply "dream castles" conjured up out of the imagination, they serve to remind us of a day that is forever gone.

It is fortunate that throughout the eighteenth century tasteful furniture was available to complement the Georgian style, even though there was a wide variation in the decorative treatments adopted. For one thing, it did make possible interiors that conformed to the great Inigo Jones's dictum that "the decoration of an important house must be essentially masculine, skilled and powerful, not merely ineffectually pretty. The structural line must be followed and a too-naturalistic treatment of anything taken from life must be avoided." Fifty years later Grinling Gibbons, in the employment of his not-too-stylized carvings of fruit and flowers as surface decoration, showed the way to bridge this gap between naturalism and art.

Ordinarily, the earlier the Georgian house the greater the

amount of interior woodwork. From the early 1700's on, the fully paneled rooms gradually gave way to those paneled on the fireplace wall only, though paneled dadoes persisted for a while longer. Then came plastered walls, with either wooden dadoes or chair rails, and cornices. The plaster was painted and, later, papered. After 1750 or so, pictorial papers with wall-sized scenes were fashionable. With the more monumental exteriors of Late Georgian, the interior walls might be of plaster molded to represent panels, with elaborate plaster cornices.

These formal and often elaborate Georgian interiors were fine backgrounds for the furniture of several periods, beginning in the North with William and Mary pieces, and those of walnut Queen Anne in the South, both progressing to Chippendale—the English in mahogany, the Philadelphian in walnut—by mid-century. These, of course, are generalities, all furniture and furnishings being subject to regional preferences and personal tastes.

Throughout this period there was always plenty of French furniture to add spice to an interior. Although the sumptuous baroque Louis XIV style was probably a bit too heavy and pretentious for the average plantation owner, with its lavish decoration, its ormolu mounts and gilded wood, Louis XV pieces were readily available with their lighter and somewhat effeminate rococo decoration and multiplicity of curves. These were supplemented by skillfully crafted furniture from the Netherlands and Italy. In many instances interiors furnished with the better European and home-produced furniture were enlivened with an occasional rare piece from the Orient, perhaps originally destined for New England but just as likely to end up on the Chesapeake.

Although snobbery may have been more prevalent in those days than in our time—a proposition open to question—and things imported considered superior to the home product, there is no doubt that by 1760 cabinetmaking had become a flourishing trade. Centers were established in Boston, Newport, New York and Philadelphia by cabinetmakers and carvers whose names were to become household words before the end of the century—such men as Townsend and Goddard of Newport, McIntire of Salem, Savery, Gillingham, Gostelowe, and Randolph of Philadelphia, and many more.

Although most of them took their ideas from Chippendale, Hepplewhite, and Sheraton they did seem to concentrate on form rather than decoration. Their pieces generally were lighter—except, perhaps, in the case of the Sheraton—with less flamboyant ornament and simpler underbracing, combining structural simplicity with graceful lines to achieve a feeling of distinction without sacrifice of comfort. By the 1780's they had caught up with the trend of English design and adopted the beautifully veneered and inlaid Sheraton and Hepplewhite styles which lent themselves so well to Federal interiors.

From this point on the furniture evolved smoothly into

William K.
Vanderbilt Residence,
New York City (1892)

Shadow Lawn,
West Long Branch,
N. J. (1928),
now Monmouth College

Andrew Mellon Mansion,
Pittsburgh, Penn. (1897),
now part of Chatham College

Henry Huntington Mansion,
San Marino, Calif. (1910),
now an art gallery

Hammersmith Farm,
Newport, R. I.
(early 20th-century),
modern country residence

Adam, English Regency and French Directoire, all of which were more or less harmonious with Greek Revival interiors. Soon thereafter homemakers had the choice of Phyfe pieces in mahogany, a style that set the pattern for the increasingly ornate Victorian with its gallimaufry of richly flowered and flocked wallpapers, damask draperies, Dresden vases, prism-adorned brass lamps, Belter laminated rosewood in plush upholstery, papier-mâché tables and bentwood rockers, on carpets of multicolored velour.

Thus arrived the Late Victorian era when it became the fashion to fill every room to overflowing with massive furniture and bric-a-brac, flourishing palms, and whatnots loaded with trivia. Since this period coincided with booming cities and rising wealth across the country, Victorian houses laden with towers and verandas soon outnumbered all other styles of architecture. And, in spite of all this, there were among them some that might justifiably be dubbed "great," such as the Carson Mansion in Eureka, California, which carried the decorative possibilities of wood to their ultimate conclusion.

Luckily, the better-quality American Chippendale, Hepplewhite, Sheraton, and Adam styles continued to be available long after the day of the *chaise percée*—the handmade pieces which alone were suitable for the great houses that still flourished. With the turn of the twentieth century even the best of furniture succumbed to the machine, with only the finishing touches and the fitting together reserved for the skilled craftsman.

The point to be noted here, then, is that in furniture and interior design, as in all other arts, no strict line of progression is involved—or even possible—from one style to another. Rather, design proceeds from phase to phase and fashion to fashion, with little necessary relation between any two. Normally, of course, the poor design will prove ephemeral and the good one will be lasting, as the Chippendale, the Sheraton, the French Provincial and the early Phyfe—among a dozen others—have proved, despite the modifications and the torturings they have undergone at the hands of individual furniture makers and designers throughout the years.

And so it is also with architecture, a noble art whether confined to the external structure, to its interior shaping and ornamentation, or both, from the first great mansions styled in the current imported fashion to the latest of modern Italian Renaissance adaptations. Between the two we note the violent breakings away from Roman inspiration to the Greek, to the Adam of Herculaneum, and the neo-Gothic that lent itself so well to the industrial revolution that fathered it. Throughout all these phases the means were available for combining the best of both arts—often with astonishing good taste—into the superior dwelling places that have earned acclaim as great houses of America, some few of which are presented here, an assembly of much that is of timeless beauty, enchanting both in concept and achievement.

Friendship, Maryland
HOLLY HILL

A Mansion with a Fabulous History and Irresistible Charm

Few houses have so dramatic a history as Maryland's Holly Hill; few are so lovely inside and out, in spite of unpretentious architecture, or are so deceptive as to size. Although it is a story-and-a-half house, it has upper chambers that are fascinating with their old-time decoration and paintings, and main-floor rooms that are both surprisingly large and charmingly furnished with American and French pieces dating back to the late sixteen hundreds.

Not all of the house, however, is that old. It was 1667 when a planter named Richard Harrison built a story-and-a-half, two-roomed frame house on Holland's Hill which lay between present Friendship village and Herring Bay on the Chesapeake. Several years later he added two more rooms, one downstairs and one upstairs, and in 1704 bricked in both ends and one side. By 1716 Harrison gave the house and the plantation on which it stood to his son, Samuel. History then becomes vague, but, sometime before 1733, a brick wing was added, and finally an outside brick kitchen, giving the house its present T-shape.

During these years, the legend goes, a pirate dug a half-mile tunnel from the house to Herring Bay through which he could smuggle his ill-gotten treasures. Today there is only ten feet of the tunnel open and accessible from the cellar. There are, however, other interesting relics of early days. On some of the original panes are the diamond-scratched names of the early owners and important guests. Though there is no pirate loot on the premises there is treasure of another sort—fascinating early features such as the paneling, fireplace and archway moldings, the lined doors and the extraordinary decorated woodwork and seventeenth-century paintings over fireplaces and door, the exterior trim, partly dentiled, and the double ogee arches of brick over one door and two windows, surmounting the wooden trim. The chimneys, too, are quite ambitious, with arched panels and decorative tops, one of which accommodates five flues. Thanks to the low eaves there

Holly Hill (1667-1720)
as it appears in a contemporary painting
of the house and estate.

The dining room with its
original plank floors
and woodwork, and the
added charm of early
18th-century furniture
of inlaid mahogany.

Holly Hill today. At left, the
1720 wing joins the 1667 house
alongside the original entrance.

is no fancy doorhead to the principal entrance. Instead, the
entrance from the driveway is sheltered by a small porch
with a rounded soffit and peaked roof. To have used a pediment here would have been a little pretentious, especially
with the turned pillars and wooden rails and steps. On the
garden sides there are single and double doors, the former
with an eight-pane rectangular transom window to help illuminate the stair hall.

Today the entire building is of brick of an attractive old
red and pink color, made locally. Large areas, however, are
whitened by efflorescence from the lime mortar. In 1936 the
property was bought by Captain Hugh P. LeClair (U.S.N.
Ret.), and Mrs. LeClair from the Fred W. Scrivener family
who had owned it for almost a hundred years. The LeClairs
spent much time and effort in research before restoring the
house to its eighteenth-century appearance and condition.
Because of this its interiors today form pleasing and natural
backgrounds for the seventeenth- and eighteenth-century
French and American furniture, every piece of which was
acquired primarily for use rather than mere show. Even the
warming pans come in handy on chilly nights! The house also
is now surrounded by well-kept gardens and gravel walks, the
lawn and driveway borders harboring boxwood clumps that
have been there many years.

Few entrance halls are as interesting as that of Holly Hill

Alongside the original rear entrance
hall door of 1667 is a later archway to the 1720 wing.

Over the doorway to the dining room
is this wood scenic panel believed to have been
painted by Gustavus Hesselius
in the 17th century.

either for themselves or their furnishings. This is a wide stair hall, with one door opening onto the carriage ring, the other onto the gardens. Both are framed and paneled, lined with diagonal planks, and hung on very heavy H-L hinges with decorative ends. They are also fitted with massive brass-cased locks. Though there is no cornice, the walls, painted a soft gray-green, have dadoes held out by deep bolection moldings. Here also are heavily molded, paneled doors to the withdrawing room, a closet, and the library, plus an arched opening into a short passageway to the dining room.

The walnut stair rail, like the rest of the woodwork, is particularly sturdy, the square newel having sunk panels—the only portion painted a soft gray-green to match the woodwork. The balusters are beautifully turned, with occasional square sections, two to a step. The hall furnishings are few but of obvious quality—a seventeenth-century carved and paneled-oak chest, and a walnut chest of drawers; an eighteenth-century upholstered, open-arm French Régence chair with hoof feet in walnut; an Aubusson tapestry; and Oriental rugs. Pewter candlesticks and a salver stand on a Queen Anne walnut lowboy with slipper feet.

Most elaborate of the rooms is, as might be expected, the withdrawing room whose off-white walls and ceiling are outlined by a paneled dado and cornice painted the original color—a delicate silvery green. The furniture here is in the Louis XV style: a tapestry-covered fauteuil, a marquise in gold and plum damask, tripod and kidney stands, and a splendid bombé vernis-Martin commode, over which is displayed a large Aubusson tapestry. On the commode are four-light candelabra in bronze and crystal. Across the room is a *canapé-à-corbeille* in a rose pattern brocade and flanked by fauteuils in damask. The draperies are of Louis XV design, with swags and pelmets in brocade of the same silvery green as the room's dado. On one wall are displayed portraits of early owners in gilt, ogee frames. Another decorative note is supplied by a four-panel screen bearing a painting of an Italian seascape, dated about 1800. On the floor is an elaborately patterned and colorful Aubusson rug, of the late eighteenth century, whose colors are predominantly yellows and grays on red.

Notable features of the dining room are the very wide, one-piece panels of the two-panel doors, and their old-time T-hinges and oval brass knobs. Here the illumination is provided by mirror-lined wall sconces, and candles in hurricane glasses on the mahogany Maryland sideboard which is reminiscent of Hepplewhite with its bell-husk inlays and oval brass escutcheons. The chairs are Philadelphia interpretations of Hepplewhite intersecting shield-backs, with green velvet seats. Over the sideboard is a Flemish verdure tapestry, which stands out against a sympathetic background of off-white walls with a light buff trim, as do the curtains and pelmets of a richly patterned chintz. The round-cornered dining room table is of inlaid mahogany.

In the stem portion of the T-shaped house is a downstairs bedroom with two adjacent paneled walls—one incorporating the fireplace and two closed doors, and one a pair of windows. The third wall, incorporating a window and a door, has a dado and a chair rail. The fourth wall is of plain plaster. All walls and woodwork are painted medium green, the original color. The bed is a double-sized folding type with two pencil posts, a copy of one in the Metropolitan Museum of Art in New York, with a spread and valance of crewelwork, the same design and material being used for the window pelmet. The background linen of the bed and window fabrics gives the room a light and gay air without destroying its look of well-preserved antiquity.

Among the furniture pieces are a Pennsylvania mahogany four-drawer chest with reeded corner pillars, a Queen Anne drop-leaf table, a Virginia wing chair in red, a small mahogany tripod tilt-top table with a scroll top, a spider-legged lamp table, and Chippendale side chairs and armchair. The floor is covered with large Oriental rugs in tan, red, and blue. An interesting sidelight is thrown on the restoration work required in this room by the fact that three later fireplaces had to be removed to uncover the original Jacobean rounded-back fireplace. This turned out to have a wide brick arch which involved renewing the paneling to match the curve.

Upstairs, in the 1720 wing, is one of the prize rooms of Holly Hill—a bedroom with marbleized fireplace paneling and doors. This calls for quite a different graining pattern than usual, and the colors used are blues, beige, and green. It is probably the most complete and unretouched example of this style and technique to be found in the thirteen original states. The overmantel panel is of almost equal interest, being painted with a lake scene showing a castle flying the flag of Saint George. The artist, unfortunately, is not known.

This room is furnished with earlier pieces than the others, including a Queen Anne daybed, c. 1720, which has eight turned maple legs, a reeded bottom, and a fixed back with turned posts and vase splats. There is also a saddleback, vase-splat chair with Spanish feet, turned stretchers, and a reed seat; and an interesting unfinished Connecticut-type maple lowboy of about 1760 which has four cabriole legs, and four drawers. The light Dutch foot is distinctly unusual on such a piece. Over this lowboy is a small Queen Anne looking glass in a painted frame, and nearby an inlaid maple chest of drawers.

Although the foregoing does not complete the catalog of furniture and decorative features of Holly Hill, it is sufficient to show that discretion in remodeling and taste in furnishing and decorating can result in the perfect adaptation of a centuries-old house and early furniture to gracious modern living. In achieving this, Holly Hill has the further distinction of demonstrating that the elusive quality of charm can easiest be recaptured if it is never deliberately sought. In this lies its greatness.

The intricately marbleized woodwork around this bedroom fireplace encloses an overmantel panel painted to depict a lakeside castle flying the flag of St. George.

The downstairs bedroom with its folding pencil-post bed, crewelwork spread and valance to match the window pelmet.

The stately 200-foot façade of Carter's Grove looks
out across terraced fields to the James River.

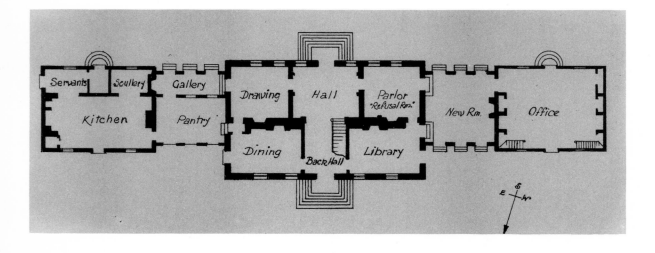

This floor plan shows
how the "hyphens"
added service space.
The stair hall faces
the river.

Williamsburg, Virginia
CARTER'S GROVE

Two Centuries of Magnificence

Carter's Grove, six miles southeast of Williamsburg, marks the pinnacle of early Georgian design in America. Much of its appeal lies in its masculine simplicity of design, and the slightly Queen Anne flavor that still clings to it, both inside and out, despite the changes made to its fabric thirty-odd years ago. Its paneled interiors are superb.

The original structure, completed sometime between 1750 and 1753, consisted of a two-story main house flanked by a pair of single-story gabled dependencies. The main section had a moderately low hipped roof with slightly flared eaves, dominated by a tall, square chimney at each end of the ridge. Sometime later the eastern dependency was connected to the main house. Between 1927 and 1930, this connecting "hyphen" was removed, and both dependencies were tied to the central block by the present linking sections which have small hipped dormers to match the larger ones of the dependencies themselves.

At this same time the rooftree of the house was raised six feet and dormers added on all four slopes to provide light for the new attic rooms. These changes combine to give the whole mansion an added air of distinction which compensates for any loss of antiquarian flavor, and increased livability besides.

The original mansion was built by Carter Burwell, a grandson of the famed and fabulously wealthy Robert "King" Carter, though Carter Burwell's father, Nathaniel Burwell, apparently launched the project some years earlier by erecting the east wing. The west wing was put up prior to 1750, but the design of the main section demanded the services of a great deal more than local talent. There is evidence to suggest that the design may have been the work of architect Richard Taliaferro, who was responsible for several notable buildings at Williamsburg. In any event both a master builder, David Minetree, who had been working at Williamsburg, and Richard Baylis, a master carpenter brought from England, were employed, and this

Focal point of this back hall grouping is a portrait of John McCrea (1789-1869).

The northwest room, with
original paneling, was enlarged
in 1928 by removal of a partition.

may account for the fact that there are certain striking re-
semblances between the original Carter's Grove and two
English houses—Rutland Lodge at Petersham, Surrey, and
Ormond Lodge at Kingston-on-Thames.

As usual in this era, bricks were made on the plantation,
and lime for the mortar was derived from oyster shells delivered
at the James River landing. Apparently much of the wood
—mostly pine, poplar, and walnut—was cut on the site, a
fact that may account for the mixture of woods in the paneling.
The red bricks are set in Flemish bond, without benefit of
quoins at the angles, using flat-arch brick lintels over the
windows and doorways. The main floor, set above a high
basement in the manner of an Italian *piano nobile*, is set off
by a molded-brick water table, and the second-floor level by
a rubbed-brick belt course.

The north and south entrances are almost identical, with
pedimented doorways and six wide, graduated stone steps.
Apart from these, the only deliberately decorative feature is
the heavily molded and modillioned cornice. On both north
and south roof slopes there are now five hipped dormers, and
two on each main-roof hip. The principal difference between
the two main façades is that on the north (garden) front there
are only nine windows as opposed to thirteen on the south
(river) front. The reason for this will be apparent on examining
the floor plan which shows the variation between the entrance
hall and the stair hall exterior walls.

The entrance hall is noted for
its exquisite pine paneling, the
sweeping stair arch, and
detailing

In connecting the wings to the main block the gaps were filled by ridge-roofed, one-and-a-half-story "hyphens," each with three small dormers front and back. Three arched openings for French windows, each with a semicircular fanlight, were formed in the front and rear walls. In order to provide for fireplaces in these connecting rooms, extra chimneys were built into the inner gables of the wings. So carefully was all of this done that the mansion exterior today presents a wholly harmonious appearance. Inside it is equally delightful and the architectural detail little short of awe-inspiring.

The glory of this house is its paneling which differs in detail from room to room. Originally the whole of the ceiling-high wainscoting was painted, but in recent years a natural finish has been substituted in several rooms, unfortunately revealing variation in the woods, unsuspected joints, and poor grain. Thanks, however, to an excellent job of staining and finishing, these discrepancies are not particularly noticeable on casual inspection. As far as the detail is concerned, the finest paneling of all is in the main hall. In this entrance salon, as it is alternatively called, the paneling incorporates fluted pilasters surmounted by the complete Ionic order, including a cornice supported by carved modillions.

Separating this area from the stair hall is a tremendous elliptical arch supported on heavy molded imposts over wide, paneled jambs. The arch tympanums are paneled but the soffit is plain, and relieved by a twin molded keystone. Above

This window seat in the drawing room overlooks the broad James River.

The plantation office was built soon after 1700, and the house erected between it and the kitchen, 1750-1753.

Visible here is some of the second-floor hall woodwork, executed by the Englishman Baylis.

The Refusal Room with its exquisite mantel of Siena marble.

this the overhang of the architrave is beautifully carved with an endless rosette band.

Equally striking is the staircase with its paneled wainscoting, richly turned balusters—three to a step—the walnut handrail ramped over the posts and forming a volute atop the spirally turned newel. The step ends are nicely molded, and supported by carved brackets. Both stair landings are of pine and walnut laid in a geometric pattern, and even the stair soffits are covered with fielded panels.

Quite as elaborate is the bare paneling of the west drawing room (the so-called "Refusal Room" in which Mary Carter is said to have rejected the marriage proposal of George Washington, and Rebecca Burwell that of Thomas Jefferson). However, the fluted pilasters here have molded tops instead of formal caps, although there is a full entablature, including triglyphs and guttae on the frieze, plus a dentiled cornice over the projecting mantel. This mantel is of white and Siena marble with a carved frieze panel and crossettes.

In the dining room the cream-painted paneling is comparatively plain above a paneled dado, and the shelfless, eared mantel of white marble is held in a simple, square-edged bolection molding. At ceiling level is a simple molded box cornice. The connecting room between the office and the main block is somewhat similar but has a fluted pilaster on each side of the mantel, plus a dentiled cornice.

In every formal room of Carter's Grove the furniture and furnishings are in keeping with the setting, displaying eighteenth-century elegance without detracting from the atmosphere of a comfortable home. In the west drawing room, for example, the subdued wood tones of the stripped paneling, and the delicately carved mantel form a perfect background for the polished mahogany of Chippendale armchairs, tea tables, and galleried urn stand; there are lively touches of gold in the Chinese Chippendale looking glass and the gilt gesso of a seventeenth-century ancestral portrait's frame. Equally at home are the crystal and marble girandoles, the silver candlesticks on the tea-table slides, the rich green brocade of the William and Mary wing chair, and the *tête-de-nègre* color of the Chippendale sofa—all cry for the sateen breeches and powdered wigs of an earlier day.

In the dining room there is a somewhat less formal atmosphere, and touches of a later era in the prints on the walls and the eagle-crested convex mirror, though the armchairs are Queen Anne pieces in mahogany with gold damask seats; the table is a three-pedestal Phyfe creation. Also in mahogany are the sideboard table and sideboard with knife boxes, and a wine cooler and other appurtenances of gracious eighteenth-century living.

Quite different from either of the foregoing is the connecting room (or New Room), a cozy spot for informal conversational groups and old-time games. This has soft-colored chintz curtains over the round-topped French windows, with antique brass

From the drawing room the view extends through the hall and parlor to the far end of the office. Note the dentiled cornice and carved chair rail.

tiebacks; a Hepplewhite sofa in striped satin, a pair of smaller sofas in pale-green damask; two chairs in gold damask, Hitchcock chairs with colorful seat pads, and a walnut, flat-topped secretary-desk whose glass-fronted cupboard displays antique porcelains. Standing under the crystal-and-bronze chandelier in the middle of the room is an exquisite mahogany pedestal table with brass feet, adorned by a large English pewter bowl ever full of blooms from the gardens, and silver-and-crystal table lamps with shades of ivory silk.

This, then, is Carter's Grove today—a house not without its historical associations. Most leading families of colonial Virginia enjoyed its hospitality, and, according to legend, a fatal duel was fought in the east drawing room. In war days, Colonel Tarleton of the British Light Horse Brigade occupied it in 1781 and left his mark upon it. For some unimaginable reason either he or one of his officers, it is said, rode up the stairs, hacking the handrail with his saber. The mark is still there for all to see.

In 1964 Carter's Grove came into the possession of the Sealantic Fund and is now open to the public under the management of Colonial Williamsburg.

27

Stratford, Virginia

STRATFORD HALL

Historic Home of the Lees

The massive H-plan of Stratford Hall crowned by twin groups of arched chimneys relies on texture to counteract the rigidity of its lines.

One of the greatest, and certainly the most unusual, of all colonial mansions of the Early Georgian period is Stratford Hall, home of the fabulous Lees of Virginia. Built in 1725-30 by Thomas Lee, Council President and Commander in Chief of the colony, on his 6,500-acre estate bordering the Potomac, Stratford became the property of four descendants in turn, ending with Henry Lee, Jr., whose half brother, Robert E. Lee, born there in 1807, was to become the greatest of Southern generals. The mansion passed out of the family's ownership in 1829, and was acquired in 1929, with an estate of 1,100 acres, by the Robert E. Lee Memorial Foundation as a national shrine. It was then restored to its approximate condition as of the late eighteenth century, with some of the original furnishings, and (where possible) duplicates of those dispersed.

Built on the H-plan, so popular in eighteenth-century England, with the central section one-room deep, Stratford copies the *piano nobile* style of the Italian villas, with its raised main floor. On the other hand its massive proportions and the crowning groups of four chimneys tied together by arches above the low-pitched hip roofs, all suggest the influence of Sir John Vanbrugh's much larger Blenheim Palace whose chimneylike pillars were coupled by arches atop apparently functionless towers. But the Lee mansion is of brick throughout, innocent of pilasters and columns and rusticated stone, therefore imposing instead of overpowering.

Austere to a point of severity, the exterior relies on texture rather than decoration to counteract the rigidity of its lines. The exposed basement wall is built of oversized bricks laid in Flemish bond with glazed headers up to the molded stringcourse. Above that the bricks are smaller and of a uniform rubbed red until the chimneys are reached, when the glazed headers are again introduced.

The eight chimneys are arranged in squares of four, their tops joined by arches, with balustraded wooden platforms at roof-peak level to form roof decks. Other important features of, the exterior are the stone staircases at the north and south entrances. These have heavy stone balustrades and diminish in width from bottom to top. Doors at the east and west ends also give onto outside stairs, that on the east leading to the kitchen outbuilding nearby; the dog-legged stair on the west end arches down over the ground-floor entrance.

Each of the wings contains four rooms in the raised basement and four on the main floor. On both floors the two front rooms are separated from the rear ones by a lateral hallway. On the ground floor there are five bedrooms, a schoolroom, spinning room, housekeeper's room, and in the center section a large room probably for servants, and two small ones for storage. On the main floor the center section is devoted to the great hall, the wings providing space for a dining room and its service alcove, a parlor, parlor closet, library, library closet, and a room known as "Mother's Room" with a connecting nursery. The closets, incidentally, are of normal room size. Connection between the two floors is by a single narrow stair in the east hall.

The great hall is monumental in both size and architectural detail. Twenty-eight feet six inches square, it is seventeen feet four inches high, with a tray ceiling, the walls sloping in above the cornice to a flat center. Flanking each door and window are fluted Corinthian pilasters on plinths, all the flat wall spaces being paneled. Above the pilasters a full entablature is carried right around the room, and broken out, *en ressaut*, above each capital. The window draperies are of crimson damask, with deep tasseled pelmets, and on the floor is an almost room-size Oushak rug. The walls are adorned with Queen Anne gilt-framed mirrors, and portraits of Thomas Lee, his wife, Hannah Ludwell, and Richard Henry Lee, while below the mirrors six-legged folding mahogany card tables serve as consoles. Other furnishings consist of exquisite Queen Anne settees upholstered in hand-tooled leather, embossed in gold; seven-

Properly austere is the little schoolroom for the younger children on the ground floor of the east wing.

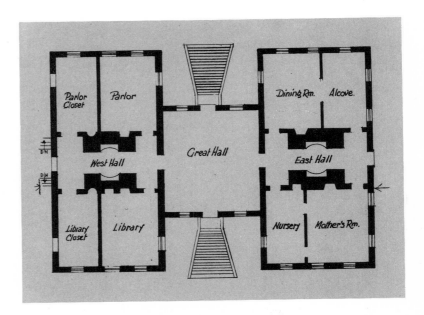

The main floor plan shows how the chimney grouping was effected, the great hall being innocent of any fireplace.

Used for a variety of important functions, the great hall accommodated both front and rear entrances and doorways to the transverse halls.

Adjoining the nursery and opening into the east hall is the Mother's Room in which Robert E. Lee was born.

teenth-century cane-back, scroll-foot, Spanish-style armchairs; Queen Anne side chairs; a spinet, a harp, and a handsome tall clock in William and Mary style by William Clement.

The library is another delightful room though it has none of the classical air of the great hall. The fireplace wall is paneled from floor to ceiling, the others are of plaster tinted a warm beige or light peach between the high baseboard, the wide dado, and the deep cornice, all the paneling and trim being painted a deep blue. The chandelier is similar to that of the great hall but has only half as many sconces. The formal window draperies and pelmets are of a cinnamon color which matches that of the handwoven mohair upholstery of the Queen Anne walnut chairs and the cane-back, turned daybed (c. 1690). The rug is a Ghiordes in yellows and blues on a rose background.

Light-Horse Harry Lee was responsible for changing the décor of the parlor to late eighteenth-century style. For this reason there is a stunning Adam mantel in wood, painted a delicate gray, the mantel reeding being carried right around the room dado above its panels. The plaster walls and ceiling are of a creamy peach tint, and from the ceiling hangs a handsome crystal chandelier. The rug is an Aubusson of 1780-90 with floral designs in tints of rose on a light ground, and the draperies are of lampas in soft gray-blue, adding the final touch to a restful color scheme.

Over the mantel is a Charles Willson Peale portrait of Lafayette, who presented it to Light-Horse Harry Lee. The

largest piece of furniture in this room, and one of the most handsome, is a delicate Sheraton secretary-bookcase, formerly the property of General Robert E. Lee. The chairs are a mixture of Sheraton and Hepplewhite, and there is a Sheraton card table used as a console, a scrolled-top tea table, and a Chippendale card table with round tray corners for candlesticks and counter dishes. The tall clock is an extra fine piece in mahogany, dated 1740, by John Johnson of London.

Of all the bedrooms at Stratford, the one known as the "Mother's Room" is perhaps the most interesting and colorful. This is the southeast chamber in which several members of the family, including Robert E. Lee, were born. This room and the adjoining nursery have been restored to the condition they were in at the time of the Confederate general's birth. Here, the walls are of a dove-gray color with an oyster-white ceiling, and the trim a dull matte white. Against this background the toile de Jouy in faded rose and white stands out boldly. This fabric is used in the 1790 pattern known as "America's Homage to France" for the tester bed, and in another pattern, "Four Quarters of the Globe," for the draperies and the wing chair. The rug is an eighteenth-century Persian Tabriz in shades of rose on a light ground. Between the windows is a delicately beautiful 1790 American gilt mirror in the Adam manner, and below it a Sheraton bracket-foot chest of drawers. The mahogany bed itself is a particularly fine example of Sheraton design.

The spacious dining room with its three windows and a wide

The stately dining room opens into an alcove where informal meals were served.

On the ground floor, beneath the library, is a bedroom called the Blue Room with its oversized fireplace and canopied bed.

North of the west hall is the parlor
with its Adam mantel installed
by Light-Horse Harry Lee.

Off the west hall is the library closet—
a cozy nook for games or study.

arch into the service alcove seems even larger than its 16½ by 21 feet, an illusion helped by the paneled dado which is painted gray-green to match the rest of the trim. In contrast, the walls are a light peach color which emphasizes the feeling of openness, accented by window draperies of gold damask trimmed with red velvet, the pelmets having a somewhat geometrical strapwork border to add a note of formality. In the center of the polished wood floor is a large oval drop-leaf table in mahogany, its four cabriole legs ending in horse-hoof feet. The Queen Anne side chairs and armchairs in walnut, elmwood, and beech have shell-carved knees and leather seats.

Through the wood-trimmed, keystoned arch connecting the dining room with the service alcove (later called the dining alcove), can be seen a life-size portrait of Queen Caroline, painted by Charles Jervis. (The Queen had made a gift of three hundred pounds sterling to Thomas Lee when his former home burned down.) Flanking the portrait are windows whose draperies match those of the dining room. The alcove has its own dining furniture, presumably for informal meals, the larger room being reserved for state occasions.

Adjoining the library but not opening from it is a smaller room known as the library closet—a cozy nook for study, a game of cards, or a quiet pipe. With its tall ceiling, its bare plaster walls, chair rail and wooden cornice, its charm is enhanced by the colorful damask draperies at the three windows and the gay rug. Besides the comfortable armchairs and deep wing chairs, it contains four Philadelphia Chippendale chairs, a Queen Anne spoon-foot gaming table, and a two-drawer bracket-footed mahogany chest dated 1774.

Beneath the library is the Blue Room whose much lower ceiling and tall, canopied bed give it a feeling of intimacy and warmth despite the blues of the wood trim and bed hangings. The arched brick fireplace, plastered and whitewashed, is quite large and forms an interesting architectural feature.

On the east wing ground floor is a schoolroom for the younger children. Its interior is perfectly plain, the door and single window set well into the brickwork, exposing deep reveals and the plastered-over brick arches. Here are a pair of entrancing juvenile Windsor chairs with one-piece bow and arms, and a small oval gateleg table for the young students, along with the master's desk and bamboo Windsors, a mahogany tavern table, and a large high-backed pine settle, all of which seem quite at home with the whitewashed walls.

Today Stratford Hall is once again the center of a thriving plantation—this time concerned with farming, stock raising and horse breeding. The main dependencies, however, can still be seen as they were. One is the great kitchen, with the laundry, smokehouse, and herb garden close by, another is Thomas Lee's law office, the third a schoolhouse and master's quarters, the last housing a workroom and storehouse. All of these help to recapture the atmosphere of Stratford Hall as it was in the days of its hero-patriot owners.

OPPOSITE: A corner of the library with its portrait of the mother of Thomas Lee's wife, Hannah Harrison Ludwell, by Sir Godfrey Kneller.

New Bern, North Carolina
TRYON PALACE

The Governor's Residence and Government House

Few newly reconstructed buildings dating from colonial times are capable of recapturing the atmosphere of history and splendor that Tryon Palace achieves. Here is a building, at once a governor's residence and a government house, that has great esthetic value as well as historical and architectural importance. And though it has risen anew in recent times from the ashes of its destruction in 1798, so beautifully has it been re-created both in fabric and content that it is possible to imagine this is the original group of carefully preserved buildings.

Here, then, we have an imposing English Georgian mansion, one of the very few built in this country whose plan is that of a Palladian villa. There is the two-story central block with its hipped roof, and an eaves parapet—rare at least before the American Revolution—on either side of a pedimented pavilion. Connected to this main structure by curved colonnades are the twin, two-story dependencies. These buildings, in turn, are joined by a rounded wrought-iron fence atop a stub wall in the center of which is the inner gate, also of iron, with brick pillars and semicircular brick sentry boxes, completing the entrance courtyard. This opens on to a formal approach, at the outer end of which is a pair of handsome wrought-iron gates from a London house dated 1741.

Today we need have no doubt that Royal Governor William Tryon knew exactly what he wanted in his official residence— a mansion splendid and imposing, dignified enough to impress the king's colonial subjects with their homeland's might and majesty. It seems that he achieved his ambition, since the original mansion, which was begun in 1767, has been widely praised as "one of the most elegant and noble structures erected in colonial times"; and it apparently has lost nothing of its original impressiveness in the reconstruction. The reason for this acclaim is that Governor Tryon was perspicacious enough to bring with him from England a highly competent master builder and architect, John Hawks, to design the buildings and supervise their erection.

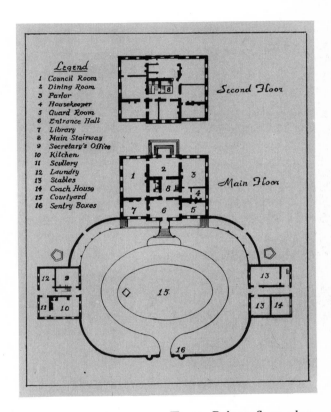

Tryon Palace floor plan.

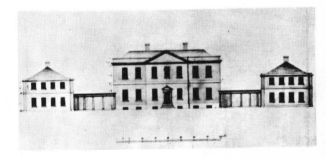

John Hawks' elevation of Tryon Palace.

OPPOSITE: Tryon Palace seen through the handsome wrought-iron gates from a 1741 house in London.

View of the restored Tryon Palace from
the waterfront with the British red ensign of 1770
and signal flags on the mast.

A 1769 painting of Queen Charlotte
with the Prince of Wales and Duke of York,
now in the alcove bedroom.

The Maud Moore Latham Memorial
parterre beyond which John Hawks' allée
celebrates the original
palace's supervising architect.

For his inspiration, Hawks seemingly turned to contemporary English Georgian houses and, for details, to the recently published (1757) book *The Complete Body of Architecture* by Isaac Ware, a London architect. Judging by similarities in the two façades, Hawks also may have had firsthand recollections of Lord Harcourt's Oxfordshire seat, Newnham, or he may have copied it from Robert Morris's book, *Select Architecture*.

It is unfortunate that Governor Tryon was transferred to New York before completion of the project into which he had put so much time and thought. Luckily, the stable and the elegant pentagonal "necessary houses" were completed before the mansion was occupied. However, there still remained to be erected several smaller structures such as a smokehouse, dovecot, and poultry house. These were arranged for by Tryon's successor, Governor Josiah Martin, who apparently left everything pretty much to the capable Mr. Hawks.

Building was still going on and little if any garden had been laid out in 1775 when revolutionary activities made it necessary for the new governor to abandon the palace. After the Revolution the palace became the state capitol of North Carolina, and four governors were successively inaugurated in it, two of them utilizing it as their official residence. In 1794 the capital was transferred to Raleigh, and in 1798 the main building was destroyed by fire.

Restoration of the palace to the condition it was in during Governor Tryon's occupancy was begun in 1952, after considerable investigation of records and digging on the site—a project aided considerably by the discovery of Hawks' original plans and Governor Tryon's inventory of furniture and furnishings. The necessary bricks were made in Virginia, including many of a particularly bright red hue similar to those used for the original main structure. The resulting contrast in color between the palace and its dependencies is not only pleasing but intensifies the architectural character of the mansion whose principal ornament is the massive reproduction in color of the royal arms of George III set into the pavilion pediment above the main entrance.

Several of the original mansion's steps were found in the ruins, and sandstone for the remaining steps and the trim was obtained from the same English quarry as the originals. Mantels, carved paneling, inside shutters, doorways, picture moldings, and similar items were acquired from important eighteenth-century English houses to contribute to the authentic atmosphere of the interiors which were to house furniture and *objets d'art* as near to the Tryon possessions as possible.

One laudable result of all this intensive investigation and effort was the creation of a reproduction that not only parallels the original in effect but also recaptures its spirit. Furthermore it needs no patina of age to give it authority and dignity, and for once we can gaze upon a historic building as it actually must have appeared, in all its pristine freshness, to the people of its early days.

The entrance hall with its marble floor
and three of the four marble statuary pieces
representing the continents.

Among the parlor treasures is a 16th-
century Turkey carpet, a walnut spinet of 1720
by Thomas Hitchcock, and a 17th-century
Claude Lorrain painting.

The library is a quiet, richly mellow room with 400 of the original 500 titles in fine bindings, and a Gainsborough portrait.

In the supper room is a tremendous gilt trumeau in delicate chinoiseries enlivened by an Oriental river scene.

This 18th-century tile-floored room is in the basement. Its equipment suggests an old-time tavern.

The Government House plan is of particular interest for the way in which the requirements of official business were combined with those of family life. Great pains were taken in both the location and size of the main stairway to insulate the first floor from the second. Downstairs, the largest space was devoted to the Council Chamber, in addition to which there is a formal, or state, dining room, a parlor, large entrance hall, a library, a room for the military guard, and a cubbyhole for the housekeeper. Surrounded by these is the central stair hall with a grand staircase for the governor, his family, and guests, and a lesser hidden stair for the servants going about their sometimes indelicate duties.

On the second floor, reserved to the private use of the family, there are eight rooms—a drawing room, supper room, three guest rooms, and two family bedrooms with dressing rooms or closets. On the third floor of the mansion are eight more rooms, six of them used as bedrooms for the indoor servants, the others serving as a sitting room and storage room. In the basement are a preparation room, coachman's room, and assembly room. Allocated to one of the two major dependencies are a secretary's office and bedroom, the main kitchen and scullery, a laundry, and three bedrooms. The other building is the stable and coach house, with a hayloft above.

All the important rooms of the mansion are provided with ample window space, the sash having large panes, thin mutins, stiles and rails, in accordance with the then latest Georgian style. In addition the stair well is provided with a domed skylight (an idea made use of in Hadrian's villa nearly 1,700 years before!) so that on bright days the mansion is flooded with light.

The Council Chamber is the most splendid of these official

rooms. It is also the most versatile since it could quickly be transformed into an elegant ballroom, sparkling with light from twin chandeliers and candelabra of shimmering Irish crystal. The upper walls are white with panel moldings of plaster, while the dado, the door and window trim, the frieze and cornice, and the folded-back shutters in the deep window reveals, are painted a delicate green, the shutter panels outlined with carved and gilded moldings.

The mantel is of delicately carved white and Siena marble, with alabaster columns and inlay. The columns are duplicated on the paneled overmantel (Ionic below, Corinthian above) to flank the coat of arms of the House of Hanover. Topping all this is a broken pediment in plaster, terminating just below the green-painted frieze. White, fluted pilasters set the projecting chimney breast apart from the great eared panels which contain life-size portraits in oils of King George III and his consort, Queen Charlotte, in their coronation robes.

How bright this room must have glowed in the mellow light of many tapers illuminating the portraits of their majesties, especially on the night of a formal ball with the colorful uniforms and gala gowns and sparkling jewels. Even with that wonderful seventeenth-century Ispahan carpet removed and the tables and the councilors' Gothic chairs gone, there was still the vivid splash of color provided by the costly draperies of Italian silk damask in deep red and the narrow George II chairs, with seats to match that bold hue, ranged along the walls.

Among the more notable pieces of furniture in this room are a pair of matching mahogany drop-leaf tables by John Goddard and Townsend of Newport, a Gothic-Chippendale side table, a Chippendale table-desk with an important master's chair in the style of Manwaring, gilt pier glasses by John Gumley, dating from about 1720, and a massive musical

Distinctive furnishings of the drawing room are an English needlework carpet, a secretary of 1765 with thirteen panels, and Raeburn open-arm chairs.

Soft gray tones form an admirable setting for a Verres seascape and Oriental Wilton carpet in the governor's bedroom.

A rare English moquette carpet and a maple four-poster with an 18th-century French quilt grace the southwest bedroom in the east wing.

Lady Tryon's dressing room has an 18th-century mantel and English carved moldings, with an overmantel painting of Margaret Hamilton by David Martin.

timepiece, made around 1736, which not only chimes but plays operatic tunes.

Only second in importance to the Council Chamber-cum-ballroom is the state dining room which opens off it. Here again stark white ceilings, and walls above a gray-green-tinted dado set off the furniture and furnishings to perfection. The fireplace surround is of blue-veined marble, surmounted by a painted lintel decorated with carved ribbons and swags in the Adam manner (probably the first in America), with heavy scroll consoles supporting the shelf. A crossetted panel above this, shaped in the plaster and outlined in gold, enframes a portrait of Mary, Queen of Scots.

From the ceiling's center hangs an eight-branched English cut-glass chandelier of 1740, centered over a three-section mahogany dining table whose legs and apron are decorated in the early Adam manner. The chairs are English Chippendale with pierced splats and cabriole legs. A Philadelphia Chippendale tall-case clock, also in mahogany, and with its dial silvered by James Warne of London, occupies a fireplace alcove. On the floor is an eighteenth-century hand-tufted Savonnerie carpet of strapwork design made in Turkey. Opposite the fireplace is a large portrait of Queen Anne, who was ruler of England when New Bern was founded in 1710.

The parlor is the third main-floor room whose air of spaciousness is emphasized by white walls and ceiling. The most prominent feature of the room is the carved Siena-marble fireplace and paneled chimney breast. The latter, complete with a broken pediment and basket finial, is elaborately carved and molded, its central panel occupied by an exquisite seventeenth-century pastoral painting by Claude Lorrain.

Chief among the furnishings is a set of seven George II mahogany chairs with four cabriole legs; the seats and backs are upholstered in rich Soho tapestry. The colors of the sixteenth-century Turkey carpet of Hispano-Moresque design blend delightfully with those of the chair tapestry background and the green of the tasseled silk lampas draperies that adorn the four windows. The largest piece of furniture in this room is a wide mahogany breakfront bookcase holding many eighteenth-century volumes in fine bindings. This bookcase is flanked by a pair of William and Mary carved and gilt sconces, and nearby a homelike touch is provided by a 1720 Hitchcock walnut spinet which is still playable.

One of the more astonishing things about the palace is the furniture and equipment to be found in the service quarters. In the housekeeper's room, for example, there is a delightful shell-top corner cupboard (c. 1765) with decorated spandrels and a curious folding circular bottom shelf. With the doors ajar, this half-shelf can be opened out so that objects removed from the upper shelves can be assembled on it. It is also surprising to find in the guard room a Queen Anne walnut secretary with mirrored doors, together with some examples of eighteenth-century Whieldon pottery.

The governor's library is a quiet room and a comparatively small one, designed for study or mild recreation such as chess or the discussion of a bottle of port with a crony. Daytime lighting is amply afforded by three large windows and artificial illumination by the six-branched brass chandelier, the candle brackets on the mirror, and the hand candlesticks supplied for use on desk, chest, or tables or to search for some particular title in the bookcase which houses more than four hundred original copies of the five hundred finely bound, eighteenth-century books listed by Governor Tryon as belonging to his library. The window draperies and the upholstery of the Gainsborough Chinese-Chippendale armchair are of eighteenth-century Genoese cut velvet in rich shades of gold and brown; the only rug—a Savonnerie "Lion of Leon" design loomed in Madrid—in beige and faded red, with touches of blue and black, contributes a pleasing pattern without overaccented color. Well-distributed golden highlights are supplied by the gilt frames of paintings and mirror—the large architectural seascape of the Claude Lorrain school that dominates the mantel; the Gainsborough portrait of Philip Bowes Broke; and

The Council Chamber-cum-ballroom is equally impressive in either role thanks largely to the huge portraits of royalty dominating the fireplace wall.

The essential dignity of the drawing room owes as much to its architectural features—pediments, pilasters, and cornices—as to notable antiques and well-chosen colors.

The Mauve Bedroom is named from the rich color of the woodwork matched by that of the draperies.
The rug is 16th-century Persian.

the carved George II looking glass with its delicate, hinged candle brackets.

The rooms in the private apartments are warm and intimate, revealing the cultivated tastes of the governor and his lady—rooms with subdued colors, soft lighting, polished woods to reflect the firelight and candlelight. Such a chamber is the drawing room whose essential dignity stems largely from its architectural features despite the fact that it is furnished with what are rare antiques to us but to the Tryons probably were simply the best of the latest and most fashionable of household effects available in England at that time.

Some of the important items that have earned for this room a reputation for exceptional beauty and harmony are: the distinctive English needlework carpet of the 1760's in soft blues, pinks, greens and beige on a *tête-de-nègre* ground; a pair of inlaid harewood and fruitwood console tables; a mahogany secretary of 1765 which has a swan-neck pediment and doors with thirteen panels; a pair of Adam-style mahogany elbow chairs; Chippendale side chairs; two Raeburn open-arm chairs; a pair of carved and gilded Chippendale mirrors; a spider-legged drop-leaf tea table; sundry pieces of crystal and porcelain and other appropriate appointments.

Somewhat more colorful and gay is the supper room, with its white walls and pale green dado, where an oversize gilt mirror in delicate chinoiserie, with a Chinese river scene in the upper section, vies for attention with the colorful Chippendale mahogany sofa beneath it. This sofa, which once belonged to the Dowager Duchess of Marlborough, is worth special mention since it still has its original needlework upholstery.

The six Chippendale chairs in this room are upholstered in antique red velvet. Against one wall is a fine George II mahogany china cabinet; elsewhere Gothic mahogany hanging shelves display colorful and rare porcelains—exquisite figurines of 1760 gold-anchor Chelsea and Dr. Wall Worcester pieces in the Kylin or unicorn pattern.

As a final example of the delights that have been preserved in the Tryon Palace restoration, nothing can excel the governor's own bedroom. Here the soft gray tones of the plain walls form an admirable foil not only for the splendid Dutch seascape by Verres that adorns the overmantel, but for the gleaming brass of the eight-branched chandelier; the Queen Anne bonnet-top highboy in burl walnut; and, best of all, the English mahogany canopy bed with its hairy-paw feet, and the richly bordered plain hangings which so effectively contrast with the Oriental-patterned Wilton carpet, made in 1750 for the Duke of Newcastle, in which dull yellows and blues disport on a background of red. Another piece which should not be overlooked is a kneehole dressing table which, together with a shaving chair and basin stand (the latter, oddly enough, complete with a Dr. Wall Worcester blue-painted basin and matching water bottle) identify it as a room designed for a gentleman of both means and taste.

OPPOSITE: The dining room with its portrait of Mary, Queen of Scots. The rug is a 1770 Savonnerie, the chandelier is English (1750).

THE JEREMIAH LEE MANSION

Regal Dignity in Colonial New England

Built in 1768, during prosperous times, Colonel Jeremiah Lee's great pre-Revolutionary mansion may seem, at first glance, more like a London town house than a New England colonial residence. Actually it is mid-Georgian Palladian in style, and though its walls seem to be faced with smooth ashlar, complete with light-colored quoins and keystoned lintels, its siding is of rusticated wood disguised by limestone-gray paint to which a modicum of sand was added to give the surface the required texture.

The center bay is projected slightly to represent a pavilion, and this is topped with a pediment enclosing a large semi-circular window to light the attic. The roof is of a gable-on-hip design, centering on a tall octagonal, domed cupola flanked by two large chimneys. Over the impressive ten-paneled door of the main entrance is a well-proportioned Ionic portico atop half a dozen wide freestone steps. The total effect is one of massive dignity which suggests the palatial scale and grandeur of most of its sixteen rooms.

The slightly off-center hall is almost sixteen feet wide and extends the full depth of the house—a distance of forty-three feet. Against the right wall, from halfway to the rear, the great stair rises at a gentle angle, its risers low and its treads genteelly wide. The huge mahogany staircase is almost eight feet broad, and richly adorned with elaborately turned newels and balusters, its paneled and pilastered wainscoting matching that of the hall itself. The open-string end of each step is paneled and carved, and large panels enclose the closet under the stairs.

At the top of the first landing is a wide, arched window that floods the stair with light. From this point the stair turns back on itself to reach the second floor, adding more gleaming wood tones to the hall below its paneled soffits. Originally the walls of both lower and upper halls were covered with a fabulous wallpaper which was carried right up the stairs. The wallpaper in the lower hall has disintegrated, but from

The Jeremiah Lee Mansion
is mid-Georgian Palladian of rusticated wood
finished to look like ashlar.

OPPOSITE TOP: Detail of the reception room, its native pine walls grained to resemble oak; the furniture is a mixture of 18th-century Queen Anne and Chippendale pieces.

OPPOSITE BOTTOM: The staircase of mahogany, with its elaborate turnings, carved brackets, and pilastered wainscoting.

The great drawing room displays large panels
reproducing paintings of Roman
ruins, possibly by Pannini.

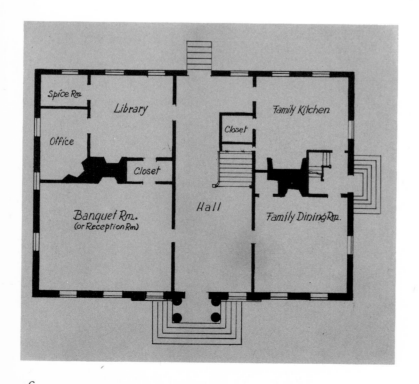

The first-floor plan suggests
the importance of the wide hall and stair leading
to the great drawing room above.

the foot of the stairway up, the rest remains intact. This wallpaper, brought from England, is painted in tempera on 21-by-27-inch sheets of watercolor stock, the scenic panels being copied from engravings of paintings by eighteenth-century French and Italian artists. The equally splendid wall covering of the great drawing room on the second floor displays large panels in which are reproduced paintings of Roman ruins (possibly by Pannini) inside wide scroll borders in the rococo style. The egg-and-dart border matches that of the woodwork.

Returning to the main floor, the reception or banquet room owes its magnificence to its woodwork. The elaborate raised paneling in native pine is grained to represent oak. The whole is tied together by a highly detailed entablature, and centers on a fireplace resplendent with carvings in the Grinling Gibbons manner—though the usual pea pods are missing. The white marble fireplace surround is framed by a carved molding upheld by scroll-type consoles. Above the lintel, carved brackets support the mantel shelf, and between them is a carved swag in high relief. The eared overmantel panel is supported by another pair of consoles and topped by a baroque cresting. All of this is flanked by carved festoons to form an amazingly beautiful grouping derived from Plate 51 of Abraham Swan's book, *British Architect*, published in 1745.

The tall windows, with their paneled shutters and seat bottoms, are draped in figured and fringed pure silk lampas of a rich red. Here, as elsewhere in the mansion, the furniture is a mixture of eighteenth-century Queen Anne and Chippendale pieces, including two side chairs which belonged to Colonel Lee, while the rug is a Bergama of the period.

On the opposite side of the main hall is the family dining room with painted, wood-paneled walls that are given architectural character by fluted Corinthian pilasters flanking the fireplace. Held in the fireplace's bolection molding are scenic tiles, signed by their English maker, John Sadler. On the other walls the paneling is confined to the dado. The rug is of needlework of the period.

At all three windows the pelmets and draperies are of eighteenth-century scarlet silk damask, which forms a strong contrast to the light blue painted woodwork, including a complete entablature with a heavily dentiled cornice. The dining table is a square, gateleg, Chippendale piece with ball-and-claw feet, but the chairs are shield-back Hepplewhites, with brass-nailed seats of black leather. These once belonged to John Hancock with whom Colonel Lee served on the Committee of Safety in 1774-75.

The "Pannini" wallpaper of the second-floor drawing room has already been mentioned. These scenic temperas, however, are but part of the stately background that sets off the walnut and mahogany furniture. The fireplace surround of white marble contrasts nicely with the gray-tinted woodwork of the mantel which is a simplified version of that of the banquet room, minus the carved swag, festoons, and consoles. This gives

Detail of another painted panel at the drawing room's west end.

The splendid woodwork of the reception room is climaxed by the fireplace replete with carvings in the Grinling Gibbons manner.

General view of the first-floor reception
or banquet room whose raised paneling
is of native pine "grained" to represent oak.

The paneled walls of the family dining room
are given architectural character
by fluted Corinthian pilasters framing the fireplace.

it a starker air better suited to the "Pannini" ruins whose heavy borders are already sufficiently ornate.

The fireplace and chimney breast project an inch or so, as do the window architraves, a treatment carried up through the cornice to ceiling level to produce an *en ressaut* effect. The windows are hung in green damask set inside the reveals so that some of the trim in addition to the cornice shows. Into this setting are introduced various groupings of eighteenth-century furniture, such as a large, round, drop-leaf Queen Anne table with spoon feet centered on a large Persian rug; a Queen Anne wing chair and side chairs also in green damask; Chippendale ladder-back side chairs in black leather; a mahogany ball-and-claw-footed drop-front desk; and an early English piano on a Chippendale frame.

Very similar is the interior detail of the upstairs parlor except that the pilasters are Ionic, and the fireplace tiles, also made by Sadler, are extremely rare ones in color. The fireplace wall is paneled, but the others are covered with scenic wallpapers, one bearing a figure of King Neptune, another an antique seascape. There is also a decorative paper panel over the door. The chairs are shield-back Hepplewhite pieces which had been given to the daughter of General John Glover as a wedding present. The general was that famous commander of the amphibious regiment of Marblehead and Salem fishermen who ferried Washington across the Delaware on his way to Trenton in 1776.

Off the stair hall is what is known as the guest bedroom, the woodwork painted green in happy complement to the soft orange of the Sadler tiles surrounding the fireplace. The bed is dressed in a rare and complete set of coverlet, valance, curtains and backdrop of mid-eighteenth-century American crewelwork in which occurs the same soft orange tone of the tiles. Off the bedroom is a dressing room or powder room, as well as sitting room containing a small fireplace.

Behind the upstairs parlor is the master bedroom, which is somewhat simpler in style than the other rooms of the mansion. It is interesting to note how little charm depends upon display, and how much feeling of comfort is supplied by the homey atmosphere of the furnishings.

Here the plaster walls are of a light yellow which harmonizes so well with the original green of the trim, the paneling of the fireplace wall, the door and even the corner posts. The fireplace is enlivened by gay tiles, the rest of the color and pattern being supplied by the beautiful chintzes of the bed coverlet, valance, and curtains in their soft yellows and browns, with accents of brick red. The bed itself is a thing of beauty with its tapering, carved and reeded posts, and its mahogany tester frame. A Hepplewhite secretary, with finely grained mahogany drawers and folding top, diamond-paned doors and neat brasses; a Queen Anne lowboy and a Sheraton table flanking the bed; a Chippendale mahogany, crested mirror; a gold-framed family portrait, and even a gold-stenciled, black-

The fireplace walls of the parlor are paneled;
the others are covered with scenic wallpapers.

painted chair with curling arms contribute to the intimate atmosphere that spells home in even the most imposing mansion of wealth and authority.

Colonel Lee died in 1775 in the service of his country, and some years later the estate was taken over by the Chief Justice of the Massachusetts court, Samuel Sewall. Sold in 1804, it was used as a bank for the next 105 years. In 1909 it became the property of the Marblehead Historical Society which proceeded to rescue it from dissolution. The Lee furnishings were scattered at the time of the sale, but the Society has succeeded in furnishing the mansion with fine authentic pieces of the period which are more than sufficient to re-create the general appearance of the interiors as they were in their heyday—and that in itself is surely no small accomplishment. Today the mansion is pretty much as it was in Jeremiah Lee's day at the outbreak of the Revolutionary War in which, as a member of the Committee of Safety, he played an important part.

Charming in its simplicity
is the master bedroom, much color and pattern
being supplied by the soft yellows,
browns, and brick-red of the chintzes.

Monticello in the summer— exquisite architecture in a perfect setting.

Jefferson's first design for Monticello (1771).

Charlottesville, Virginia

MONTICELLO

The Home of Thomas Jefferson

It would be difficult anywhere to find a house more thoroughly permeated with the character of its builder than Thomas Jefferson's Monticello. This is a mansion unique in many ways and thoroughly individual. Its interior may not be so strikingly beautiful as the exterior yet it is unforgettable, permeated by the spirit of one of the most remarkable men in American history—the man who wrote the Declaration of Independence and was, among so many other things, Governor of Virginia and two-term President of the fledgling United States. And so, to know the house it is necessary to know this man, to observe him over the years as his mind conceived and planned, remodeled and, in part, rebuilt his home "ever nearer to the heart's desire."

To go to Monticello is to feel his presence; to study its history is to watch his dream come slowly true as his knowledge of architecture widened and his ideas changed, and he ruthlessly tore down what he had so meticulously put together to make way for the new.

In spite of the wife and the family who shared this home with him, and of all the notable personages who enjoyed his hospitality there, Jefferson seems to have conceived and carried out his ideas without reference to anyone, keeping his dreams to himself. The one exception, perhaps, might have been that New Year's night in 1772 when he and his new bride, Martha Wayles Skelton, their coach stranded in a blizzard, rode up the steep, winding path, cold and wet, only to find the partially completed mansion in darkness and the servants asleep. Ever considerate of others, Jefferson stabled the horses himself, and he and his wife retired to the small pavilion that had been the first building erected on this site—the single, main-floor room he had used as bachelor quarters while the building was going on. Because of this incident the pavilion has since come to be known as "Honeymoon Lodge."

This, of course, was but a small incident in the history of Monticello, plans for which were first begun in 1767 when

Thomas Jefferson—a copy of the Rembrandt Peale portrait of the man who drafted the Declaration of Independence and was twice President of the United States.

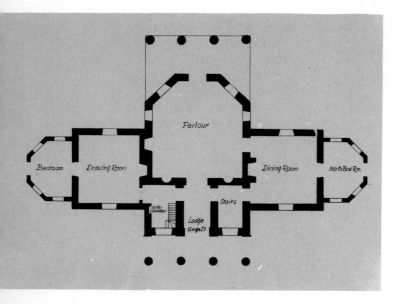

Floor plan of the original house.

Monticello as finally completed, together with its dependencies, in 1809.

Jefferson was a young man of twenty-four. Already a lawyer as well as a substantial landowner, he was also intensely interested in architecture, and had long planned to build his dream house atop the 857-foot hill adorning the Shadwell estate which he had inherited on his father's death in 1755. Here one was almost literally on the crest of the world, looking out over the Piedmont to the Blue Ridge Mountains and "the beautiful blue hills of Albemarle"—a prospect that he loved—and a mansion designed after Robert Morris's simplified interpretation of the Palladian style seemed exactly suited to the location and his needs. He was soon to reconsider.

It must have been about 1769 when Jefferson first acquired a copy of Leoni's *Palladio*, a book that apparently changed his ideas as to the kind of house he wanted. At any rate he made the drawing pictured (on page 50) of the main façade as he planned it according to Roman classical principles. As he had remarked on several occasions, he saw little to admire in English architecture and the colonial adaptations of the Georgian style left him cold. Here was his chance to create something different—incorporating Palladio's ideas without copying any of his designs.

The original house, therefore, was Palladian in style, with hipped roofs on the wings, and a central, two-storied portico back and front, each topped by a wide pediment that actually constituted the gable of the main roof. Apparently realizing that this massive portico was somewhat overpowering for so

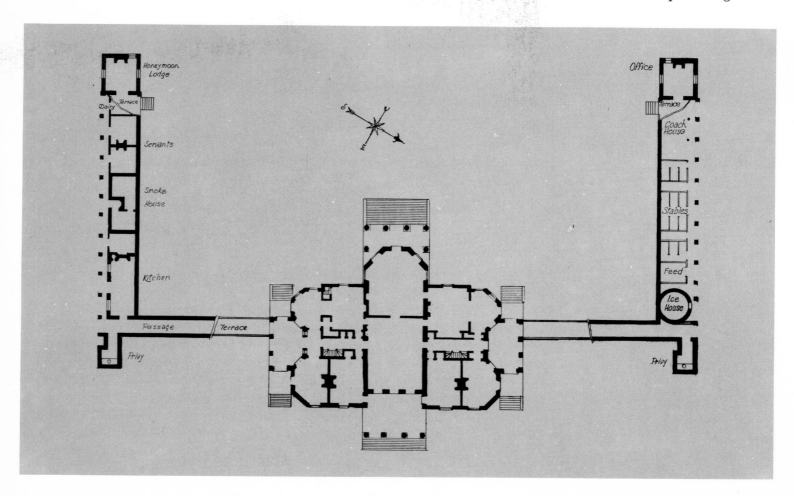

OPPOSITE: Watercolor painting of Monticello by Peticolas (1826) showing Honeymoon Lodge at right.

small a house, he later added polygonal extensions to the wings, an idea that may have been culled from Robert Morris's *Select Architecture*.

In 1769 a start had been made by leveling the top of the "little mountain"—this "monticello" as Jefferson called it—and building was begun in 1770. By 1772 the small house was ready for occupancy, but the two-story porticoes apparently were never completed. Ten years later Mrs. Jefferson died, and in 1784 he was sent to France as Minister, an appointment lasting five years. During that period in Versailles he studied French architecture intensively at first hand, undoubtedly stimulated by the perusal of such books as Antoine Desgodetz's *Edifices Antiques de Rome* and similar works. In any event he became vastly intrigued with the French adaptations of the Roman style, his admiration aroused by the single-story mansions with high-ceilinged rooms whose lesser apartments, though two stories high, were calculated to disguise the small overall difference in height.

Enamored of this idea, Jefferson returned to Monticello in 1789 to begin drastic remodeling. He tore down the unfinished portico on the east front and took out the great stairway together with a smaller one on the other side of the entrance. New, high-ceilinged rooms were added on the garden side, almost doubling the house's original depth. Over the western, central room—the parlor, whose polygonal bay projected well into the western portico—he erected a large dome with a stepped, octagonal base. Below the dome was a second-floor room, also eight-sided, which Jefferson referred to as the "sky" room or "dome" room according to the impulse of the moment. Despite his distaste for English houses, this dome does bear some resemblance to that of Lord Burlington's Chiswick villa which, in turn, may have been inspired by Palladio's Villa Rotonda.

Along the west façade, separated by the high-ceilinged hall (and now connected by a balcony across the hall), were the original rooms of lower height, all two stories tall, with attics above. Throughout these two-story sections the upper windows were brought down to the tops of the lower ones in order to maintain the appearance of a single-story building.

In place of the earlier main staircase which Jefferson considered a space waster, small winding stairs from passages between the hall and the piazzas give access both to the basement and the upper rooms—stairs so narrow (two feet) that it is inconceivable that even small furniture could be carried up them. From Jefferson's bedroom another tiny stair ascends to his clothes closet. Because the windows to the second-story rooms are low and terminate under a complete entablature carried right around the outside of the building, they are too close to the floor and of insufficient height to afford a view in comfort. The attic rooms have to be content with skylights located in the roof, and these are hidden from view by a balustrade above the cornice. Behind the dome, the roof

The tea room as seen from the dining room.

OPPOSITE: The entrance hall showing the seven-day clock designed by Jefferson.

Jefferson's bedroom, the bed occupying an alcove between the bedroom and the study.

ridge is crowned with a wooden railing which effectually hides it.

On its main floor, a couple of feet above ground level, the mansion sits astride the main hall and large parlor which, with their respective porticoes, form its lateral axis. Much smaller chambers are the study, library, dining and tea rooms and the four downstairs bedrooms. Upstairs are the mezzanine and attic rooms, with the sky room under the dome. These, together with the end piazzas, and the twelve basement rooms, form the main building which is of mellow red brick, its pillars, pediments and entablature painted white—the total structure having the appearance of a single-story mansion of exquisite proportions and style.

The building and rebuilding of this mansion was actually spread over a period of forty years, and when finished it was both architecturally and structurally as perfect as Jefferson could make it. The solid masonry walls were up to sixteen inches thick, depending on the load they were called upon to carry, the floors supported by heavy oak joists, closely spaced, with brick laid between them in a mortar of clay and straw, an excellent fire-retardant as well as insulation against both cold and noise. In the "restoration" of the building, however, it was apparently considered advisable to replace the deteriorated wooden joists with steel members, and eliminate the brick nogging—some 100 tons of it—entirely. Steel was also used to support the main floor. Apart from this, and extensive reconstruction of the terraces and outbuildings, the mansion is today pretty much as it was in Jefferson's time.

From the west lawn nothing is seen of the dependencies except the terminal pavilions. These groups of outbuildings consist of two rows of rooms at right angles to the house, one to the north and one to the south, connected to the main building by covered passages. The roofs of the rooms and the passages, which are approximately at ground level, form the north and south terraces respectively. This U-shaped arrangement of the dependencies owes something to Palladio, but the manner in which it has been adapted to the site is evidence of Jefferson's genius. The rooms are set back into the hillsides, the exposed fronts forming arcades that face downhill.

The L-shaped terraces carry white-painted wooden railings of a Chinese lattice pattern along each edge, the inner ones setting the limits to the front (west) lawn in a most attractive manner. Besides its terminal pavilion—the aforementioned Honeymoon Lodge—the southern wing takes in the dairy, two servants' rooms, the smokehouse, and the kitchen. In the northern one the pavilion served as Jefferson's office, with the coach house, stables, feed storage, and icehouse under the terrace. Connected to the inner end of each wing is a privy, while handily located in the connecting passages are rooms for wine, beer, rum, cider, and wares, each calling for special storage arrangements and, no doubt, strong locks.

Although Thomas Jefferson was skilled as an architect he was also extremely inventive, as the visitor immediately discovers on entering the eastern portico. Here, on the portico ceiling, is a dial indicating the wind direction, the pointer being actuated by a "weathercock" wind vane on the roof. But this is nothing to what awaits him inside the hall. Here, on the front wall, is a clock operated by two sets of "cannon-ball" weights—iron balls threaded on a pair of cables running over pulleys at opposite sides of the room. While the clock dial registers the hour, the vertical position of one group of weights indicates the day of the week. When the weights finally vanish through a hole in the floor the clock needs rewinding.

At the opposite end of the hall is a pair of large glass doors which are also out of the ordinary. Opening one of them causes the other to swing wide automatically—a mere matter of pulleys under the floor connected by chains! Other symbols of the statesman's ingenuity are to be found in his suite which consists of a library, bedroom, and study. Here is the polygraph he used—two pens linked by levers to write letters in duplicate—an invention of a Mr. Hawkins of Philadelphia which Jefferson improved upon; a portable desk similar to the one on which he drafted the Declaration of Independence, serving, with a simple adjustment, for either reading or writing; and a chaise longue with a revolving seat and a table for writing while semirecumbent.

The entrance hall, looking through the automatically opening doors Jefferson himself designed.

Displayed in the library are Jefferson's "Vice-President's" chair, his "polygraph" writing device, and portable reading or writing desk.

Jefferson's bed is set in an open alcove between the bedroom and study, no doubt a convenience on rising and retiring, and making for better ventilation than the usual three-sided bed recess. Between the passage from the kitchen stair and the dining room, a revolving door with shelves enabled food to be passed through without a kitchen servant entering. Finally, a tunneled conveyer from his private toilet to a sewage cart eliminated the need for covered pails being carried through the rooms. Altogether there was little his active mind overlooked, even the design of the window draperies for which he made sketches that are now on view alongside the individual windows.

For the most part the rooms at Monticello are of interest as much for their architectural details and decoration as for their furnishings. Few, unfortunately, are exactly as they were in Jefferson's time, much of the original furniture having been dispersed on his death. On the other hand some important pieces have been recovered by the Thomas Jefferson Memorial Foundation which owns the property, and others replaced by duplicates or acceptable substitutes. In any case, the interior architectural features, which reflect the classical purity and simplicity of the exterior, are well worthy of study. The entrance hall, for example, is extremely pleasant with its triple arch over the glass doors and flanking floor-length windows, and the molded and paneled woodwork in gleaming white against the pale blue-green of the walls. The ceiling center is decorated with an eagle in a circle of eighteen stars, all in white plaster.

The balcony rails, the dadoes, the trim and the oversized carved brackets that support the structure are also white. The

Wedgwood-blue walls and white trim together with a massive arch form a dramatic setting for the dining room pieces.

floor is the original one of pine. Once this room was lined with trophies of the chase and relics of the Lewis and Clark expedition, which Jefferson sent out in 1804 to explore the newly acquired Louisiana Territory. Today only the moose and elk horns, and several bones of some unknown mammal remain, and on their pedestals below stand copies of the missing marble busts of Jefferson's contemporaries—Voltaire, Turgot, Hamilton—and of himself. Here also are a few pieces of furniture of moderate distinction—chairs, tables, and a console—together with some prints and oil paintings, including one of the Marquis de Lafayette, and an original by Thomas Sully of Jefferson's daughter, Martha Jefferson Randolph. Over the fireplace hangs a copy of the Rembrandt Peale portrait of Jefferson.

Happily some other rooms are more elegantly furnished. In the parlor, for example, where the floor is the original beech and cherry parquet, is a fine suite of Louis XVI furniture, together with an inlaid mahogany table, and an English piano with satinwood inlay, made about 1800 by Astor of London.

Another particularly effective interior is that of the dining room with its walls of Wedgwood blue and white trim, its massive three-centered arch spanning the opening to an alcove undoubtedly intended to receive a handsome sideboard. This tall room with its coved ceiling repeats the frieze and cornice pattern used on the exterior walls of the mansion to good effect. The Wedgwood motif is carried further with jasperware plaques let into the face of the white mantel. A two-section table with ball-and-claw feet, and a set of Hepplewhite side chairs are all original Jefferson pieces. The acces-

A corner of the tiny room of Honeymoon Lodge where Jefferson and his wife spent their first night at Monticello.

sories include a nice Waterford epergne, French bisque figurines, and an ormolu clock. The room, incidentally, has small dumbwaiters built into the ends of the mantelpiece, one for the delivery of full wine bottles, the other for the removal of the "dead" ones.

Adjoining the north piazza is the tea room, semi-octagonal in shape, with a wide doorway to the dining room spanned by the usual massive arch. A normal-sized door opening leads into a passage accommodating a stairway both up and down, while the exit to the piazza and the terrace steps is via floor-length, triple-sash windows. Here, too, the woodwork is on a monumental scale—the heavy arch and the frieze and cornice from which it springs, all painted white, with heavy brackets between the windows supporting marble busts of Jefferson's favorite eighteenth-century American heroes and patriots.

The three rooms of Jefferson's personal suite are all quite plain except for the cornice, the delicate marble fireplace in the library, and the great archway between the library and the bedroom. All these rooms depend largely upon bright color for their attractiveness, the window and bed-alcove draperies being of red damask lined with green linen, and having gold-tasseled borders. The chaise longue and the tall mahogany ceremonial chair (known as the Vice-President's chair because Jefferson used it while holding that office) are both upholstered in red leather.

The three other bedrooms on this floor follow the French fashion of putting the beds in alcoves and diminishing the openings with heavy, festooned draperies—attractive but claustrophobic. The room in the south wing, once occupied by Jefferson's daughter, Martha, still contains its original highboy, as well as Louis XVI side chairs which are similar to the armchair in the north square (Monroe) room. These two rooms are quite similar in décor, with white-painted walls, while the north octagonal (Madison) room is papered above a pale blue dado.

One of the better rooms, architecturally speaking, rarely seen by visitors because of the difficult stairs, is the previously mentioned "sky" room under the dome. Below the coved ceiling are six circular and two semicircular windows which produce an interesting effect.

In looking over the plan of Monticello as it is today, it is at once obvious that the hall (24 by 32 feet) and the parlor (24 by 28 feet 6 inches) are the only rooms large enough for formal entertainment. It is highly probable, therefore, that either or both of these rooms may on occasion have served a dual purpose, especially in the matter of banquets, balls, or receptions. Whether this is so or not, the fact remains that in spite of inadequate stairs and diminutive rooms, Monticello is as fascinating for its architecture as for its history, and for the remarkable mind that conceived it as much as for the interiors where comfort takes precedence over display.

Towson, Maryland

HAMPTON

A Mansion in the Wilderness

Within one mile of Towson and ten of Baltimore stands Hampton, one of America's most imposing late-eighteenth-century mansions, the elegance of whose interiors suggests that it was designed for something more than simple gracious living.

Building was begun in 1783, at the close of the Revolutionary War, by Charles Ridgely who had inherited not only 2,000 acres of land "in the wilderness" but a prosperous ironworks and the bulk of the family fortune. The design of the mansion apparently was undertaken by Ridgely himself, a much-traveled and erudite gentleman, in consultation with a master carpenter named Jehu Howell, and probably with the help of books on architecture which were then more readily available than architects themselves. The result was an exterior that has a certain nobility and much charm, even though the design details leave something to be desired. Most obvious of these concerns the massive portico with its closed and fenestrated sides, the pillars of which are too far apart, a fault emphasized by the horizontal line of the balcony, and the narrow portal that should be a wide and welcoming front door.

Apart from such things, however, the main building is extremely interesting with its great domed cupola and decorated dormers, the nicely molded chimneys, and the well-scaled vase finials at the roof corners and on the pediments. The solidity of the structure is emphasized by the stucco finish to the stone walls, a feature carried over into the somewhat undersized and irregular wings which house the domestic offices. The only changes made to the house since its construction were the substitution of colored glass for plain in the hall windows, and the replacement of the north portico steps and floor by marble ones in 1867. After being inhabited by the Ridgely family for six generations, Hampton, together with forty-five acres of land, was purchased by the Avalon Trust, and turned over to the National Park Service in 1948. Included

Hampton—one of the most elegant mansions of its day and little changed either outside or in.

The great hall which often served both as a ballroom
and a dining room for 51 persons.

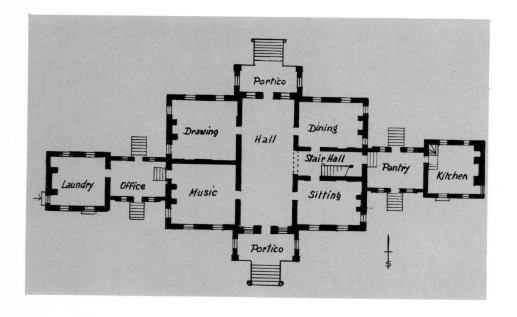

The plan emphasizes the value of
the great hall and minimizes
the importance of the stairs.

OPPOSITE TOP: Two prominent features of the music room are a
portrait of the Duke of Wellington and
an enormous French chandelier.

OPPOSITE BOTTOM: The northeast bedroom, now named the
Needles Bedroom, after the noted Baltimore craftsman
John Needles (1820-1860) who made its forniture.

were many original furnishings and portraits. The Society for the Preservation of Maryland Antiquities was then appointed Custodian and has been responsible for its restoration and furnishing.

Inside the house there are many fascinating architectural details. These, together with the large size of the rooms and their rich furnishings, suggest that Hampton was designed not merely as a comfortable home but also as a background for elaborate entertaining. This might well be expected in the residence of an important family whether its head was engaged in making cannon and shot for the Revolutionary Army or was a general and governor of the state.

Although the balanced façade suggests a Georgian interior, the plan actually goes back at least a hundred years to a time when, in the moderate-sized English mansion, a grand staircase was not its most important feature but was relegated to a side hall. This has some obvious advantages, as is immediately apparent on entering the huge central hall which is 22 feet wide and 53 feet long. This is a room that could serve equally well as a ballroom for state banquets such as some of the succeeding Ridgelys delighted in giving. Unfortunately, the Charles Ridgely who built the house lived only six months after its completion in 1790.

At both ends of the hall there are large windows which leave no room for a wide doorway, but do provide ample daylight under normal conditions. The more important artificial lighting was supplied by a pair of many-branched crystal chandeliers whose place has been taken by equally handsome Waterford pieces. The dignity as well as the beauty of this room is enhanced by the decorative hand-carved woodwork of the cornice, the paneled dadoes, the pilasters, and moldings of the screened-off archway to the stair hall. All five doorways in the side walls have eared architraves and finely paneled doors. The pilasters, incidentally, are fluted and topped by complete architectural orders, and the semicircular fanlights over the exterior doors, added about 1850, display the family crest in varicolored glass.

The hall furniture, which flanks an immense Serape rug, includes a pair of convex mirrors with crystal sconces, both original to the house, and a pair of large, gold-framed Empire mirrors, two Empire love seats, a Hepplewhite serpentine-fronted sideboard, a mahogany tall clock by Benjamin Chandlee of Nottingham, Chippendale and 1820 Sheraton-style side chairs, and a piano by H. Kisting & Sons. Flanking the sideboard is a pair of colorful Chinese warmers. By the south entrance there is an almost life-size portrait of Eliza Ridgely, daughter-in-law of the second owner of Hampton, Governor Charles Carnan Ridgely (1760-1829). This picture is a copy of an original by Thomas Sully (1783-1872), as is a smaller portrait, also in the hall, of the governor himself. The window draperies, suspended under beautifully carved and gilded pelmets, are of silk damask in green and gold which contrasts

One corner of the great hall features a Sully portrait of Eliza Ridgley, daughter-in-law of the governor.

A corner of the music room, featuring a portrait of Mary II, Queen of England, and a harp of Eliza Ridgley's.

OPPOSITE: Black and gold Empire furniture sets the keynote for the palatial drawing room with its impressive architectural detail.

An Hesselius portrait of Charles Ridgley, the builder of Hampton, hangs over the Maryland hunt board in the dining room, which once served as sitting room.

delightfully with the pale gray of the walls and the off-white of the trim.

The black and gold of its Empire furniture sets the keynote for the drawing room, which is almost palatial in its splendor. The architectural details include a pedimented and eared overmantel frame whose tiny dentils are repeated in the shallow mantel, the eared fireplace surround, the room cornice and the heavy window architraves. The door, too, is pedimented, and the windows are balanced by wall niches. Paneling is used to good effect in the inside shutters, the dado, and even the sides of the projecting chimney breast. The draperies are of gold silk damask.

The Empire pieces, which are credited to Phyfe, include a pair of black and gold, marble-topped consoles, a gilded-bronze mounted sofa upholstered in gold with black painted designs on the frame and gold swans on the arms, a round table with a leaf-carved and gilt pedestal and feet, its porcelain-on-marble top exuberantly decorated with a scenic painting. There is also a game table in black lacquer and gold, and a small, black Chinese tilt-top occasional table, its papier-mâché top inlaid with mother-of-pearl.

In contrast, the dining room is almost commonplace yet it too has notable architectural features, and some excellent pieces of furniture. Here is the same dentiled cornice and pediments, though the latter are broken in this case, and the same paneled dado and shutters. An air of richness is supplied by the voluminous silk damask draperies and swags, and a fine "wedding-cake" chandelier with its prisms and globes, which once graced the great hall. Of the three portraits adorning the walls, one of Captain Charles Ridgely, the builder of Hampton, and another of his wife, Rebecca Dorsey Ridgely, are originals by John Hesselius; the third is an unattributed painting of Lafayette, who was a guest of Governor Ridgely at Hampton in 1824.

The massive, two-piece mahogany dining table is a Phyfe

A Turkey carpet and chandelier
are original furnishings
in the north bedroom.

adaptation, but the serving table with tapered and fluted legs is pure Sheraton. The sideboard is an inlaid Sheraton (probably English), flanked by Hepplewhite chairs, whose delicacy contrasts strangely with the Late Sheraton, Gothic-arch-backed chairs made in Baltimore about 1820 and used at the table.

One of the most striking upstairs rooms is the northwest bedroom where most of the pattern is concentrated in the floor-fitting Turkey carpet, which was ordered by Eliza Ridgely from Paris, and the English chintz appliquéd and quilted bedspread. The architectural features of the room were accented by painting the pilasters, the overmantel panel and its flanking pilasters, the fireplace surround and the baseboard, in the same white as the walls and ceiling. The cornice, baseboard, and window architraves and fireplace background are all in a light blue-green. A rather peculiar effect of decapitation has resulted from the painting of the entablature above the pilasters white only up to the cornice which is blue-green—even though that section of the cornice is projected *en ressaut*.

The chandelier in this room is particularly interesting because its body is made of decorated porcelain. This supports three clusters of gilded bronze candle branches, all with prism-laden bobêches. There are only three paintings—one of them an original portrait by Thomas Sully of Eliza Ridgely's husband, John (1790-1867).

The second floor of the mansion is noteworthy because of the elaborate architectural features of the upper hall. Here is no simple cornice but a complete classic order with dentiled cornice, frieze triglyphs and guttae, fluted pilasters, each door and closet opening crowned with a broken pediment, and the dadoes, doors, reveals, and soffits paneled. This in itself constitutes a fitting commentary on the careful design that went into the whole mansion and sets it apart from others of its date which have little to recommend them except old age.

THE WILLIAM CORBIT HOUSE

Architectural Elegance on Appoquinimink Creek

The Corbit House in Delaware
is a pre-Revolutionary architectural gem.

The plan is simple,
the details exquisite.

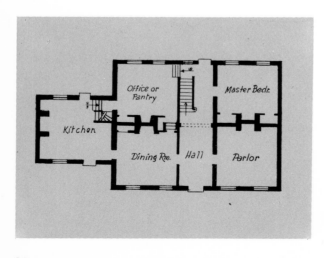

A smiling pre-Revolutionary house that recalls the flavor of its times—a mansion so much "all of a piece" inside and out, so warmly inviting that it gives the impression of harboring a host of friendly ghosts—that is the home William Corbit built for himself at Cantwell's Bridge on Appoquinimink Creek, Delaware, in the years 1772 to 1774. A splendid example of Late Georgian architecture, its present excellent condition is largely due to the expertise and enthusiasm of H. Rodney Sharp who, from 1938 on, so skillfully and painstakingly remade it into the house it must have been in its early days.

William Corbit himself was a surprising young man. At twenty-seven he had become master of his trade—the manufacture of leather—and proved himself a shrewd businessman with an urge to cultivate a taste for the better things of life. It is not known who the house's architect was, but undoubtedly Corbit had definite ideas of what he wanted in the way of a residence, having lived in Philadelphia where fine architecture was the concern of every cultivated man, and Abraham Swan's books on the art of building were readily available. In any event the house is a city dwelling in appearance and plan. The exterior decoration is confined to the main façade, and the interior architectural features and joinery are considerably modified from Swan's original, rather flowery designs.

The house itself is of red brick laid in Flemish bond, two and a half stories tall, with a low-pitched hipped roof sporting a massive square chimney on each shoulder, pairs of dormers on three roof slopes, and a balustraded roof deck straddling the ridge. The end of the house facing the highway is a blank wall; the other end has only two upper windows, and these overlook the two-story kitchen wing added in 1790 to replace the original cellar kitchen and provide extra bedroom space. What apparently were lower-floor windows in this end of the house were then converted into connecting doorways which remain to this day.

Importance is given to the hallway by architectural features that complement the furnishings.

The drawing room is the house's most elaborate chamber with its pediments, pilasters, and marble-faced fireplace—a perfect setting for the Chippendale pieces.

Less elaborate, more homelike is the parlor, the Spanish needlework rug and the armchair's brocaded silk repeating the soft moss-green of the walls.

The Pine Room with whitewashed walls and brick tones has a rustically simple aspect all its own.

The main façade of the house proper, facing east, owes much of its beauty to the proportions of its elements which emphasize the horizontal. The molded-brick water table is not continued around the ends, and neither is the heavy granite belt course—an unusual feature of Georgian houses innocent of quoins or corner pilasters against which to stop it. On the other hand, the decorated cornice with its mutules and carved soffit is found on all four sides. The two dormers over the entrance façade differ from the rest by having arched tops with pointed Gothic lights and decorative consoles. Above them the deck rails of intricate latticework add a note of proud gaiety to the whole structure.

The modest eight-paneled door is framed with Tuscan pilasters, the arched fanlight, set deep in the doorway reveal, rising into a mutuled pediment. The lower windows are twelve-over-twelves, the upper ones twelve-over-eights, all crowned with carved granite lintels. Those of the ground floor are flanked by white-painted paneled shutters, the upstairs windows with green louvered blinds—an old Delaware custom that has much to recommend it. Originally, the house was perched on a terrace, with five granite steps down to a road leading to Corbit's tannery and to the boat landing on the creek. The roadway, as well as all but one of the outbuildings—a square brick smokehouse near the kitchen—have long since disappeared.

The elegant main façade of William Corbit's house is no false front. Each room has been designed with the same meticulous attention to detail. And, thanks to the sober treatment of the decorative features, they and the architectural embellishments complement the furnishings rather than overpower them. As a result, each room has a personality of its own, giving the impression of a decorative whole with no violent contrasts or disturbing anachronisms.

The restrained beauty of the details becomes evident on entering the hall. Nicely proportioned, it is given importance by pedimented doorways and a central flat arch with frieze and cornice, supported by fluted pilasters. The mutule-decorated cornice, duplicating on reduced scale that of the house, is carried around the ceiling on both sides of the arch. Here also is a paneled dado which continues on up the stairs. With a white ceiling, dado, and trim, the walls a warm yellow and the rug a mixture of buff, tan, and blue, the hall not only has plenty of reflectance to make the most of available daylight, but provides an unobtrusive yet colorful background for the mahogany pieces, mirror, and oil paintings that furnish it.

Most of the rooms have the same feeling of rich delicacy. The parlor, to the right of the hall, for example, is predominantly pale green, with the same dado, but a molded dentiled cornice and paneled fireplace wall. Fielded paneling of this type, incidentally, is common to all fireplace walls in the house. The overmantel panel is crossetted, as is that around the marble facing below. The cornice dentils likewise are repeated under the mantel shelf. The soft moss-green is also found in a Spanish needlework rug and the brocaded silk of an armchair.

The dining room is quite different from either of these, contrasting the red-brown tones of the fireplace-wall paneling and cupboard, the doors, cornice, and trim, with an eighteenth-century Chinese-pattern wallpaper of creepers and butterflies on a white ground. The wallpaper also fills the space between the baseboard and chair rail, and its green touches are reflected in the silk chair seats and the sixteenth-century Ispahan rug.

On the second floor is the drawing room—the most elaborate chamber in the house. Its formality is emphasized by the pedimented doors and overmantel, the fluted pilasters flanking the fireplace, the paneling formed by applied moldings on the plaster walls, the carved chair rail, the baseboard molding, and the stepped modillions and tiny pierced mutules of the cornice. But even here, evidence of the restraint exercised in modifying these decorative features is obvious when they are compared with Swan's designs. Not only is the ceiling plain, but the cornice and chair-rail moldings are considerably simplified, and a finial is omitted entirely from the overmantel pediment. Nevertheless the room is both large and impressive, occupying the space of one chamber plus the width of the upper hall. Here, again, the ceiling is white, the woodwork blue-green, and on the floor are eighteenth-century Kulah and Ghiordes prayer rugs in myriad yellow tints.

Opening off this room is the southeast bedroom which, like the rest of the private chambers, is comparatively plain. In this one there is a molded cornice, but minus the running fret. The fielded panels of fireplace and wall and doors are dignified, and on the mantel a narrow fret emphasizes its delicacy as against the solidity of the wide mantel facing. Both walls and woodwork are painted blue-green—an effective foil for the dark red raw silk of an armchair and the medley of colors in Oriental-patterned bed hangings.

Since inventories of the house contents were available, the problem of refurnishing the house was simplified, and the interiors today fairly approximate the originals. In the hall, for example, there is an English hanging lamp of 1770, a Georgian looking glass in mahogany with moldings in gold leaf (c. 1760), a marble-topped Queen Anne table, a Queen Anne three-back settee, and Philadelphia Chippendale side chairs—all good and comfortable pieces in keeping with the solid gentility of their surroundings.

The parlor presents a livelier aspect, displaying mostly mahogany pieces against a light green background. There are Queen Anne and early Chippendale chairs, a late-eighteenth-century Philadelphia desk-bookcase with broken pediment and basket finial, a New England pad-footed easy chair, a Philadelphia bird-cage table, an adjustable tripod windshield candlestand with a drawer, and a brass six-branch chandelier.

In the drawing room are two upholstered armchairs—a

In the southeast bedroom walls and woodwork are blue-green, the armchair dark red, the bed hanging a riot of Oriental pattern and hues.

The kitchen is pleasantly inviting with its old pine and pewter around the hearth's segmental arch.

Equally inviting is the dining room with its Chippendale chairs, its Queen Anne table, and ancient Ispahan rug.

Philadelphia-Queen Anne piece in eighteenth-century, pale blue silk brocade and a New York easy chair in blue and white lampas. The side-chair seats also are covered in brocade. There is, in addition, a Queen Anne stool with a cushion of brown velvet. None of these colors seems to clash unduly with either the green of the woodwork or the multicolored Persian rugs. The crystal chandelier is a vase-stem type with eight ogee glass arms, brass sockets, and tall glass globes matching those of the wall sconces. On one wall is a George II gold-leaf, urn-topped filigree mirror—practically the only purely decorative piece in the room. In contrast there is also a plain-looking spinet made in 1791 by Charles Taws of Philadelphia.

The early Chippendale chairs in green silk, and the walnut Queen Anne oval table in the dining room again emphasize the essential restraint of the furnishings of the house, a mood set by the color of the woodwork and the plain paneled doors of the built-in fireplace cupboard.

The creek at the William Corbit house is still there, but the barges and shallow-draft boats no longer bring traffic from the Delaware to the town wharf, and thriving Cant-well's Bridge long ago declined into placid Odessa. As to the mansion itself, its future preservation is assured in the hands of its present owners, the Winterthur Museum.

OPPOSITE: The northwest bedroom contrasts green-gray walls with mulberry curtains and bed hangings.

STRAWBERRY MANSION

Individuality on the Schuylkill

The Philadelphia mansion called Strawberry not only has a fascinating personality arising out of its harmonious combination of architectural styles, but also an interesting history. In 1797-98, William Lewis, a noted Philadelphia jurist, built what is now a part of this mansion on the site of an earlier house called Somerton which was destroyed during the Revolutionary War. It is believed that one chimney wall of Somerton was incorporated in the new building. This new house, which Lewis called Summerville, departed considerably from the Late Georgian style so popular in pre-Revolutionary days, being set low, with an unadorned but balanced façade with end chimneys and a ridge roof. It stood a simple two stories, with a pair of handsome arched dormers, front and rear, to light the attic—a simple country summer home, as Lewis called it. Though built of fieldstone it was stuccoed smooth, the stucco scored to represent ashlar blocks. Long and shallow in plan, with a central hall, it was in recent years given a certain added importance by a pedimented porch with simple round columns and flat pilasters.

In spite of this noncommittal exterior, the interiors displayed some of the more obvious classical revival features then coming into vogue—the wide entrance hall with four arched niches, the delicate arched swag, and curved muntins of the rectangular fanlights over the main and interior doorways, the punchwork decoration of the dado cap, the trailing vine ornament of the cornice, and similar features.

In 1820 the house was acquired by Judge Joseph Hemphill who, five years later, added two three-story flanking wings in the Greek Revival manner to complete the present mansion which was still called Summerville. A major feature of the added wings is the decorative though somewhat monumental parapet with a central panel and flanking scrolls that crown each one of them. The top story is set off by a sill-level stringcourse and a plain frieze, between which the low third-floor windows are located. So well did the new and old units blend

Once a late-Georgian mansion, Strawberry acquired its Greek Revival air through the addition of the parapeted wings.

OPPOSITE: The music room is Greek Revival in period and Empire in style with its pink velvet causeuse below a crystal chandelier.

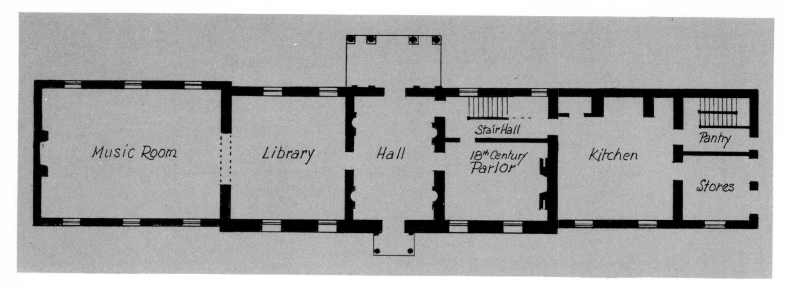

This plan of the present house shows the changes effected by extending the façade. (The Jefferson dining room is over the 18th-century parlor; the Empire bedroom above the music room.

The banquet room has its original parquet floor and French Empire furniture in reproduction.

The Empire bedroom gets its name from the 1810 bed.
The colors are pale green, plum, and gold.

Features of this end of the Empire library
are the display of Tucker ware in an English
Regency cabinet, an 1820 pier table
and trumeau, and upholstered pieces
in black and gold.

The library's southeast corner is dominated
by curtains of lavender and gold against deep
window reveals with paneled shutters
in gray-green and white.

that the mansion acquired not only a certain distinction, thanks to its unusual façade, but grace and dignity besides.

This addition naturally involved some structural changes to the original house, the most important being the elimination of one fireplace between the library and the new music room. Fortunately, it was not necessary to remove the second-floor fireplace since access to the wings was through a rear corridor. Other fireplaces were, of course, added in the new wings. On the main façade, the central block was allowed to project a few inches, breaking up the long face of the building. The center cornice, however, returns slightly at both ends, tying the three units together and giving the entrance section added importance despite its lower elevation. The main façade faces east; to the west is a terrace, the garden, and the Schuylkill River.

Some years after these changes had been made, Hemphill's younger son, Coleman, made a name for himself as a strawberry grower, so that, in 1842, when the property was sold to a Mrs. Grimes and became a dairy farm, strawberries and cream were featured. From this the place became known as Strawberry Mansion. In 1867 the city bought the estate and leased the building as a restaurant for some fifty years thereafter, its wharf being known as Strawberry Landing. In this manner the name Strawberry Mansion has been perpetuated to this day.

The entrance hall is notable for its architectural features, the most prominent of which are the four niches with their projecting bases. Their trim consists of fluted pilasters, below and above the dado, with a keystoned round arch. The base is paneled, the corners decorated with fancy quarter-round molding, and the dado molding which caps it is enlivened with punch-and-gouge work typical of Philadelphia interiors of this period. Besides the eight-paneled front and rear doors, similar but double-leaved ones open into the eighteenth-century parlor on the right and the library on the left. With their delicately molded trim and decorative fanlights the doors add an air of elegance to the hall. Another narrow, louvered-type door gives access to the stair hall at the rear. This is accommodated in a paneled reveal, with a louvered panel in place of a fanlight. All of the wood is painted gray to contrast with the white of the plaster.

The hall furnishings include a handsome hanging lantern of a simple classical design of gilt bronze and clear glass, a pair of English 1810 gilded wood bull's-eye mirrors, two Chippendale side chairs, once the property of George Washington, upholstered in burnt-red silk damask, a colorfully patterned piece of Chinese export porcelain in each niche, and antique Oriental rugs on the pine floor.

In the eighteenth-century parlor, the outstanding architectural accent is provided by the Robert Wellford mantel which has cheeks and facing of Valley Forge marble. The mantel is of wood, with fluted pilasters, its architrave decorated with figures and swags applied in gesso, and the cornice enlivened with punch work. The chair rail, level with the window bottoms, is also decorated with punch work and gouge carving. The simple window trim, with paneled shutters in the reveals, is surmounted by molded wood pelmets, and all this wood, including baseboard and doors, is painted the same soft gray-green as the plaster walls, but the ceiling and cornice are white.

In stunning contrast is the soft salmon color of the curtains which are of a heavy antique satin. In the boldly patterned Oriental rug, the predominant colors are a deep blue and rust on a beige ground. Other color accents are the brilliant burnt-red of the seat pad on a fancy Sheraton painted armchair, and the deep beige of a Sheraton tub chair in brocatelle. There is also a Hepplewhite balloon-back side chair in mahogany, dating from about 1800, and a Sheraton card table below an odd-looking mirror that is probably French. On this table is an Oriental export bowl in porcelain. The tea table here is a Hepplewhite design in mahogany with a single drawer. On it is an English Sheffield-plate hot-water urn, with a teapot, creamer and two cups and saucers of export porcelain. Pieces of English porcelain form the mantel garniture, together with a pair of Sheffield-plate candlesticks.

Still in the William Lewis part of the mansion is the library, now minus a fireplace. The molded cornice is quite simple, as is the window trim with its shallow aprons punch-and-gouge decorated. As elsewhere on this floor, the window reveals accommodate paneled shutters. The background here again is gray-green and white, while the curtains, hung with deep swags, are of lavender satin with a long gold fringe. These hang from gaudy Empire rods adorned with rams' heads at one end and elaborately curled rams' tails at the other. The rug is modern, in a light green with medallions in gold and lavender. Against it, the black and gold Empire sofa in plum-colored satin, and a gilded Empire chair in light blue with yellow and beige stars, form a delightful contrast. There is

In the hallway are four niches enlivened with punch-and-gouge work of the Classic Revival period.

The parlor's main architectural accent is the Robert Wellford mantel with gesso ornaments and marble facings.

A gilt-bronze, clear-globed hanging lantern,
gilt bull's-eye mirrors,
and Chippendale chairs furnish the hall.

also a pair of small Empire side chairs in a fine-cut velvet of green on gold.

The French Empire style is also represented by an 1820 pier table and the mirror over it. The latter is a trumeau type with a reversed gold-leaf picture, plus a pair of three-branched bronze candle sconces. On the table is an epergne of amethyst glass supported by three bronze figures on a marble base. Joseph Hemphill having been a partner of William Ellis Tucker, maker of the fine Tucker porcelain, it is no surprise to find here a handsome English Regency cabinet displaying examples of Tucker chinaware.

Beyond the library is the music room which is distinctly Greek Revival in period and Empire in style, from its Greek-key ceiling decoration and crystal-and-ormolu chandelier to the pink velvet causeuse below it, decorated in gold on white with neoclassic designs. The window surrounds are strongly architectural, painted white, and consisting of pilasters with very flat pediments decorated with egg-and-dart moldings, and repeating the neoclassic motif of the causeuse. The draperies are pink with gold swags and bronze tiebacks and brackets. The black marble mantel also continues the theme with its Ionic colonnettes and square, mirrored overmantel with the emblem across the frieze.

The seated pieces include a pair of gilded armchairs in pink velvet, carved in acanthus and palmetto designs, with griffins as the arm supports, and white-painted chairs and settees with gold accents and flowered-brocade upholstery. Though twin-type Argand lamps stand upon the mantel, for auxiliary lighting dependence is placed upon semicircular iron wall brackets, each holding three candles, with decorative filigree in gold leaf, and crystal drops and swags.

Other equally fascinating rooms which can only be briefly mentioned are the Jefferson dining room, so called because of a letter and portrait of the great man displayed there, the second-floor banquet room, and the Empire bedroom. In Lewis's time the Jefferson room was a bedroom. Today it is gay and light with colonial blue woodwork and white walls, the chairs—reproduction transitional Chippendale-Hepplewhites —in blue and ivory brocade. The sideboard is a New England Hepplewhite, and the table a two-pedestal English type with brass feet and edge-banded in satinwood. The rug is a Kirmanshah in deep blue, wine red, and light blue on beige, and the mantel a nice Wellford with the delicate air of an Adam design.

The banquet room has an original parquet floor, and contains French Empire furniture in reproduction. The dining and sideboard tables have columnar legs with brass trim and heavy bases. The solidity of these pieces and the dark blue-gray mantel with colonnettes is offset by the lively curtains in bright yellow and the gold medallions of the white wallpaper. The saber-legged chairs are likewise lightened by green satin seats with Napoleonic bees in beige and white.

Once a bedroom, the
Jefferson dining room gets its
name from a letter and portrait of
the statesman displayed there.

The bedroom is notable for its French Empire bed (1810) draped in a baldachin of pale green satin with pale blue tassels and plum trim. Its inner side is a deep gold moiré with a woven medallion, matching the bed cover. Other touches of gold are supplied by the ribbed silk of a walnut French chair and tôle urns on the mantel; the walls are also a golden yellow and the ceiling medallion is gilded, as are the baseboard and door trims. The curtains are of a green satin with a maroon braid. A somewhat lugubrious note is struck by a Spanish needlework picture illustrating "Love" and "Death" —a fitting note on which to take leave of lovely, time-bound Strawberry Mansion, one of the fairest of all . . . even in its latest character as a Fairmount Park historic house now restored and open for public inspection.

Garrison, New York
BOSCOBEL

Adam Perfection on the Hudson

Boscobel—America's finest Adam survival, built 1805-1807.

The mansion which States Morris Dyckman began to build at Cruger's Point in 1805 has long been considered by connoisseurs as one of the most beautiful examples of Adam architecture in the United States. In spite of its air of fragility, its slender pillars, its somewhat theatrical swags and tassels, and the fanciful trim of its semicircular pediment window, there is nothing flimsy about the structure of this mansion which has so recently been rescued from an ignominious fate. Some of its timbers are actually among the largest on record, and the construction, in keeping with the Adam design, is without fault. In any event it has withstood more than 160 years of sun and storm, and experienced vicissitudes to which few great houses are ever subjected unless entirely abandoned to ruin and decay.

That this noble house should have reached the point of demolition before being removed, in fragments, to another site, and undergone re-creation so triumphantly forty miles from its original location is hard to believe. Nevertheless, today it stands as proudly as ever on the riverbank at Garrison-on-Hudson, its delicate beauty undimmed thanks to a marvel of reconstruction and restoration, inside and out, performed by its new owners, Boscobel Restoration, Incorporated. Apart from its external appearance, the house is also unusual in that it has a unified personality, as a dwelling in which the interiors are in keeping with the character of the exterior to a greater degree than was customary in formal residences of its day. It was, and once more is, a house made for sunshine, from the glowing exterior with its great windows to its airy, spacious rooms decorated in the Adam manner and made gay with graceful detail and delicate colors. Even the end terraces flanking the main façade are, whether by original design or not, free of overhanging roofs that would have deprived the adjacent rooms of adequate light.

Boscobel was one man's dream which he did not live long enough to enjoy. Staats Morris Dyckman (1755-1806), an

OPPOSITE: Set off by a triple archway, the front hall features a Moorfields carpet in Adam design and ball-type crystal chandelier.

The entrance hall after dark. Sparkling with crystal and enriched by the glowing beige-on-blue Moorfields carpet of Adam design.

OPPOSITE: The music room is 18th-century French. Dyckman's portrait hangs over the mantel.

The music room opens into the drawing room through an arched and fanlighted double doorway. Over the mantel is a portrait of the owner-architect States Morris Dyckman, who died before the building was completed.

85

A striking grouping in the
upper hall is a pair of painted
chairs believed to be by
the Seymours of Boston.

Even this guest room is endowed with an air
of luxury by the colorful patterned fabrics,
a striking tôle chandelier, and yellow-painted
Hudson River dressing table.

American of Dutch descent and apparently of loyalist sympa-
thies, had spent many years in England, and it was during the
last of these extended visits that he planned the mansion he
proposed to build on one of his properties along the Hudson
River. On his return—at which time he anglicized his first
name from Staats to States—he brought with him not only
many of the smaller household furnishings and accessories,
such as silver, glassware, china, and minor pieces of furniture,
but also a clear idea of the plan and structural details of the
house, and even the name, which he had borrowed from an
English mansion of a far different period and style.

A man of cultivated taste and of adequate means, Dyckman
was content with nothing but the best both in the house and
its furnishings. He wanted a home that would not only be
elegant but totally unlike any of its most fashionable neighbors.
And his wife, Elizabeth Corné Dyckman, seems to have con-
curred, judging by the manner in which she condoned his
apparent extravagances. Like others of his class and education
at that time, Dyckman was a competent student of architecture, and he was fortunate in having as cousin a New
York builder, William Vermilye, who was happy to undertake
the construction of Boscobel. Work was begun in 1805, but
Dyckman unfortunately died a year later, leaving the mansion
to be completed according to his ideas by the faithful Vermilye.
Mrs. Dyckman, with their son, Peter Corné, took up residence
at Boscobel in 1807, and the family occupied it for the next
hundred years.

In 1955 the vacant house, whose lands had become public
property, was well on the way to disintegration. Sold to a wrecker,
it was taken apart and removed into storage. Shortly afterward a
group of local residents undertook to salvage the mansion, and
acquired a suitable tract of land on which to re-erect it. From
the stored materials they rebuilt the house on its new site,
and furnished it as close to the original as possible. This job
was considerably simplified by their coming into possession
of an invaluable collection of family papers and records. These
included many invoices for building materials and bills for
the furnishings acquired both in England and America, together with records of purchases of prints and pictures, and
even of seedlings and trees for the gardens. The restoration
was completed in 1961, the plasterwork and other missing
details being duplicated from carefully preserved original
fragments.

Today the house in its new and splendid location stands
pretty much in its original condition, exactly as it appeared
in the later days of its occupation, and as bright and charming as it must have been when it was first erected. There is
the same flat roof with a brick chimney at each corner; the
same decorative parapet rail whose design is repeated in the
balcony of the two-story portico. There, too, are the original
wooden pillars which had been turned in one piece; the narrow,
flush siding; the brackets and swags and Gothic panes in the

OPPOSITE: In the high-ceiled drawing room a vivid
Directoire Aubusson rug sets the stage for the painted Adam
armchairs, the Sheraton shield-backs and mahogany sofa
under a chandelier of amber glass.

The second-floor library opens onto a pillared portico through three floor-to-ceiling windows.

mutule-decorated pediment. Below a dentiled and mutuled cornice on either side of the recessed portico are the two-story pilasters which separate it from the wings into whose great sunken panels the square triple windows are set.

Under the portico roof the tall windows are one sash wide, the upper ones which face to the front extending to the floor to give access to the balcony. Below is the handsome doorway, its semi-oval fanlight spanning the side lights; its trim and the door panels are ornamented with roundels and ovals in Adam design—the whole perched on a four-foot-high foundation of tooled sandstone now half-hidden by plantings and approached by nicely proportioned wooden steps. The two end terraces are at main-floor level, and are retained by stout brick walls surmounted by wooden railings, with wooden steps duplicating those to the front door. The exterior walls are painted a light gray and the trim white, including the edge moldings of the pilasters, emphasizing the architectural quality of the whole façade. The basement, which extends beneath the whole of the main floor, provides space for storage and for servants' quarters, with open-air access by steps at the rear.

The rooms are light and spacious, the first-floor apartments having ten-foot ceilings. This results, among other things, in a charmingly proportioned entrance hall, with two large windows, door side lights and a fanlight, all uncluttered by draperies except for a pair of swagged velvet lambrequins above the windows. So much glass makes possible an almost unrestricted view of the front lawn and the hills beyond West Point across the river. All glass areas, except for the fanlight, have paneled shutters folding back into the window recesses. Below them the front wall is paneled.

From the front hall, two doors give access to the drawing and music rooms and the dining room, and, at the rear, the central grand staircase leads up to the second floor. Within three feet of the stair foot, the front hall is divided from the rear section by a triple archway with Tuscan columns. Between this and the entrance, the hall is almost square, with a ball-type crystal chandelier in the middle of the ceiling centered over a large, square Moorfields carpet. This rug is of Adam design with a circular pattern in tints of beige on a deep blue ground, flower baskets in the corners, and a bound cable border. At either side of the hall is an inlaid Hepplewhite console from England, with an urn-topped pier glass of Adam design above it, and an urn-backed chair at each end. From the central arch hangs a blue-tinted candle globe to light the stairs. The pillars and the trim are white and the walls a pale gray, giving the hall an almost ethereal air.

This hall constitutes an inviting introduction to the rest of the rooms on this floor, most of which carry out the Adam theme. The drawing room, in particular, emphasizes this quality of grace with dignity, and has the further advantage

A small chamber furnished to represent the 1806 tastes and interests of an adopted son, States Brewer Dyckman.

The Ashlar Bedroom, named for the wall finish, has an English bed, India print hangings, and a Phyfe chair which was among the original Boscobel pieces.

of being connected to the music room by an arched and fan-lighted double doorway which is usually open so that the general air of roominess is greatly increased. Each of these rooms contains an excellent example of an Adam mantel, that of the drawing room having attached pillars with paterae and bands of Greek-key ornament, and both with inset Wedgwood plaques. Also in the drawing room is a huge waterfall chandelier, its tall candle globes, crystals, and sparkling ring of prisms all in amber glass. Above the mantel is an especially fine gilt chimney glass with figures in the round.

Other important pieces here are a satinwood-inlaid Sheraton secretary in mahogany, attributed to John Aitken of Philadelphia; a New York mahogany pembroke table; painted English open-arm chairs in the Adam style, satinwood side chairs in flower and medallion designs, and a Sheraton sofa believed to be by Stover & Taylor of New York. The rug is another Moorfields in bright green, beige, and browns.

The music room is given individuality by the Louis XVI painted fauteuils which are quite at home with a tall Muzio Clementi piano, and a Sheraton half-round commode, dated 1800, by John and Thomas Seymour of Boston. The harp is by Evat of London, and the rug is a late eighteenth-century Aubusson, while the portrait over the mantel is of States Morris Dyckman.

The dining room acquires a somewhat regal air from its

LEFT: From the window end, the architectural character of the drawing room is emphasized by the arched opening of the music room with its leaded fanlight and the pedimented frame of the side door.

RIGHT: The drawing room as seen from the music room.

OPPOSITE: A landscape by Thomas Doughty hangs over the fine Adam-style dining room mantel. The pedestal table is English and the shield-back chairs are Hepplewhite with rare pearl and scale carving.

globe-style, eight-branched, crystal-trimmed glass chandelier. This is centered in the yellow-tinted ceiling whose step-molded cornice is painted white along with the trim. The wide triple window, which extends almost the width of the room, has very heavy mullions dividing the main sash from the side lights. It is given extra importance by the outer stiles which are treated as pilasters, and the deep window head with its carved Adam decoration, all projecting from under the plaster cornice.

On the opposite side of the room is the newly retrieved original Dyckman sideboard made by one Robert Wallace, "joyner at the sign of the Three Trees in Beaver Street." Around the mahogany twin-pedestal dining table are Hepplewhite shield-back chairs which were made in New York in 1790, and are now upholstered in a dark blue fabric trimmed with silver nails set in swag form. These, and the mahogany board set with a Herculaneum dinner service in the urn design with blue borders on white, make a brave showing, and typify the taste and quality of the whole interior where the early atmosphere has been recaptured as well as the style.

Elizabeth Corné Dyckman's bedroom. Over the mantel hangs a portrait of the Dyckmans' son, Peter Corné.

93

Chillicothe, Ohio
ADENA

Seductive Simplicity on the Scioto

Adena from the southeast,
simple but substantial in its
stone and slate exterior.

Architecturally chaste to a point of severity, Adena is one of Ohio's earliest mansions and among the most important historically. It was designed by none other than architect Benjamin Henry Latrobe for Thomas Worthington, a native of Virginia and man of culture and substance who moved to Chillicothe in 1798 when the town was a mere two years old and he a distinctly mature benedict of twenty-five. Eight years later the erection of the twenty-room stone mansion was begun by two masons from Virginia—the Morris brothers—and completed a year and a half later in 1807. In 1803 Worthington had become one of the first two United States Senators from Ohio, beginning a distinguished political career that was to include two terms as governor. He had also found time to accumulate a large estate while adding substantially to his already sizable fortune.

The house was built on wooded high ground with magnificent views of the Scioto Valley and the distant foothills of the Alleghenies. It is a two-story structure of locally cut freestone whose mottled yellow-brown, under a later blue slate roof, comes to warm and vibrant life in the sun. Of great simplicity, it has neither quoins nor modillioned cornice to suggest Georgian aspirations—only balanced façades, the principal one partly hidden by corner wings, reduced in significance by a single-story porch between them, but saved from mediocrity by the dignified informality that careful design and sturdy solidity of construction can give.

Between the wings is an impressive raised "courtyard" with flagged paths and lawns, enclosed within the sweeping curve of an iron-railed stone wall. Both the main block and wings are crowned with bold hipped roofs and massive stone chimneys between which a flat deck is all that remains of the original balustraded captain's walk which is accessible from the attic.

The interiors are free from architectural embellishment except for some of the fireplace mantels and the paneled dado

The house's impressive main façade with its columns,
massive wings, and roof deck.

As befits a house designed
by Benjamin H. Latrobe,
Adena's plan is compact,
convenient, and totally suited
to the family's needs.

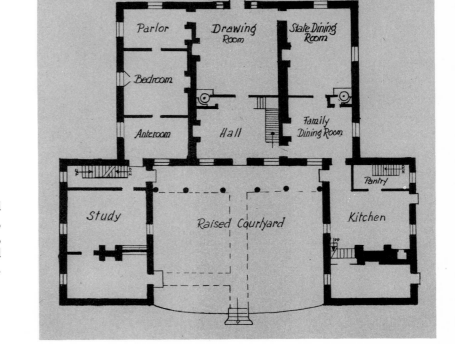

In the state dining room, where architectural detail is minimized, color is emphasized, the walls painted a light gray-green, the ceiling blue-green, and the woodwork white.

of the family dining room. In spite of this, most of the rooms are positively enchanting, thanks to the décor and furnishing which leave little to be desired.

The plan is interesting for a number of reasons, one of which is that it is distinctively "different." From the courtyard, the entrance door opens into a large hall, wider than it is long. To one side is a fireplace; at the other the main staircase, and, between them, a doorway to the drawing room centered in the south façade. To the right, along the next wall, are the two dining rooms—a larger one for state occasions, a smaller one for the family.

At the other side of the hall there is a small anteroom leading to the master bedroom from which another door opens into a tiny parlor. The thing to note here is that access to this parlor is possible only through the bedroom or the drawing room, and that guests can enter the state dining room from the drawing room, while the servants reach the state dining room from the kitchen via the family dining room. The kitchen is located nearby, in the west wing, the east wing being devoted to what was the study, library, and personal office of Governor Worthington. Both the kitchen and study wings have other doors to the exterior.

A useful feature in the case of both the drawing room and the state dining room is the installation in a corner of door-high dumbwaiters—revolving shelves reminiscent of Jefferson's Monticello—by which beverages and food can be passed through without the servants entering the rooms. Upstairs, the floor space was originally divided into two sections by a through wall. On one side are two bedrooms, reached by a stair from the study hall; on the other are three bedrooms and a boxroom, a great deal of space being taken up by a landing from the main stair. The two basement rooms, one under each wing, were reached by steps from the kitchen-wing pantry and the study passage. In all, there are eleven fireplaces in the main block served by two large chimneys. The wings contain four fireplaces, both kitchen and study having a small additional room with an exterior door.

In spite of their lower roofs (and ceilings) the wings do have an upper floor, that over the kitchen wing being set aside as a lumber room, the other dedicated to spinning and weaving—activities one would suppose not particularly conducive to study on the floor below! This floor plan carries out the impression given by the exterior view, of compactness and efficiency, even though closet and storage space was unimportant when movable wardrobes were the fashion.

The Worthingtons had ten children, and although Thomas died in 1827, Adena remained in the family until 1903. At that time it was acquired by George Hunter Smith, whose daughter, Elizabeth S. Fetterolf, presented it to the state in 1946. Since that time the Ohio Historical Society has accomplished the restoration and furnishing of the mansion much as it was in the period 1806-1815, thanks largely to the vast amount of documentary evidence available and the gifts of original furniture pieces by descendants of the family.

Records indicate that most of the original furniture of Adena was American-made, in the Sheraton or Hepplewhite styles, though original pieces retrieved included later items by Phyfe. Actually, some original pieces, from chairs to clock cases, were

Looking into the state dining room from the family dining room: the latter's walls are a dusty teal blue, the dado and trim natural walnut.

In the drawing room, the woodwork is white, the ceiling blue-gray, the rug a bold patterned Kirmanshah on a background of ruby red.

made by local craftsmen, while smaller items, such as some of the silverware and mirrors, were imported. These have all been duplicated as far as possible, and the draperies made from antique fabrics typical of the period.

Some of the original wallpapers were purchased in Baltimore in 1808, and these are represented by French and American reproductions of authentic period designs which do not clash with the colors of the original paints. On this basis the interiors have regained their old-time charm and distinction.

Although there is very little interior architectural detail, the decoration more than compensates for this lack. In the entrance hall, for example, the ceiling is a dark blue-gray, and the wallpaper, in mauve and white, has a classical border resembling a carved cornice. Here, as elsewhere in the house, there is a chair rail. This is painted the same apple green as the trim and stair paneling, with the baseboards in a blue-black. The doors are white as are the stair risers, but of the twin handrails only one is in polished cherry, as is the single newel post; the other handrail is walnut. This is the only place in the house in which cherry wood was used except for the revolving shelves, most of the wood being native walnut.

The hall furniture consists of an original Philadelphia Sheraton sofa upholstered in an eggshell-striped silk damask; one Hepplewhite shield-back chair with seat covered in striped satin (1785); an exceptional Sheraton mahogany console table; and a mahogany tall clock by Elnathan Taber, Simon Willard's famous apprentice.

In the drawing room the most decorative feature is wallpaper in two shades of gray and mauve with white highlights, simulat-

The northwest bedroom is made gay with colorful chintz bed and window hangings, and oval braided rug.

OPPOSITE: The drawing room's most decorative feature is the wallpaper in two grays with white highlights. The border represents tasseled swags in grays, blues, and black.

A wallpaper with a dark rose pattern on a parchment ground and a rug of dark blue, gray, and pale green on a dark red field contrast beautifully with the study's olive-green woodwork.

ing drapery panels. This is carried from baseboard to ceiling (ignoring the chair rail) where the deep border, in grays and blues and black, represents tasseled swags—the whole thing a massive trompe-l'oeil. The woodwork is white, the ceiling blue-gray, the rug a large bold-patterned Kirmanshah, with ruby red the predominant color. Additional color is added by the upholstery fabric of a Sheraton sofa made by Phyfe—brick-red stripes on an ivory ground. Over this is a portrait of Thomas Worthington's eldest sister, Mary W. Tiffin, with Sheffield silver-plate triple sconces of English make (1785) flanking it. Here also are a pair of Sheraton inlaid card tables serving as consoles. In addition there is an original round Hepplewhite card table, and a small Chippendale mahogany tilt-top made in the East about 1795. The most imposing piece, however, is a Hepplewhite mahogany secretary made by Henry Connelly of Philadelphia around 1805.

The mantelpiece is of a simple paneled design in wood, with a facing of marble from Pennsylvania. Over the mantel is a gold-framed portrait of Thomas Worthington as he was at the time of his marriage in 1796. On either side is a gilt, Adam-style mirror made in England about 1780. The chairs are a somewhat varied lot, but strangely compatible—Sheraton lattice-backs by Connelly (1805) with round seats upholstered in beige broché, a Hepplewhite shield-back similar to the one in the entrance hall, a pair of Martha Washington-style Hepplewhites from Virginia in red satin broché, and a Sheraton mahogany armchair, also by Connelly (1805), with the seat in striped lampas.

The state dining room offers quite a contrast, the only similar feature being the fireplace. The walls are painted a

OPPOSITE: In Adena's drawing room wallpaper simulating drapery panels makes up for the lack of architectural detail.

The upstairs bedroom boasts
of matching Sheraton bed canopy and
window draperies, the bedspread duplicating
the reds, greens, and blues on a
white ground.

light gray-green, the ceiling blue-green, and the woodwork white. The rug is a Kirmanshah in an all-over flower pattern of reds, tans, and greens; the draperies are green silk damask. There is an overmantel portrait of Julia Galloway, daughter-in-law of Thomas Worthington. Flanking the mantel are a pair of Sheraton mahogany console tables with reeded legs, and above them a pair of gilt English Hepplewhite mirrors with sconces (c. 1780). The dining table is of a transitional Hepplewhite-Sheraton style in mahogany with a deep apron and turned reeded legs, thought to be a Phyfe piece dated about 1805. The sideboard is a mahogany breakfront in the Hepplewhite manner of the same date but made in Virginia.

In the family dining room, next door, the walls are a dusty teal blue, the dado and trim in natural walnut. This is the only room with unpainted woodwork and the effect is striking. The downstairs bedroom has white walls and ceiling, with the woodwork a rose-tan, and, like the rest of the bedrooms, is quite plain. The bed is a Hepplewhite mahogany tall-post style (1785) with flat tester-type hangings and a dust ruffle of yellow bourette, and the antique spread is of trapunto quilted white cotton. The window draperies match the canopy, and here is one of the only two windows with a gate-type window bottom, known as a window door, giving access to the garden.

Outside the mansion the only surviving building was the smokehouse. The washhouse was rebuilt in 1953 and plans are underway to rebuild the other outbuildings. This also applies to the walks, terraces, and gardens which contain a 125-year-old arbor vitae supposed to have been planted by Mrs. Worthington, as well as ancient catalpa trees. Forty varieties of roses known before 1830 are already growing here, together with boxwood hedges, all of which help to restore the early nineteenth-century atmosphere of one of the most interesting great houses of the Midwest.

The downstairs bedroom possesses one
of the two window-doors leading to the garden.

103

OPPOSITE: Over the state dining room mantel is a portrait
of Worthington's daughter-in-law. English mirrored sconces and
Sheraton card tables flank the fireplace.

Charleston, South Carolina
THE NATHANIEL RUSSELL HOUSE

The Fine Adam Mansion of "The King of the Yankees"

The handsome central doorway of the Russell House with its semicircular hood and oval fanlight, with a filigree of wrought iron above.

Probably the South's finest town house of the Federal period is the Nathaniel Russell mansion, which owes much of its charm and beauty to the influence of the then popular Adam style. This house was built during Charleston's post-Revolutionary era of prosperity which came to an end with the War of 1812. Russell, son of a Chief Justice of Rhode Island, had moved to Charleston about 1769 at the age of thirty-one, and in due time became one of the city's wealthy merchants. Because of his activities in organizing a group of Charlestonians of New England origin he was elected first president of the New England Society, becoming popularly known as "The King of the Yankees."

Prior to 1800 it was the custom for leading merchants of Charleston to live above their business premises opposite the wharves on East Bay. With the turn of the century, thanks to a general prosperity, many of them began building dwellings in more fashionable quarters, and in about 1807 Russell decided to follow suit. At this time, architectural and decorative innovations introduced by the brothers Adam of London had taken a firm hold in Charleston. Fortunately, the local architect-builders were competent to handle the structural and decorative problems involved in the provision of round and oval rooms and spiral staircases, and to assess the possibilities of delicate, low-relief plaster ornaments grafted to the chaste Federal interiors. And so the new house was built with its main floor at ground level, its shorter façade to the front, its entrance narrowed by eliminating side lights, and the building with its eaves parapet made a frank three stories tall.

The handsome central doorway with its semicircular hood and oval fanlight has but one window on either side of it. Above it is a filigree of wrought iron forming the second-floor balcony which runs the width of the façade. The second floor, one room wide and three deep, caters to the summer breezes, its ceiling two feet higher than those of the other floors, and its floor-level windows giving access to the balcony. On the

The South's finest town house of the Federal period—its main floor at ground level, its shorter façade to the front.

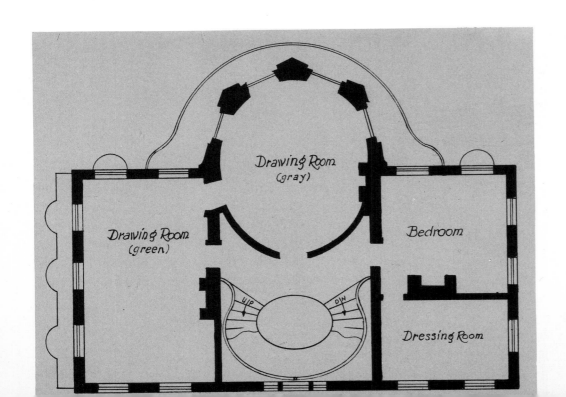

Drawing Room
(gray)

Drawing Room
(green)

Bedroom

UP

DN

Dressing Room

The Adam influence is seen in the oval rooms and spiral staircase, as indicated in the plan of the second or principal floor.

105

Even the elaborate door frames conform to the contours of the rounded walls, as in this hall.

In the rounded end of the library, three tall windows successively capture the day's sunlight.

south façade three great oval rooms, stacked one above the other, make their presence obvious by ballooning out from the center section, and carrying with them a generously proportioned semicircular iron balcony at second-floor level. Instead of following the interior curve of the rooms, however, the outside of this three-foot-thick wall has five flat faces so that it is semi-octagonal in shape. Surprisingly enough, these large rooms still leave plenty of space between them and the north wall for a wide hall and its soaring elliptical stair. Beyond this point the house is still one more room deep, and two wide, providing three principal rooms to a floor.

The external walls are of brick and the entrance façade, though narrow and tall, is beautiful in composition, each floor having its own attractive features and contrasting interestingly with the others. All window trim is set well into the reveals, except for the projecting stone sills of the first and third floors. The main entrance, though slender in proportion, is given importance by the projecting stiles and cornice and the hood with its molded ribs and keystone. The deep door reveals are paneled, with fluted pilasters decorating their front edges. The door itself has eight panels and all the woodwork is painted white, as is the window trim.

Close above the fanlight arch is the front balcony, curving outward at each of the three windows, and close below it is a brick stringcourse. These and the high balcony rail help to cut down the apparent height of the second-story windows whose tallness is emphasized by the arched recesses into which they are set. Each window is crowned by a winged stone lintel, while the arches, springing from a lipped stone stringcourse (interrupted by the recesses) have keystones of their own. Just above the arches is a twin stringcourse of brick. With all these horizontal lines played off against the vertical ones, the total effect is one of good proportion, combined with structural strength and solidity.

Interest amounting to fascination begins immediately on entering the stair hall, which, as might be expected, is dominated by the stair itself. This sweeps upward in a wide arc to each floor landing in turn, entirely independent of the walls for support. This separation of stair and wall makes it possible for a window to be included in the rear wall at each inter-floor level, thus flooding the hallway and the stair with light. The flowing curves of the twin mahogany banisters terminate in tight spiral clusters of the plain, square balusters instead of the usual ornate newels, emphasizing the purity of line that needs no decoration.

Opposite the stair is the convex wall of the oval drawing room, in which is centered the curved doorway with its deeply carved stiles supporting a frieze decorated in relief, and a projecting cornice. Against this background, the few pieces of furniture, and a small but colorful Oriental rug, make an agreeable pattern, in which a mahogany tall clock balances a large mahogany-framed portrait hung above a late Sheraton-

OPPOSITE: Up from the hall—the flying staircase is a work of art, illuminated by a great triple window two-thirds the way to the second floor.

While most of the interiors are architecturally elegant and demand no hangings or window draperies, the latter are used in the dining room to good effect.

The Green Drawing Room with its seven windows where full opportunity has been taken of the possibilities for architectural elaboration.

style railback settee. Other pieces in the group are Sheraton lattice-back chairs of the same period and a tilt-top pedestal table of Regency flavor.

While most of the interiors are architecturally elegant and demand no hangings or window draperies, the latter are used in the dining room to good effect. Entered from the stair hall, this room also has double doors opening onto the garden, with a large rectangular fanlight which adds to the daylight illumination of three large windows. After dark, the light is provided by twin crystal chandeliers, augmented by tall silver candelabra and candles in hurricane globes. The architectural features of this room are confined to a simple plaster cornice, paneled dado and shutters, all painted a creamy white. These stand out well against the deep yellow of the plaster walls which, in turn, contrast pleasantly with the citron yellow of the satin draperies whose fringes and tasseled cords are of a peacock blue. This blue, incidentally, closely matches that in the antique Feraghan rug.

The mahogany furniture is a blend of American and English pieces including a deep-cupboard-type Hepplewhite butler's sideboard, a three-part Hepplewhite inlaid dining table, circular card tables of the same style serving as consoles between the windows, and a set of Adam chairs in peacock blue and gold silk damask—altogether a room of true eighteenth-century classic elegance.

OPPOSITE: Important features of the Green Drawing Room are the gray marble fireplace, a handsome brass firebasket, and an antique Aubusson in beige and terra-cotta.

Since it is customary in these Southern mansions to utilize the lighter and airier second story for summer living and more formal entertainment, it is no surprise to find the Russell mansion with two drawing rooms on this floor. Of these the rectangular drawing room is the larger and more stately with its seven windows affording opportunities for extensive architectural elaboration. This room is called the Green Drawing Room because of the deep Adam green of the plastered wall areas and the lighter, faintly contrasting green of the woodwork.

This interior is a splendid example of the Adam style, treated with exceptional restraint—including a plain white ceiling. The deep cornice is elaborately patterned, and each of the window architraves carries a frieze in the urn-and-swag pattern and a decorated modillioned cornice complete with dentils. The pilasters are built up of twin fluted colonnettes boxed in with separating fillets, and terminating in acanthus carvings of the same diameter. At its lower end the box rests upon three balls on a base block—a definitely unusual design detail. These window surrounds and the similar double-door frame are tied together by a paneled dado with a carved top rail. The Adam mantel is of wood, with fluted Ionic colonnettes and swag-decorated architrave with a modeled center panel.

The carpet is an antique Aubusson in beige and terra-cotta, the latter tone being picked up by the scagliola tops of two tables and a pair of paintings. The chandelier is a rather simple pattern of wire-strung crystal beads and drops, with ormolu in Directoire fashion. On the wall between windows are a pair of dignified yet dainty parcel-gilded mirrors with filigrees of husks and flowers in the Hepplewhite manner. Below them are more Hepplewhite card tables.

The oval drawing room on the second floor, known as the Gray Room because of its light gray walls and darker woodwork, has an equally elaborate frieze and cornice though of a vastly different design, made up largely of geometric figures and stepped curves. The window and door entablatures, however, are almost duplicates of those in the Green Drawing Room, but the stiles are in the form of narrow, flat panels with fine horizontal reeding. Some moldings are ornamented with gold leaf. Here also is an Adam mantel of wood with an extra-wide fireplace facing of white marble. The colonnettes are of a fluted Corinthian pattern, with frieze decorated with paterae, and the central panel and ends with low-relief figures.

The general atmosphere of this early nineteenth-century house reflects late eighteenth-century taste as well as the current styles in furniture and décor of its own period. That such have been combined without detracting from the homogeneous atmosphere of elegance and good taste is no small compliment to the knowledge and skill of the restorers, the Historic Charleston Foundation, into whose hands it passed after a varied career since 1867 as a girls' school, convent and, again, a private home in 1956.

The first-floor bedroom has walls of Wedgwood blue, a four-poster in white figured muslin, and a fine Chinese rug.

OPPOSITE: The Gray Drawing Room, with an overmantel painting by Francesco Albani, a Phyfe sofa, and a Carabaugh rug of 1800.

FARMINGTON

A Historic House Planned by Jefferson

Octagonal rooms in the Adam manner and tiny hidden stairways constitute Thomas Jefferson's signature to the fourteen-room mansion near Louisville called Farmington. Master builder Edward Shippen, however, took liberties with details, thus endowing it with Kentucky characteristics and adding to its charm and individuality.

In 1808, John Speed, a widower of Danville, Kentucky, with two young daughters, married Lucy Gilmer Fry, whose Virginia family was intimately acquainted with the Jeffersons. Eight months later the building of Farmington was begun on land near Louisville that was awarded John's father, Captain James Speed, for services in the Revolutionary War.

During the building of the house the Speeds lived in a log cabin on the plantation which eventually comprised 1,500 acres. Most of the structural materials were derived from the land—ash trees were felled for the flooring, poplar for paneling; clay was dug and fired for brick and floor tile, and limestone burned to make mortar and plaster. And, as the building went up, the country craftsmen carved Kentucky variations into classic designs of the Federal period, as the doorways and mantels bear witness.

Completed in 1810, the house is of brick, one story high above a raised basement, with a hipped roof, and a portico of tall, slender wooden pillars supporting a pediment with an elliptical window in its tympanum. The symmetrical façade has tall windows and a wide entrance, the semicircular fanlight over the door being set into a blind elliptical arch that extends over the door side lights. This fanlight is repeated over the door from the front hall into the back hall, and again over the rear door. The basement has an eight-foot ceiling with windows above ground level. The first-floor ceilings are fourteen feet high except for the back hall which drops to eleven feet to preserve the beautiful proportions of the interior. All windows have flat brick arches and the trim is set into reveals.

Kentucky variations of classic Federal designs are featured in the impressive main entrance to Farmington.

OPPOSITE TOP: The octagonal parlor showing the 5½-octave piano, an English harp, and a New York coin-silver tea service of 1800

OPPOSITE BOTTOM: A corner of the Blue Room with a 1780 wing chair, a 1790 bow-front chest, and the American pencil-post bed in blue and white print.

The raised basement and deep portico give the house an air of distinction.

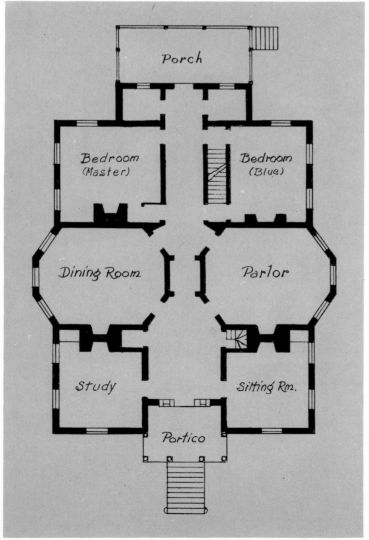

Plan of the elevated main floor, showing central through-hall.

Portraits of John Speed (1772-1840), who built Farmington in
1810, and his wife, Lucy Gilmer Fry Speed (1788-1874).

The spacious portico with its four pillars and two pilasters
projects four feet and is recessed four feet. Its walls are stuccoed
smooth and painted a soft green to set off the white door
surround and fanlight arch. Entry to the basement is through
a side door under the portico, as well as from below the wooden
rear porch.

With the house facing southwest, the northwest and southeast façades are characterized by the projecting angular bays
of the two octagonal rooms occupying the central portion of
the house. At the rear there is a lower rectangular projection
accommodating two small rooms and the entrance to the
narrow rear hall. The wooden porch is attached to this
projection.

The room arrangement is quite symmetrical, with an entrance hall the same width as the portico, and a room on
either side, each containing a fireplace in the rear wall. Opening off the hall at this point are twin recesses with doors, one
of which opens into a closet, the other revealing a very small
stairway to the front part of the basement.

Past this point, the walls of the hall, which separate it from
the two octagonal rooms, slope inward to a narrow and short
passage connecting the front hall with the much narrower
rear one and continuing through to the rear door. Beyond
the octagonal rooms are two square rooms, one of them reduced in width by the rear stairways to the basement and the

Pride of the octagonal dining room
is this English Sheraton sideboard, formerly owned
by President Zachary Taylor.

View through the house from the front hall,
showing the four American Sheraton
side chairs in blue satin and the Anatolian rug.

This English wooden birdcage (1700)
on its New Orleans iron bracket (1800)
is a feature of the sitting room.

attic. The purpose of the two small rooms in the tiny rear
wing is unclear but they may have been intended for children since they adjoin the large bedrooms. One important
feature of this room arrangement was that, in summer, opening the front and rear doors, and the one in the connecting
passage, would permit ventilation of the octagonal and rear
rooms, all of which have two doors opening into the hall
and are equipped with fanlights.

The basement floor is, of course, similar in plan, but the
rooms may have differed in purpose before the early outbuildings were done away with. It is interesting to see, however,
that the connecting passage here becomes a closet, closed off
from the front part of the house, suggesting that this area
was reserved for the family—probably as bedrooms since the
Speeds ended up with eleven children. The rear section was
reserved for a pantry, kitchen, and the inevitable dirt-floored
wine cellar and storage rooms.

As is usual in these historic houses, some of the earlier
furniture being unavailable, substitutions have been made as
near to the originals as possible. In this instance, all the furniture dates before 1825, with the exception of draperies and
chair coverings which nevertheless are of the correct period as
to fabric and design.

In the entrance hall the great thickness of the front wall can
be gauged from the depth of the cupboards under the door

side lights. This hall, because of its proportions, smooth off-white walls, white trim, and lack of cornice, is splendid in its simplicity. In the center of the plain ceiling hangs a brass chandelier with a vase stem and ball, and six glass-shielded candle sconces. Serving as consoles are a pair of English mahogany card tables of 1790 vintage with satinwood inlays. There are also four American Sheraton side chairs in pale blue satin and an Anatolian rug in beige with a flower pattern and red border. Off the hall to the right is the octagonal parlor, a decorator's dream with café-au-lait walls, and trim to match the mantel's off-white. The draperies are of English cotton damask of a French design in copper. This color contrasts delightfully with an antique Mahal rug in beige and rust. The New York-made Sheraton sofa, with its carved, rayed back panels, exposed arms, and frame with carved rosettes, is upholstered in brown, rust and yellow to match the rugs. One of the two Martha Washington 1790 chairs is covered in the same damask as the draperies, the other in a beige damask. There is also a pair of English Regency black-and-gilt side chairs with gold striped seats. Wall decorations are confined to a portrait of William Starling, a hero of the Revolutionary War, painted by Matthew Harris Jouett in 1817; a 1780 oil painting, *The Lesson*, by an artist of the Boston school; and an English needlework picture (c. 1740).

An especially interesting item is the London-made piano of

An interesting duo—the Sheraton child's chair screws to the table to make a high chair. The miniature pewter set belonged to the Speed family.

Against café-au-lait walls and white trim of the parlor stands a New York-made Sheraton sofa, under a Boston School painting, *The Lesson*, of 1780.

Also in the parlor is a Willard banjo clock of 1815 and an American Sheraton desk, circa 1800.

five and a half octaves—the extra octave making it possible to play certain Mozart and Haydn symphonies written for four hands. The only other instrument here is the English harp, signed "Meyer," which dates from 1735. Other pieces of note include a Baltimore oval-top table in mahogany with satin-wood inlay (c. 1790); a cherry drop-leaf table with fret ends from Virginia; an American Hepplewhite desk of 1780 from New York State, and a small, round snake-foot cherry table dated 1800.

Across the narrow connecting passage is the octagonal dining room whose walls are painted a warm gray-green with off-white trim. This background is vastly enlivened by formal draperies in gold cotton damask and two small antique rugs—one an Oriental of indeterminate vintage, the other a Bergama of rich and vivid color from Asia Minor. The sideboard, dining table, and chairs are all in mahogany and of Sheraton design, the sideboard having been brought from England by a member of Zachary Taylor's family around 1810.

Down the rear hall, beyond the parlor, is the Blue Bedroom, so named because of the soft gray-blue of its woodwork—the window architraves and sash bars and muntins, the dado, room and closet doors, and fireplace mantel. The walls are cream-colored, as are the fringed English linen curtains. These curtains, however, have "Medway" pattern print valances in cream and a blue pattern, matching the canopy of the 1780 pencil-post bed of mahogany-stained birch.

Among the furniture pieces are a bow-fronted chest of drawers in cherry and curly maple, marked "W. Flint." On the walls are a bird print by Mark Catesby and a pair of English prints—one by W. Dickenson dated 1784.

Equally varied are the contents of the sitting room to the right of the front hall. These curtains also are set into the architraves—a documentary toile in a variety of colors on a beige ground, separated by the off-white trim from the muted

This parlor group includes an English,
5½-octave piano, a New York or
New Jersey Chippendale wing chair, a
coin-silver tea set of 1810, and
an English Regency black-and-gilt side chair.

The parlor fireplace mantel
is of local design.

The walls of the octagonal dining room are a warm
gray-green with off-white trim; the draperies gold cotton damask;
the rugs Oriental—one a Bergama. Sheraton sideboard
and chairs are English, circa 1800.

The cream-colored fringed English-linen curtains
of the Blue Bedroom have valances in cream and blue
to match the 1780 pencil-post bed's canopy.

turquoise of the walls. The rug is another Kermanshah. The
only large pieces of furniture are a walnut secretary of 1770
with paneled doors from Virginia, and a cherry highboy, dated
twenty-five years later, from Lancaster, Kentucky. There is
also a Martha Washington worktable that once belonged to
the family of Thomas McKean of Delaware, a signer of the
Declaration of Independence.

With such things the Speed family must have been fully
familiar because of the circles in which they moved. One son,
Joshua, went from college to operate a store in Springfield,
Illinois. He became a lifelong friend of Abraham Lincoln who,
in 1841, spent three weeks at Farmington with the family.
Another son, James, became Attorney General in Lincoln's
cabinet, and was with the President when he died. It is such
associations that add to the fascination of Farmington and help
bring its history to life. This the members of the Historic
Homes Foundation, its present owners, must have realized
when they embarked upon this splendid job of restoration.

The Yellow Bedroom has a Kentucky
cherry chest of drawers, a child's tôle bathtub
of 1830, Windsor bow-back chairs and cradle.

Combining English Regency and Grecian detail,
the architect of the Owens-Thomas House
grafted lightness and gaiety onto dignity.

Nothing appeals to the viewer's
sense of beauty as much as the
cast-iron balcony
on the house's south side.

Savannah, Georgia

THE OWENS-THOMAS HOUSE

English Regency in the South

Genius was at work when William Jay, a young English architect, designed what is now known as the Owens-Thomas House in Savannah for Richard Richardson in 1816. In doing so he took architectural liberties that turned into triumphs in combining English Regency with Grecian detail and grafting lightness and gaiety onto dignity. In replacing the Late Roman of the Adam brothers with the Hellenic he anticipated the more formal Greek Revival style without running it into the ground, securing beauty with originality in both exterior and interior. Building was begun in 1817 and completed two years later.

The Owens-Thomas House and grounds occupy a city block facing on Oglethorpe Square, an estate that was bought by George Welchman Owens in 1830. The Owens family occupied the house for the next 121 years. When George Owens's granddaughter, Miss Margaret Gray Thomas, died in 1951, she bequeathed it together with many of the furnishings to the Telfair Academy of Arts and Sciences. The Academy then appointed the Owens-Thomas House Committee to renovate the building and gardens and complete the furnishing with pieces approximating the originals.

In true Regency manner, Jay covered his tabby and brick walls with stone-tinted stucco, and formed stucco architraves around the lower windows, setting the upper ones into recessed arches. The projecting stringcourse was made a prominent feature by adding bands and moldings below it in the manner of a cornice and a frieze. This is carried right around the building, taking in the flat roof of the curved Ionic portico that shelters the main entrance. From the portico sides stone steps descend in sweeping curves toward the balustraded garden wall of stuccoed brick.

At the rear of the mansion, twin octagonal bays flank a porch with two Ionic columns and two matching pilasters, but nothing appeals to the viewer's sense of architectural beauty so much as the balcony on the house's south side. Iron, ap-

The stairs of bog oak have mahogany banisters inlaid with brass; to the second floor the balusters are of painted iron representing wood.

The drawing room is notable for its striking and unusual decorative details.

parently, was Jay's favorite structural material both for exterior and interior use. In this balcony it certainly produced results that would have been difficult to achieve in any other material except wood, especially as regards the fine details.

The base of the balcony consists of four tall cast-iron pillars in the form of curling acanthus-leaf scrolls resting on stuccoed plinths. On them is set the balcony floor, and, above that, four fluted cast-iron columns of the Composite order. These, and a pair of cast-iron pilasters, in turn support an architrave, frieze and cornice, with a cresting of stylized honeysuckle and dagger-shaped pendants below. Cast-iron rails of a delicate design are installed between the columns, and spear-motif garden railings extend behind the acanthus-scroll castings. It was from this balcony that General Lafayette, a guest of the town, addressed the citizens in 1825.

Originally it was planned to duplicate the balcony on the southwestern side of the house, but the ironwork, shipped from France, was lost along with the ship in an Atlantic storm.

The low-pitched roof of the house is largely hidden by a parapet of stuccoed tabby above the eaves, with shaped recesses above each window, and a pediment surmounting the French door with its side lights and fanlight above the portico roof. Below the stringcourse the house corners have rusticated quoins, but above it plain pilasters are substituted. On both north and south sides there is also a pediment spanning a wide, central window with its side lights. To the rear of the house, below the piazza, is a garden, and in this area, close to the north boundary, are the old slave quarters and a carriage house.

An important feature of the Regency style is that interior decorative details are reduced to a minimum. The rooms can then best serve as sympathetic backgrounds to the furniture. Consequently, the room walls in the Owens-Thomas House are of plain, smooth plaster, though round-topped alcoves or niches are employed in the family rooms. Baseboard, door, and window trim moldings are all unobtrusive. Fireplace mantels are also of little note; with one exception they are of marble with simple moldings. That exception is the especially fine Italian marble mantel, carved by the English sculptor Robert Westmacott, Jr., which graces the Mauve Salon. Even the hearth is of white marble; the grate and the fender are made of Swedish steel which blends in perfectly with the pale stone.

The fireplace, however, is not the salon's chief claim to fame. That distinction rests with the treatment of the ceiling which is probably unique in the United States. Although the room is square, the pale mauve ceiling is decorated with two circular ornamental bands in a Greek-key pattern. The outer band touches each wall at the center, but the room corners are filled in with fan-shaped fluting in plaster. This curves down to a decorative, vase-shaped, bracketlike ornament in the wall angle. The ornamental bands are Pompeian red, the

A splendid Italian marble mantel and banded ceiling with corner
flutings are distinctive features of the Mauve Salon.

The dining room contains
a Phyfe masterpiece in the
five-pedestal table,
with a massive Regency
sideboard in the wall recess.

corner brackets gilded, and the walls a deeper mauve than the ceiling. The total effect is both striking and delightful.

On either side of the fireplace is an arched alcove, each containing a four-posted Phyfe card table with an English 1763 candlestick, by Ebenezer Coker, inside a hurricane globe. These are balanced on the plain opposite wall by a pair of late Empire sofas in bird's-eye maple. The mantel garniture consists of a pair of ormolu and crystal Argand lamps. On the wall between them there is a portrait of Robert Bolton (1757-1802), father of the builder's wife.

Suspended by chains from the ceiling center of gilded acanthus leaves is an English chandelier of 1810. This holds six candles in frosted globes around an amphora-shaped glass stem, with a patterned glass bowl beneath it.

Most of the furniture in this room is of mahogany by Phyfe, including cane-seated side chairs, one of which has legs of the curule style. The tea table is a marble-topped Regency piece with heavily carved feet and gold stenciling around the apron. This was once the property of Miss Thomas. There is also a small Phyfe tambour sewing table whose lid, when opened, raises a slanted writing surface into position. Here, too, is a painting of the school of Jean Baptiste Greuze (1725-1805).

Since this was the room that was meant to open onto a duplicate of the south balcony, the windows are of the gib type, with twin-paneled bottoms that hinge inward.

In entering the house, the first door to the left of the hall leads to the drawing room which also possesses a striking and unusual feature in its Greek decorative details. The plain plaster walls, tinted a delicate blue, have a deep baseboard but no cornice. In place of the cornice, a small molding is the anchor point for a continuous border of anthemia—stylized honeysuckle flowers connected one with the other by their stems. These are cast in plaster, painted white, and project four inches from the wall, just below the ceiling. Under this a recess is formed in one wall by curving the lower wall inward slightly and curving the upper two feet, from the ceiling down, outward in the same manner. In the upper bowed section is another Greek-key pattern set against the amber glass of a low strip window through which the northern light glows like sunshine. In the recess below this decorative strip stands a marble-topped, brass-railed Empire console in mahogany, supposedly carved to look like iron.

Twin windows at one end of the room have the usual deep, paneled reveals and inside blinds, but here they are draped as a unit. The silk draperies extend the full width of the wall, with overlapping swags in mauve and gold. The windows themselves are also covered by crossover curtains of white cotton voile. Under the swag which ties the windows together is a French wine cabinet (c. 1789) in rosewood with brass inlay. In the recesses are cane-seated window seats in black lacquer with gold stencil decoration and bolsters in mauve with gold tassels. Above the cabinet is a gilded Sheraton-style

The otherwise simple little girl's bedroom contains a startlingly regal Regency sofa-bed, its canopy draped from a gilded crown.

mirror with balls and bundled reeds as decorations. The room also contains a pianoforte made in Boston in 1820. Its decorative accents are gold stenciling and brasswork, with black rings painted on the leg turnings. A harp, standing close by, was made in London that same year. Two portraits grace the walls—one painted in England by the American John Singleton Copley, although the subject is unknown; the other is an oil of an early resident of Savannah named Israel Tefft, painted by Nathaniel Joselyn in 1808.

In spite of its lack of decoration, the dining room is quite impressive. The large windows have paneled bottoms and double inside louvered blinds above and below. The doors are paneled and beaded, as are the deep reveals in the thick walls. It is this wall thickness that makes possible the arched recesses, and here there is one wide alcove between two doors. One of these doors was originally a dummy for architectural balance, but it is now converted into a display cabinet for silver. The recess accommodates a massive Regency sideboard of the pedestal type. Above this hangs a Regency-style convex mirror with girandoles. Silverware, normally displayed on the sideboard, includes vegetable dishes by Kirk of Baltimore and a rediscovered tea service that once belonged to the house's first owner. The side chairs are Phyfe style, and the enormous mahogany extension table, with its twelve carved knees and brass feet, is a Phyfe masterpiece.

The entrance hall to the Owens-Thomas House is an interest-

A music box converted to store sewing materials.

The Lafayette room,
occupied by the General
and his son in 1825.

The Lafayette room, like the drawing room,
has a black marble fireplace.

ing study in form and color. It is also an epitome of what Jay was essaying in his treatment of the interiors. In the first place, the hall forms an almost perfect architectural composition with its twin white, fluted columns of the Composite order, crowned with gleaming gold capitals, and standing on marbleized stylobates that extend beneath the pilasters against the walls. Above these classical columns which frame the stair, the architrave and frieze are plain; the cornice is decorated with an egg-and-dart molding. A few feet in front of the columns hangs a hall lantern of engraved glass, and in this outer hall, or foyer, consoles formed of semicircular white marble tops on decorative carved and painted wooden brackets support busts of Sir Walter Scott and Lord Byron.

To the rear of the columns, a pair of Regency-style chairs flank the stair foot. The stairs, made of bog oak from Ireland and having mahogany banisters inlaid with twin ribbons of brass, ascend halfway to the second floor before branching right and left and reversing their course to the top. Up to that point the finely molded balusters are of wrought iron painted to resemble wood. From the center of the upper landing a stair-wide bridge arches back to connect the upper rear landing with the front one. Here the balusters are of wood—possibly to save weight. All the way up, the stair soffits are nicely paneled, and the top of the stair wall flanking the bridge has a decorative scrolled border. This structural and decorative arrangement gives perfect equilibrium to the design, a feature that the architect has ensured to the point of providing a dummy door to balance the one leading to the upper rear hall.

This principle of equilibrium has been adhered to, in both exterior and interior, with symmetry and balance the keynotes of the modified Regency design which William Jay carried to their logical conclusion with admirable results.

OPPOSITE: The finely detailed stairway is the work of architect William Jay.

Tarrytown, New York
LYNDHURST

Gothic Splendor on the Hudson

Among the finest surviving examples of the Gothic Revival style as applied to American domestic architecture is the grayish-white marble mansion known as Lyndhurst, perched on a wooded hilltop above the Hudson River at Tarrytown, New York. To the modern eye this constitutes a stately and interesting period piece, though more likely to evoke curiosity as to its origins than appreciation of its potential as a comfortable though elegant residence. From an architectural standpoint, however, it represents an exceptional achievement in a period noted for its experimentation with the early and exotic as a possible basis for a distinctive style in the American vernacular.

Lyndhurst began its existence as a modest country villa designed in 1838 by that notable architect, Alexander J. Davis, for General William Paulding and his son, Philip. At that time the house was less than half its present size, and unimaginatively dubbed "Knoll" presumably because of its elevated site. Twenty-six years later it was enlarged by this same architect—by then universally recognized as a leading authority on the neo-Gothic—for its new owner, George Merritt, a New York City merchant.

Luckily for posterity, Merritt preferred this somewhat pretentious style to the so-called Venetian Gothic, or the seventeenth-century French adaptations from François Mansart (inventor of the mansard roof) then coming into vogue. Merritt's decision to retain the style while doubling the size provided the architect with the opportunity of combining the old with the new to create a unified composition in the ultimate refined Gothic Revival manner.

The changes and additions included a new wing to the north, a new porte cochere to the east, and a square tower as part of the west façade. Over parts of the building a third story was added, and the old eastern porte cochere, now fronted by a new one, became the rear entrance lobby. Various outbuildings also were added, the most spectacular being a huge

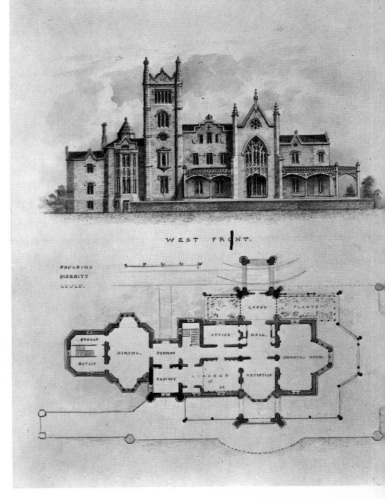

WEST FRONT.

Architect's rendering of Lyndhurst in its final form as occupied by the Gould family (1880).

OPPOSITE: Focal point of the dining room is the marble fireplace and its huge overmantel mirror spanned by tracery and clustered columns.

The mansion's principal façade.

Projected details of the
original dining room, as designed
by architect Davis for General
William Paulding and his
son Philip.

conservatory reminiscent of the Crystal Palace in its barrel-arched roofs, its central dome topped by a hundred-foot tower with a Saracenic cupola.

In 1880 Lyndhurst was acquired by the railroad magnate and financier, Jay Gould, and in 1892, on his death, became the residence of his elder daughter, Helen Shepard, who occupied it until 1938 when it passed into the hands of her surviving sister Anna, Duchess of Talleyrand-Périgord. In 1964 the estate was turned over to The National Trust for Historic Preservation, together with its remaining eighty acres and auxiliary structures.

During the entire period of the Gould family ownership no external changes of importance were made, though some buildings were added, and the greenhouse, which burned, was rebuilt in a less florid style. The few interior modernizations were confined to the installation of a small elevator, extra bathrooms, a heating plant and electric lighting. As a result the mansion remains an entirely authentic nineteenth-century architectural masterpiece, furnished in period, uniform in style and character inside and out, its pointed and decorated arches, its oriel windows, pinnacles, towers and turrets suggesting the ecclesiastical rather than the domestic edifice.

As might be expected, the interiors are equally impressive, the cavernous rooms shadowy with high, timbered ceilings, ribbed and vaulted, with tall doors, carved Tudor-arched

Grandfather clock made by Tiffany.
The walls of the hall are painted to represent ashlar.

Paulding's Gothic drawing room.

The reception room of the Gould period, with an organ added to the Merritt pieces.

mantels, Gothic railed stairs, and elaborate trim, all steeped in a cathedral-like gloom which the dark finishes and fabrics do little to dispel. Most of the windows are heavily mullioned, with elegant tracery and diamond-paned leaded glass, some of it figured or enframed in color-patterned borders. Much of the interior wood and plaster, especially that of the windows, certain corner pilasters, partition walls, and archways complete with molded labels (useful only as decoration), is painted to represent ashlar. Some of these surfaces were later covered with canvas painted in a similar manner.

Despite—or because of—these refined adaptations from the medieval Gothic, the total structure is both highly romantic in concept and picturesque in appearance, set off to advantage by its high, rolling lawns and deep copses, with magnificent vistas on every hand. Its boldly irregular outlines, its massing, and deeply shadowed façades endow it with both vitality and character as a worthy representative of a period marked by revolt against the rigid classicism and strict symmetry of the Greek Revival style earlier hailed as the apotheosis of the republican ideal.

In developing both his original design and the final concept that he was so miraculously able to complete after a hiatus of twenty-five years, Davis may have derived his initial inspiration from Lowther Castle in Westmorland (England), though much appears an entirely original modification of the English Collegiate style to a smaller scale and more delicate proportions. Many of the details were undoubtedly adapted from the published designs of A. W. Pugin, Davis's genius obviously lying in his ability to weld these elements into a triumphantly unified and compatible whole that sets Lyndhurst apart as a major exemplar of the neo-Gothic (or Gothick) style.

This house's special claim to fame rests not only upon its architectural homogeneity but also on the furnishings of its sixteen principal rooms which represent the several major phases of its history, plus the existence of many of the original pieces from each occupancy, with one important exception. With each change of ownership, much of the furniture apparently was transferred along with the house.

Though the Paulding residence was small compared with the Merritt mansion, it originally contained much interesting furniture, no less than fifty neo-Gothic designs (if one includes fire grates and bookcases) being produced specifically for it by the architect who, like Robert Adam before him, believed that house and contents should be designed one for the other. Some of these items survive today.

Other relics of the Paulding days consist of the magnificent overmantel mirror in the reception room, and possibly also the trompe-l'oeil graining of a passage ceiling and its accompanying Gothic lantern. Elsewhere much of the furniture dates from the Merritt occupancy, including an extensible octagonal dining table adapted from a design by Pugin. Its panels simulate traceried windows in the pedestal, and masks in the round at each corner beneath the top. Davis also designed the upholstered Gothic-style dining chairs (fourteen altogether) which are covered in leather. Apart from these, Merritt seems to have indulged his taste for eclectic furnishing by bringing in pieces of the then current Louis XIV Revival design for use in the reception room, together with copies of a Louis XV style for the parlor, consigning to the library an odd mixture of 1870 Victorian types to which Gould later added two chairs from his yacht.

Although Gould largely contented himself with the introduction of additional paintings, screens, bronzes, tapestries, brocades, rugs, and porcelains, he did transform the parlor with French Beaux-Arts details. In his office he installed an elaborate inlaid Wooton patent desk, whose twin front sections swing open to reveal an array of lockable compartments built into them. The chair to this desk, oddly enough, is a Davis design, and the fireplace is one of the handsomest in the house.

Though the furnishing style may vary considerably, the backgrounds are usually so well contrived that the pieces appear to blend comfortably with one another. The few exceptions are confined to those areas in which the intrusive items, perhaps of foreign origin, have been retained for sentimental reasons. The Duchess's bedroom with its Louis XV and XVI relics of Parisian days is one of these.

In many of these rooms the settings may be of even greater interest than the furnishings. A good example is the dining

Jay Gould's bedroom, later occupied by his elder daughter, Helen Gould Shepard.

In each ceiling panel of the reception room is a painting copied from Raphael's *Hours*.

The Merritt art gallery is notable for its splendid carved and foliated open-timbered roof, illuminated by a gable lunette.

room in which the chevron-patterned ceiling is supported on shaped beams. Some of these have bracketed ends resting on clustered engaged columns painted to resemble the marble of the mantelpiece; others spring from carved corbels. Between the tall brackets wooden tracery duplicates that of the bay windows, and behind them the wall is stenciled in a floral design of gold with a sandy texture, all glazed in red.

The focal point of this splendid setting is the marble fireplace, its full-width overmantel mirror spanned by the tracery and flanked by the clustered columns which rest on the mantel shelf of white marble.

This almost overwhelming room, in which everything from Gothic chairs to wall sconces contributes an overall effect of regal splendor, should be compared with a less formal interior such as that of the art gallery on the second floor, once Paulding's library. In this important room furniture compatibility has been a secondary consideration. Here it was that Merritt's art collection shared space with his billiard table, but in the Gould period, Gould's own billiard table was banished when he built his recreation hall, and the fine display of art treasures was augmented.

Today, the gallery is a tall, smooth-walled apartment with a lofty, open-timbered roof whose haunched beams are supported on cast-stone corbels depicting the physiognomies of Shakespeare, Washington, and other historic figures. The roof is pierced by twin lanterns, illuminating the upper walls, and at one end, over the enormous stained-glass window, is a lunette admitting daylight to the roof carvings.

The gallery floor displays a sprightly geometric arrangement of parquet strips in alternating colors over which Oriental rugs are conveniently disposed. The huge heating radiators are hidden by elaborate cast-iron enclosures with white marble tops; otherwise the whole floor space is left open for the casually arranged furniture which includes a library table by Davis, Gothic chairs and upholstered Victorian seating in a variety of fabrics and colors, some with high backs, some with low ones. Outstanding in this mélange is a Louis XV ormolu-mounted *bureau-à-cylindre*, borrowed to replace the missing original French piece, which is in sharp contrast to an American Empire glass-fronted bookcase now displaying bibelots. Overhead, great ring chandeliers (dated about 1865) provide the necessary illumination after dark. Indubitably, the paintings more than make up for the furnishings. Most of them are of the nineteenth-century French school, including one by the ineffable Corot.

Much more intimate than either of the foregoing is the reception room, which was Paulding's salon. In this, the far less remote ceiling is separated into plaster panels by delicately carved ribs, each of them displaying a painting copied from Raphael's *Hours*. The whole room is illuminated by a gaslight-style "chandelier" with opalescent globes. Three elaborate diamond-paned windows with an abundance of stained glass

OPPOSITE: In the entrance hall are the wheel-back chairs designed by the architect for the Paulding salon.

The art gallery, as it was
in the Helen Gould Shepard
period, with electric lighting.

can be sealed off with folding shutters, and other Gothic
touches are supplied by a fabulous gilded mantel mirror original to this room and by the carved paneling of a turn-of-
the-century organ. The furniture, however, is Renaissance
Revival acquired by Merritt in 1865, and it is the upholstery
—lovingly duplicated by hand from the original machine-
made fabrics—as well as the Oriental rug on a nicely patterned parquet floor that bring the room to life and create
its cozy, intimate air.

The ceiling of this room, and the equally elaborate one of
the Paulding state bedroom (the latter lighted by a stained-
glass lunette), are indicative of the importance attached by the
architect, if not the owners, to this aspect of the interiors in
carrying out the promise implied by the exterior of this neo-
Gothic gem.

138

OPPOSITE: The elaborate ceiling of the Paulding state
bedroom is lighted by a stained-glass lunette.

Rochester, New York

THE CAMPBELL-WHITTLESEY HOUSE

A Canal Town Greek Revival Mansion

The Campbell-Whittlesey House in Rochester is notable not only as an excellent example of Greek Revival architecture, but also for its interior detail and coloring, which have been faithfully restored to an unusual degree. Built in 1835-36, the mansion was first owned by Benjamin Campbell, a merchant and miller whose rise to wealth was no doubt largely accelerated during the boom times following the opening of the Erie Canal in 1825. Unluckily, the collapse of the grain market in 1841 forced him to sell. The buyer was Thomas Rochester who, shortly thereafter, resold the mansion to the Whittlesey family who were to occupy it until 1937.

Since there is no record of any architect being involved, it is assumed that the house was designed by a master builder according to Mr. Campbell's ideas, with the help of Minard Lafever's book, *The Beauties of Modern Architecture*, published the year the building was started. The house was constructed of brick with plain stone lintels and sills, the window trim being of wood set well into the reveals. The four fluted Ionic columns are of wood, with wide, decorated necking and added ornament below the abacus. The columns, incidentally, are not accompanied by pilasters on the house corners, nor was stucco used to emphasize the templelike characteristics of the design.

Above the columns, the whole roof structure is of wood, the architrave, frieze, and cornice undecorated except for the Greek-key pattern of the gratings in the side friezes. All woodwork is painted white. An interesting and unusual feature is the recessing of one side of the rear portion of the house as far back as the servants' entrance. This leaves that part of the roof cantilevered out and supported by a single bracket, in appearance much like an oversized modillion. Beyond that point the house is reduced to one and a half stories under a hipped roof.

In studying the exterior it should be noted that the pedimented gable, with its elaborate portico, does not incorporate the main entrance to the house. However, steps are provided at

The tall Ionic columns of the Campbell-Whittlesey House were given a wide necking to reduce the apparent height, and pilasters were omitted as unnecessary, both with obvious success.

OPPOSITE: In this twin parlor is the carved and stenciled table, a Sheraton chair with swan-neck arms, and a Wilton carpet in gold, gray, and green with a bold red border.

141

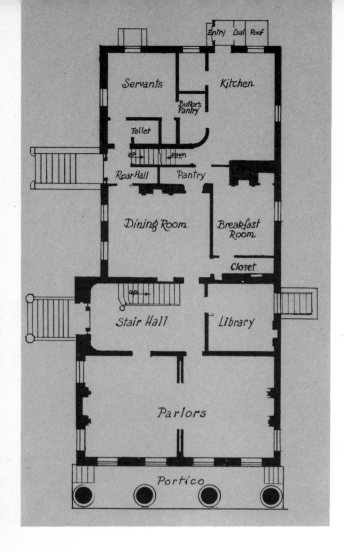

The eared window architrave, heavily paneled
shutters, and strong moldings emphasize
the classic lines.

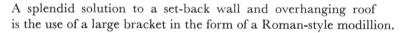

A splendid solution to a set-back wall and overhanging roof
is the use of a large bracket in the form of a Roman-style modillion.

Probably unique
in its floor
arrangement, the
house has no formal
entrance under
the portico.

142

each end of the portico, and the four ground-floor windows are of the triple-sash type, reaching to the floor, enabling them to be used for access via the portico on special occasions.

The interiors are even more individual and exciting than the exterior, thanks largely to the architectural features and the decoration. The delightful decorative designs of Lafever are even improved upon by being somewhat simplified, as becomes immediately apparent on entering the hall. The principal eye-catching feature here is, of course, the stair which sweeps upward along the wall. At a point about seven feet from the floor it swings into a graceful curve that ignores the angularity of the hall, presenting the designer with a number of problems susceptible of solution only by compromise. Since part of the stair wall must curve to keep the stair company (and support it), that, too, rounds off the inside angle up as far as the landing and as far down as the top of the doors. Two of these doors are in a corner under the stairs, and they are accommodated perfectly except for the classical overdoor consisting of an architrave, frieze, and cornice.

The door in the stair wall loses everything above the capitals of the pilasters; the other one, at right angles to it, manages to salvage two-thirds of the cornice and much of the architrave and frieze. These die into the curve of the wall, and the result is not particularly attractive. On the other hand, the door pilasters and the reveal and soffit of one of them more than compensate for the splintered entablature.

The decorated doorway between the double parlors is based on a design by Minard Lafever.

This Empire card table inlaid with brass and satinwood, with a Sèvres covered urn in blue and gold, stands in the west parlor.

The nursery wallpaper in blue, red, and beige is reproduced from one in the Cooper home in Cooperstown.

A corner of the downstairs sitting room, called the Grandmother's Room.

The open string of the stair itself is a thing of beauty with its geometrical borders and applied jigsaw band of creeper climbing gracefully to the top. The mahogany handrail and angular tapering balusters add their quota of appeal, climaxed by the strip of molding which emphasizes the curve at the top of the stair wall where the right-angled surfaces again break through. Here, the final accent is provided by a marble bust of Washington resting in the niche thus formed. The walls are finished off with a plaster cornice and a high, molded baseboard. On the opposite side of the hall two more doors stand complete with full entablatures and the same decorative pattern in the plaster. This woodwork is painted in various tints ranging from gray to lilac so that it stands out boldly against walls of a delicate gray.

Furniture in the hall includes an interesting musical instrument consisting of "singing glasses" which emit a musical tone when their rims are rubbed with a moist finger—the forerunner of Franklin's armonica. These are mounted in a lidded rosewood case with a dummy drawer and ogee legs in Empire style.

Doors in the wall facing the stair lead into twin parlors which in turn face onto the portico. These rooms, each with its own fireplace, are connected by a wide, flat-topped opening with sliding doors. This doorway is one of the major decorative features of the mansion. Simplified versions of a Lafever design embellish the architrave, and decorative panels are sunk in the plaster flanking the stiles. The eared architrave around the opening bears a decorative molding in relief of a simple, delicately flowing honeysuckle pattern confined to the upper portion. This is painted the same gray as the doorway trim. Set into the sunken panels alongside are carved anthemia bronzed to contrast strongly with the lilac tone of the background.

The walls in both rooms are tinted a warm gray, and the tops of all door and window architraves are embellished with geometrical and scrolled patterns. The window blinds and the panels below the window are painted lilac, with shadow-simulating gray borders to suggest moldings. Directly above the woodwork is a shallow frieze formed by a band of grayish purple, ornamented with a row of bronze-colored paterae. This is separated from the cornice by an egg-and-dart plaster molding in the same bronze color. The shallow top molding of the cornice is painted a dark blue which contrasts with the intense Prussian blue of the wide ceiling border. This border is separated from the central ceiling panel of light blue by another bronzed egg-and-dart molding.

In both parlors the furniture is predominantly in Empire style. Both the handsome mahogany piano, dating from around 1800, and the heavily carved center table are stenciled in gold. The mantel garniture, consisting of a pair of gilt-bronze French Empire candelabra, and a black and gold clock of the same period are suited perfectly to the black marble

In the front hall is this "petticoat" table (so called from its low mirror), stenciled in gold, and a china piece by David, *Napoleon Crossing the Alps*, from a painting at Malmaison.

146

Two prominent features of the hall are the unusual stair which ignores a wall angle and the door architrave which dies off into the curving wall.

The dining room features a Huard copy
of Louis-Philippe paper whose upper border
incorporates American-Indian heads.

Important dining room pieces
include a serving table by Phyfe,
a tôle wine cooler, and a portrait
of one Sarah Butlar, born 1822.

A corner of the library with its
heavy "pillow-block"
mantel well suited to the
massive Empire furniture.

fireplace. Both likewise are complementary to the early Sheraton armchair in gold and green brocade. Of special note are an open-arm Sheraton chair with its swan-necked arm supports, and Empire ottomans in a modern gold fabric of an old-time pattern.

Decorated in quite a different fashion is the dining room, its most striking feature being the French hand-blocked paper from the studios of Baron and Baroness Charles Huard. It is a copy of an original of the Louis-Philippe period, 1830-1848, with elaborate upper and lower borders—the former incorporating American Indian heads, doubtless intended for the American market. On the floor is an Aubusson carpet in shades of red and green and dating from the First Empire (1804-1814). The doors are of oak, and the arrangement of two large panels in the middle and two small ones above and below is unusual, and quite attractive. The furniture is especially fine, and includes a butler's sideboard with reeded corner posts in the Sheraton manner, a sunken center, and high back.

On the second floor are seven bedrooms whose style and furnishing is well exemplified by the west bedroom. This is papered from baseboard to ceiling, the pattern in pink and gray on white reproduced from an original dated 1832. The woodwork accordingly is a light gray, and the velvet carpet is of a floral design with red roses on a blue ground. The bed is a massive and finely carved mahogany four-poster with pineapple finials (c. 1825) attributed to Phyfe. At its foot is disposed a curly-maple daybed with a cane back, head, and seat. The legs are claw-footed, with an eagle's head and

The elaborate west bedroom's
four-poster is attributed to Phyfe.
Its companion piece is a
claw-footed curly-maple,
cane-paneled daybed with the
familiar eagle heads and wings.

Featured in the east bedroom
is the New Hampshire "Bird"
wallpaper here contrasted with
the mantelpiece of black marble.

wing at the top—a familiar Late Empire motif.

One of the smaller bedrooms, set aside as a nursery, has wallpaper reproduced from one in James Fenimore Cooper's home in Cooperstown. This is a diamond pattern in blue, red, and beige on a light beige ground. The woodwork is painted in two tones of beige to match. The floor is covered with straw matting, with an occasional throw rug of juvenile interest. The principal piece of furniture, besides the low four-poster bed, is a bureau in bird's-eye maple with opalescent knobs, which was made in Albany in 1816. An assortment of early nineteenth-century toys, including a particularly fine doll's four-poster bed, occupies the floor.

Thanks to the fidelity with which the Campbell-Whittlesey House has been rehabilitated by the Society for Preservation, it affords an exceptionally reliable insight into the taste exercised by a prosperous American citizen of the mid-nineteenth century in decorating and furnishing a town house on whose architectural character he had lavished so much care.

149

The Shadows, dappled with sunlight filtering
through the moss-hung trees.

New Iberia, Louisiana
SHADOWS-ON-THE-TECHE

Classic Revival Adapted to Climate and Culture

Dusky patches dappling the white walls where sunshine filtered through the trees and the cool gloom of deep loggias on hot summer days undoubtedly inspired David Weeks, a wealthy Louisiana planter, to name his new mansion The Shadows or, more properly, Shadows-on-the-Teche because of its proximity to that famous bayou. At any rate this was the Weeks town house whose building was begun in 1830 on its four-and-a-half-acre plot fronting on the highway which passes through the town of New Iberia, then known as Attakapas.

Beyond specifying that the house conform in appearance to the neoclassical style then sweeping the country, Weeks seems to have left the design and construction pretty much to a master builder named James Bedell. His confidence was apparently well justified since Bedell successfully blended French and Spanish architectural features with Grecian elements, the result being a tall, ridge-roofed house with graceful two-story columns spanning deep loggias and ample roof overhang to cope with the hot suns and torrential rains common to this subtropical climate. Today this lovely façade is sheltered by giant moss-draped oaks which invest it with an aura of enticing mystery and charm.

David Weeks, with his wife and six children, took up residence in the new home in 1834, but within a matter of days, Weeks, who was in failing health, departed by steamer for Connecticut, hoping to recuperate in the milder climate. A few months later he was dead, but in the meantime he had bought, and shipped south, furnishings for The Shadows, some of which are in the mansion today. In 1841, his widow married Judge John Moore, who shortly afterward was elected to Congress and later to the Senate, and the family continued to occupy The Shadows.

Damaged during its occupation by Union officers in the Civil War, the mansion was later allowed to fall into disrepair. In 1922 it was rehabilitated by a descendant of the builder who later willed it and its contents to the National Trust for

This stairway leads to the upper gallery on the bayou side of the house—the only enclosed staircase in the mansion.

A watercolor painting of The Shadows by Adrian Persac, 1861.

The portico stair on the land side of the house.

Historic Preservation, which took over the property on his death in 1958. Thanks to that organization the exterior is now in its antebellum condition, and the interiors much as they were up to about 1865.

As far as its external arrangements are concerned, the twin-chimney gabled roof has three dormers on each side. At the front, the eight columns support a classical frieze and cornice which are continued around the building. The columns, which suggest the Tuscan style minus the usual necking, are mounted on cubical plinths in order to retain their classical proportions in face of their unusual height. These plinths and columns are built of brick stuccoed over. The frieze is decorated with the usual triglyphs, complete with guttae, and the cornice soffits with perforated mutules. Although the gable rakes have the same flat cornice and mutules, they are not set at a low enough angle, nor properly tied into the main cornice, to transform the gables into classical pediments. The wide overhang, however, counteracts this effect visually to some degree.

The front wall of the house is set back far enough to form a deep, brick-paved portico, with a gallery above. At one end of the portico a stair leads up to the second floor, and this is almost wholly hidden by a trellis filling the space between the first and second columns and between the gable wall and the end column. In order to balance the façade, the other end is treated in the same manner although there is no stair. On the upper level the trellis gives way to jalousies.

The master bedroom and the sitting room are connected by sliding doors.

The rear façade is free of columns but the recessed center section which forms a small loggia has three arched openings. Here also is a stair which gives access, through a door, to a second-floor loggia and the upper rooms. The front and rear stairs are similar in style, with tapered newels and upswept rails, showing how simple, honest design can sometimes prove entrancing.

All walls and gables are of brick made on the premises from bayou clay and, in spite of having once been whitened, are today a beautiful mellowed pink. The timbers, too, were a product of the well-wooded estate, and even the original jalousies, which are of cypress, are still in use. Apart from these jalousies and the trelliswork which are painted a dark green, all exterior woodwork is white, including the dormer, door, window trim, balcony edge and rail, matching the great columns on which the total character of the mansion so much depends.

On its main floor The Shadows has six rooms, if one includes the rear loggia, most of them converted from their original uses since the house was built. At one time the kitchen was in a separate building; later, when the outbuildings were abolished, it was transferred to a rear corner of the main floor, adjoining the dining room. Next to this was the larger room with a marble floor then designated as the drawing room. Today the original dining room is called a studio and the former drawing room has become the dining room, which

Several of the interior doors in the house are grained to represent some more exotic wood.

153

The bayou façade also was the subject of a watercolor by Adrian Persac which now hangs in the dining room.

opens onto both the front portico and the rear loggia.

Upstairs there were originally four bedrooms and a sitting room, and the present loggia was a hall. One of these rooms (above the downstairs dining room) is the new drawing room, and removal of the rear windows converted the hall back into a loggia. The house today therefore has ten rooms, two loggias and a portico, and an open gallery, all with high ceilings and distributed to take advantage of every vagrant breeze.

The furniture and decoration of these rooms reflect changes in the fashions and styles during a period of thirty years from 1834 to 1864 or thereabouts, though some accessories are of a later date. Much interest attaches to the present dining room, largest of the ground-floor apartments and entered through the middle one of the three doors from the south portico. Besides having the only marble floor, this room has two windows and a door at each side, one opening onto the portico, the other onto the rear loggia. In common with most of the other rooms, these walls have wide molded cornices, decorated at each corner with a stylized acanthus ornament. The window and door trim (the latter including paneled reveals and soffits to both door and fanlight) are molded, with decorative ears applied. The windows are paneled below the sash frame. These, and the painted wood mantelpiece with its paneling and pillars, all contribute to the fine architectural quality of the room, a feeling emphasized by its decoration. The walls are papered in a pale green with a documentary border producing a rich paneled effect, a pleasantly dignified setting for the formal furnishings which include gold moiré draperies and a Waterford crystal chandelier. On the wall are two watercolors of The Shadows painted in 1861 by Adrian Persac. The furniture includes Sheraton dining chairs with black horsehair seats; a pair of Phyfe mahogany three-drawer servers with swash-turned legs; and a carved, ten-legged extensible mahogany dining table.

Upstairs there are two other rooms of note, the drawing room and master bedroom, which further illustrate the changes in furniture styles over the years. In the drawing room is the only marble mantel in the house, dating from its construction. The room cornice here is somewhat more elaborate than that of the dining room, and the wood trim, except for the shallower reveals, is almost the same. The chandelier, however, is of gilt pewter with crystal prisms, its sockets holding special candles of an indigo hue. The wallpaper design consists of gray flecks on a white background against which the hand-painted border in an elaborate design with touches of green, white, gray, and red stands out boldly. These and the red damask draperies and family portraits combine to create an atmosphere of restrained antebellum opulence well suited to the elaborately curved and carved furniture. On the mantel are a pair of French Argand lamps and a gilt clock, and over the brass candlestick on a side table is a hurricane globe of considerable antiquity. This table has a grotesquely carved, bulbous

The marble-floored dining room,
originally the drawing room. It opens onto both
the front portico and rear loggia, a practical arrangement when
the kitchen was in a separate building.

Portrait of David Weeks' daughter, Frances
Weeks Magill Prewitt (1820-1856),
attributed to John Beale Bordley,
which hangs in the drawing room.

In the so-called Girl's Bedroom
is this French armoire of mahogany veneer with
finial hinges and feet of brass.

pedestal, with four furry animal feet, all in brown mahogany. The piano is a Pleyel of 1855 in cherry wood, its chair being one of a set of Phyfe design. There is also a particularly fine Sheraton card table with a serpentine top, having carved and reeded legs and a deep apron accommodating a drawer. Used with this were somewhat plainer chairs of an American Empire style known in New Orleans as cinarettes (apparently a corruption of Seignouret) while rose-carved armchairs in velvet, dating from 1850 or later, were provided for fireside dreaming.

Next to the drawing room is the master bedroom from which sliding doors open into a sitting room. Fluted pilasters flank these doors and support a molded architrave, and the rest of the trim and window-bottom paneling in both rooms is in keeping. All woodwork is painted white to contrast with the gray-green walls, and simple muslin curtains hang at the windows. The bed is a massive creation with heavily turned and carved posts and a large-diameter blanket roll. The wooden tester frame is draped in scalloped linen, and a Marseillaise spread covers the bedding. At the foot of the bed is a walnut daybed of the spindle type with elegantly shaped posts.

In the sitting room, whose floor wears a dress of straw matting in the summer, the most interesting piece of furniture is a bookcase which David Weeks bought in New Haven and shipped down to the wife he was never to see again. Today it is filled with books from the family's library. Another stylish mahogany piece in this room is a Baltimore Sheraton sofa inlaid with satinwood.

Somewhat more prim, in the absence of wide colorful borders and formal paint, is a smaller bedroom set apart for a young girl. This has a wallpaper of blue-green flowers on a white ground, with a narrow, rope-pattern border in brown, yellow, and blue-green. The bed is a Sheraton four-poster with cup-and-cover and fluted turnings. From its cloth-covered tester hangs a muslin mosquito bar, and it has a white bedspread that was hand-loomed in the Cajun country in an old-time pattern. For storage purposes the room is equipped with an armoire of French design in mahogany veneer. Its doors have brass finial hinges, and its interior is divided into shelves, while the short fluted legs have brass feet. Against another wall is a bow-fronted Hepplewhite chest of drawers. This room was lighted by a glass whale-oil lamp which rests on the fireplace mantel. The door of this room, in common with several other rooms, is grained with paint to represent some exotic wood, a common conceit of mid-Victorian days known in Louisiana as *faux-bois*.

These, then, are some of the things that give The Shadows its nostalgic interest outside and in, illustrating as it does the way of life of a wealthy but unpretentious Southern family in the earlier days of the nineteenth century—a home that combined elegance with everyday living for a family that placed homelike comfort before display and is responsible for the mansion's air of tranquil charm today.

OPPOSITE: In the drawing room is the only marble mantel
in the house. The chandelier is of gilt pewter with crystal prisms.
The Sheraton card table has a serpentine
top and carved and reeded legs.

Austin, Texas
WOODLAWN

Classic Columns on the Colorado River

Woodlawn's front entrance hall. The red stair runner's stunning border is repeated in the hall rugs, in vivid contrast to the white woodwork and grisaille walls.

A Greek Revival mansion built in 1853 became one of the showplaces of Texas when it was renovated and furnished in 1957 by the state's long-time Governor Allan Shivers and Mrs. Shivers as their permanent home. Today it stands as a superb example of how classical architecture and century-old interiors can be converted into a dazzling modern home without losing the antique flavor or lessening its historic value.

This house was built for James B. Shaw, the Irish-born State Comptroller, by master builder Abner Cook who was also responsible for the governor's mansion and other important buildings in Austin. In 1857 the house and its 365 acres of land was sold to the retiring governor, Elisha M. Pease. During the Civil War it was, for a time, headquarters for Union troops, and later was occupied by General Custer. The Pease Mansion, as it came to be called, remained in the Pease family until 1957 when, with its remaining four acres of grounds, it was occupied by its present owners.

In the building of the mansion the bricks were made on the banks of the Colorado River, about a mile from the site, and the lumber felled in nearby Bastrop. The entrance portico, which parallels the roof ridge, is floored with brick. On this low terrace six two-story Greek Ionic columns of wood, delicately fluted, today gleam like white marble in the Texas sunshine. Above them the entablature is severely plain, smooth and chaste. In the portico's shadow the strongly textured brick façade of the mansion is painted a roseate pink, throwing into relief the white trim of the stone-linteled windows and their blinds, and the pilastered doorway with its side lights and transom.

Above the entrance, and enclosing another pilastered and glazed doorway, is a delicate wrought-iron balcony with a ribbonlike rail—a grace note in the mellifluous composition. Windows in the end walls have relieving arches, up and down. Toward the back of the house these end walls project to provide

Built in 1851,
Woodlawn was
renovated in 1957 to
become a dazzling
modern home
without loss of antique
flavor or historic
value.

Exquisitely blended
in the north parlor
are the Greek
classical setting
and French antiques,
its focal point an
overmantel portrait
of Mrs. Shivers.

159

From the white-beamed ceiling of the dining room a Baccarat chandelier casts a magic glow over the polished mahogany creations of Chippendale, Adam, and Phyfe, and the silver, cut glass, and porcelain that adorn them.

extra floor space in the rear rooms. Behind the mansion a family room of old brick has been added. From this point a breezeway leads to a patio with a pool, around which are arranged a playroom, dressing room, and large garage. Close by are the old slave quarters, now painted pink and converted into a guest cottage. Here, as elsewhere, the well-wooded grounds allow room for spacious lawns, statuary-studded gardens and brick walks, with flower beds and fountains and sculptured urns.

In their up-to-date décor, the interiors of Woodlawn have lost all suggestion of Victorian gloom or overcrowding characteristic of the later nineteenth century. On the contrary, backgrounds and colors are calculated to act as catalysts in rooms where a variety of furniture styles is assembled—a frequent happening at Woodlawn since Mr. and Mrs. Shivers have been avid antique collectors for many years and possess quantities of fine heirlooms. At the same time the classical spirit of the exterior has been emulated indoors wherever the function of the room would permit. A good example of this is the north parlor which is exquisite in both form and color.

The room itself carries out the Greek classical motif, its white ceiling decorated with an architectural border in gold, featuring paterae, and a circular medallion utilizing the Greek-key and anthemion motifs. Its white walls are paneled with gold molding, the horizontal panels over the windows enclosing another style of Greek decorative design. The mantel is French, of white statuary marble, delicately carved with floral swags and pendants, and a young Pan piping in the central panel. Water-white and gold is the magnificent Venetian crystal chandelier which came from Sharyland, Mrs. Shivers' childhood home. The curtains are austrian shades in ivory,

At the hall and library end of the dining room, twin breakfronts display rare pieces of china and silverware.

One exquisite grouping of the master bedroom is that of the twin mahogany dressing table with its large trumeau-style mirror and antique bronze, twin-candle appliqués.

Eclectic is the style of the master bedroom with its carved Victorian chairs, French mantel garniture, and tôle and crystal chandelier.

Among the important pieces in the south drawing room is this Chinese Chippendale cabinet displaying Meissen Zodiac figurines and Chinese snuff bottles. Flanking it are Louis XVI chairs covered in Aubusson tapestries.

Alive with gay colors, twin crystal chandeliers, and painted French furniture is the daughter's bedroom, its twin beds tied together by a shallow wall-hung canopy.

with overdraperies in a darker gold. On the parquet floor is a petit-point rug which has an overall repeated pattern and border of multicolored carnations on a beige ground. The chairs and sofa are of the Louis XVI style, painted and gilded, and upholstered in gold velvet.

Over the mantel is a huge Wayman Adams (1956) portrait of Mrs. Shivers, with an atmospheric background and enframed in a gold fillet—a splash of gay pastel colors that forms the focal point of the room. Against another wall is a transitional Louis XVI marquetry desk, and elsewhere a tall vitrine in gold leaf displaying antique china.

Far less formal but equally interesting is the entrance hall. Here a major transformation was effected by revamping the backgrounds. Even the front door was improved by replacing glass panels with wooden ones, and installing a massive brass lock. The floor is the original parquet, enlivened by red wool rugs with petit-point borders on a white ground. These match the stair runner which stands out boldly against the oyster white of the staircase trim, balusters and stair risers. The massive newel posts, adorned with glass pineapple finials, and the dado paneling of the hall are also white, but the walls are covered with a *gris* damask paper, which, however, does not diminish the dramatic effect of the glossy black stair rails and treads.

The red of the carpet and rugs, and their border pattern, tend to unify the whole area, one carrying the eye up to a wall niche where the stair turns. In this is displayed a Sèvres urn in cobalt blue. The others tie in the massive inlaid and ormolu-mounted credenza and early eighteenth-century Italian mirror. From here there is a fascinating glimpse of the back hall with its Belgian crystal chandelier casting its light on a tall chiming clock, a flat-topped armoire with a dummy broken pediment, and Victorian armchairs in a Fortuny print of red and gray, all on a rich Oriental rug.

To one side of the back hall is the dining room where formality again reigns. Here, the white beamed ceiling reflects the light of a twenty-candle Baccarat crystal chandelier on antiqued white walls paneled from floor to ceiling. Over the windows are antique gauze glass panels with fringed valances and draperies of white damask. On an antique Oriental rug, which has a formalized flower pattern on a claret background, stands the great dining table—an eighteen-foot, four-pedestal Phyfe creation in mahogany which was made in England. The dining chairs are Chinese Chippendale pieces covered in red silk. There is also a sideboard table in the Adam style, flanked by heavy pedestals on which stand huge white Meissen candelabra, in place of the more usual knife boxes. Above this table is an almost ceiling-high trumeau with a French pastoral scene over the mirror. The fireplace in the end wall is of *verde antico* marble, with brass andirons and wine warmers. Above the mantel is a portrait of Governor Shivers by John Moranz.

Still another aspect of the furnishing plan is revealed by

Comfort is the keynote of the library with its beamed ceiling, paneled walls, and massive classical fireplace.

the south drawing room which combines a variety of elements that influence the degree of formality in any room. This salon, which was originally two connecting rooms, has a plain oyster-white ceiling and walls, the simple molded cornice being imitated in the painted wooden pelmets over the windows. This severity faces a sharp contrast in the two exceedingly decorative fireplaces, one of which is a duplicate of the other. These actually are Louis XV style with ormolu trim, probably made in New Orleans. Each has an identical gilt-bronze screen, and a French fender of solid brass with cast figures.

The window draperies are of silk, in a pale turquoise, over oyster-white austrian shades. From the ceiling hangs a graceful twenty-light crystal chandelier of Italian design, auxiliary illumination depending upon a pair of five-branched candelabra and a single French candelabrum, all in gilt bronze with pear-drop crystals, in addition to odd table lamps contrived out of Dresden figurines.

The rug is a French petit-point creation. Gold lines form tilelike squares upon its black surface, and in each square is a floral design. This gives the room a somewhat exotic appearance, well suited to the large seventeenth-century, Chinese-style secretary made in England and lacquered vermilion in

In the first-floor guest room a Victorian carpet of floral squares permits the use of plain bed fabrics with a frieze of colorful swags.

163

The family room emphasizes the informal with its polished wood and plain brick, beamed ceiling, huge fireplace, combining a bar, display of firearms, and a grand piano.

From the south drawing room a vista extends across the hall to a portrait of Governor Shivers over the dining room mantel.

China. Between windows is a tall Louis XVI pier glass with a leafy crest and swags and, beneath it, a gilt console of the same period, on which stands a large Sèvres urn from the Hearst collection. Another massive mirror in gold leaf, of the same type as that in the entrance hall but even more elaborate, hangs over one of the mantels, flanked by Sèvres urns.

Of equal interest is a Louis XV *bureau-plat* in red *vernis-Martin* with ormolu trim which includes masks in the round. Among the chairs in this room are two Louis XV bergères, and two Louis XVI fauteuils, all done in blue velvet. The sofas are also Louis XVI in style but covered in tapestries. The remaining pieces include an extraordinary round pedestal table credited to the Louis XVI period. This is inlaid with Sèvres plaques depicting the monarch and some ladies of his court. The top is bound in pierced brass which also forms a short apron, and the table itself has all the air of a museum piece.

The rest of the rooms in Woodlawn have been renovated in the same manner, with furniture and furnishings often older than the house itself. There is therefore no reason why this splendid mansion should not survive as a comfortable home as well as a historic landmark for a very long time to come. No other great house deserves a better fate.

OPPOSITE: In the south drawing room are the twin fireplaces, a French petit-point rug, and Chinese patterned secretary.

THE BEEHIVE HOUSE

A Miracle in the Desert

In 1854, a mere seven years after reaching the Great Basin with his Mormon followers in a mass migration from Illinois, Brigham Young erected this splendid mansion in the pioneer settlement that was to become Salt Lake City. Designed by Young, himself a competent carpenter, with the help of Truman O. Angell, the three-story residence was built in the style of certain Vermont colonial houses with which he was familiar— houses with deep porches and balconies, tall pillars and cupolas, with more than a suggestion of a Southern plantation house before the days of the Greek Revival flood.

The Beehive House (so called from the gilded hive, symbol of industry, that crowned its cupola) was built with thick outer walls of adobe brick. The main-floor ceilings were high, the principal rooms large for the entertainment of distinguished visitors, and ample bedrooms provided for overnight guests. Young himself, with one wife and their children, lived in this house, the rest of the family occupying the Lion House next door so that there was ample room for all. Here the great Mormon leader lived for twenty-three years until his death in 1877. Eleven years later, extensive changes were made to the structure, including the rebuilding of the rear section into a three-story extension, the remodeling of the dining room, and the addition of an upstairs sitting room and parlor. Further alterations were carried out in 1893 when the house became the official residence of the Church presidents. Still later, other changes were made to adapt it for use as a residence for women.

In 1961 the clock was turned back almost a century by restoring the Beehive House to its original condition as of 1854 to 1877. Its exterior walls were once more a pale yellow over the smoothly plastered adobe, the shutters a dark green, the pillars, the trim and the doors a sparkling white. Its white southern entrance door is adorned with a specially designed silver knob and escutcheon featuring the symbolic bee. The rooms once again are decorated in the original colors, and

Characteristic of the lavish Beehive décor is this silver doorknob with a bee on the escutcheon.

OPPOSITE: A unifying feature of the long hall with its twin fireplaces and five windows is the square-patterned carpet.

The resplendent
Salt Lake City
mansion known
as The Beehive was
designed by Brigham
Young in the Vermont
Colonial style,
but of adobe brick.

Not only were
ceilings high but
the principal rooms
were large as the
main-floor plan shows.

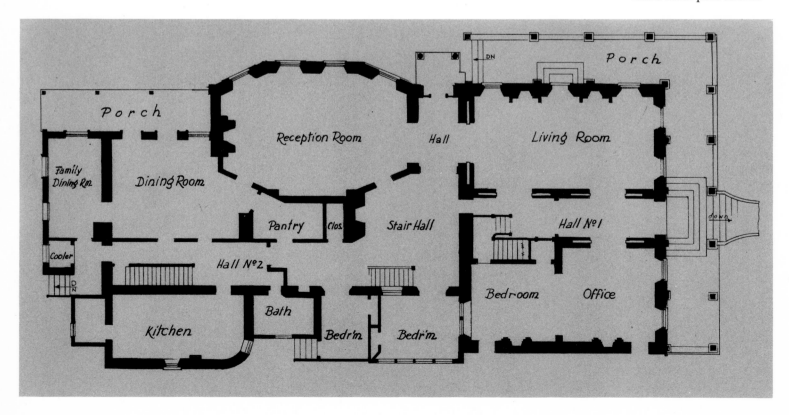

furnished in the comfortable but not overcrowded Victorian style that includes many of the original pieces, some of them made by the pioneers themselves.

From the outside the Beehive House is not only striking, but in many aspects beautiful and architecturally satisfying. Here are eleven tall, white pillars supporting a deep extension roof along the whole of the south façade and part of the east front, together with a continuous balcony that shelters the porticoes below. Each pillar has its mating pilaster against the house wall, flanking the wide windows and doors. Above the pillars is a bracketed frieze and the dentiled cornice of the porch roof. Behind this the main walls of the house rise another foot or so to the roof eaves. This is the main roof of the house, its gables facing west and east. Halfway up the slopes four tall chimneys form the corners of a roof deck whose front and rear walls are decorated, in the manner of a frieze, with Greek-key panels. This is finished off with a cornice surmounted by a delicately beautiful wrought-iron balustrade. Centered on this deck is a large, cubical, windowless tower, with the beehive-domed cupola on its wooden balustraded roof.

In this portion of the house are Brigham Young's bedroom and office, and a large living room. On the north side of this square part of the building is a larger section with bays and dormers, and a small porch tucked away in a corner. This unit incorporates a long eight-sided reception room, the family and formal dining rooms, two bedrooms and the domestic offices, all on the ground floor. Upstairs are more bedrooms, a sitting room and parlor—the latter called the Long Hall and probably the most delightful chamber in the house. Here, too, is the Victorian Room, added in 1888 by Young's son, together with a sewing room and a richly furnished octagonal room (over the first-floor reception room) called the Gardo Room, and a schoolroom for the children above the kitchen.

The main entrance hall, in the east façade, is notable for its pine paneling, mostly of tall, narrow panels with raised centers. This is given an unusually substantial air by the wide, flat stiles and rails. The door frames are relieved by a small bead-and-reel molding, and the archway posts by elaborate carved panels and reeded sections, with decorative brackets supporting a panel over the flat arch composed of reel and spindle turnings. The ceiling is white, set off by one wide and one narrow painted border line.

The principal furniture pieces in this hall are a very large, square beveled mirror in a gilt architectural frame; a long Empire sofa with scroll ends and winged claw feet, upholstered in red velvet; a bracket-footed, marble-topped rosewood commode; a scroll-footed love seat in red silk, and a General Lee armchair in horsehair. On the commode a pair of crystal-hung Argand lamps illuminate an oval-framed portrait of Brigham Young. These are all well suited to the elaborately patterned carpet in reds and browns which, alas, covers the floor that once was painted in squares to represent Tennessee marble.

The main stairway in this impressive house is modest in size.

Added in 1888, the Victorian Room contains a heavy-legged carved piano, elaborate picture frame, sculptures and draperies of the period.

The octagonal Gardo Room is a luxurious drawing room in the rococo manner, gilded and overpowering.

Off this hall is Brigham Young's bedroom with its huge closet and extraordinary carved door frames and overdoors reaching up to the plaster cornice. The fireplace mantel with its triangular raised back is almost plain by comparison. The bed, however, is a massive mahogany piece, heavily carved, with vase finials at the head flanking Gothic panels, in the center one of which is the inevitable bee. There is also a bookcase-secretary with a sliding drop-front writing surface and glass doors. This has a large cresting over the coved cornice and turned finials over tiny brackets, plus scrolls at the bookcase base—a handsome piece with brass rails and spindles on the sliding section. From the ceiling hangs an oil lamp in its white-painted cradle of cast-iron tracery, beneath a brass-rimmed glass shade with sparkling crystal drops. The secretary, the carved washstand, the swivel desk chair, all apparently were made by the Church's cabinetmaker, William Bell, and their execution leaves nothing to be desired. The walls here were painted subdued pink to match the original.

The downstairs sitting room likewise has a homey air, in the Victorian sense—the walls a soft green, the wood trim all white, and the windows hidden beneath curtains of Nottingham lace, with a colorful ingrain carpet on the floor. The furniture also is massive—a ceiling-high walnut bookcase with a busy carved cresting and a projecting drawer section at the bottom, all as solid as Gibraltar; a piano with eight-inch

Brigham Young's bedroom, shown with his hat and stick on the bed, was comparatively subdued despite the extraordinary carved door frames and the massive mahogany bed.

On the hall commode a pair of Argand lamps illuminate an oval-framed portrait of Young.

tapering legs and sturdy heart-shaped pedal bracket; a round table draped with a floor-length Paisley shawl; a horsehair-covered open-arm chair, and round-back side chairs in dark red velvet. Here, too, is another life-size portrait bust of Young in a wide gold frame, and a fine four-branched brass chandelier with crystal-decorated oil lamps and translucent yellow glass shades—a mellow room for evenings of music with the piano, harp, and violin.

How strangely this all must have contrasted with the later Gardo Room, octagonal and "arty" with porcelain busts and ormolu-mounted painted vases on bombé commode and pot-bellied vitrine, both with decorated panels in the Louis XV manner! In this luxurious drawing room gold is everywhere—in the ceiling-high frame of the pier glass with its overpowering crest and rocaille ornamentation; in the overmantel mirror with its mass of delicate golden leaves and flowers crowned with a giant acanthus leaf, a telltale cockle shell in the bottom center; in the ornate gilded brass chandelier and the metal fire screen before the white marble mantel whose sole garniture is a pair of gilt ormolu and crystal Argand lamps.

In the long hall the effect is rich but comfortable despite its thirty-two-foot length, its twin mantels and chandeliers and varied assortment of furniture pieces. Its unifying feature is the overall square-patterned carpet with its panels of flowers on a background of black, tied in with its five pairs of draperies

In the downstairs sitting room,
besides the omnipresent
portrait of the Leader, are massive
furniture pieces such as the piano,
with 8-inch legs,
a ceiling-high walnut bookcase,
and a Paisley-shawl-draped table.

in red damask topped by molded pelmets of pressed brass and glass curtains of lace. With all these sound-absorbent surfaces, and the coved ceiling, the room was highly suitable for the music of voice, piano, and harp with which the family entertained such notables as President Grant, General Sherman, Mark Twain, and others.

The furniture here is Victorian again; one of the sofas a carved and pierced open-backed Belter piece and another a triple-arched Belter deeply tufted in red satin. The side chairs are tall balloon-backs with carved crestings. The piano, the oval and marble-topped tables all are deeply carved, as is the gilt frame of an oval mirror. Here, indeed, is opulence at its most genteel as befits the residence of a pioneer who created in the desert a home of comfort, distinction, and architectural merit that would do credit to any long-established community of high cultural standards anywhere. That is the miracle that makes the Beehive House unique in American annals.

Asheville, North Carolina
BILTMORE

Sixteenth-Century France in America

In the perfection of its sixteenth-century French Renaissance architecture, Biltmore is a superb representation of a château translated, as if by magic, from the Loire Valley to the North Carolina hills. Designed by a great American architect, Richard Morris Hunt, for George W. Vanderbilt, it was built not merely as a *maison de plaisance* but to serve both as a country home and a repository for the fabulous treasures for which Mr. Vanderbilt had combed Europe and the Orient.

Taking for his inspiration three famous French châteaux—vast Chambord, delicate Blois, and river-straddling Chenonceaux—Hunt spent the five years from 1890 to 1895 building this masterpiece. Into it has gone all the skill and craftsmanship of modern artists and artisans, European and American, much of their work equal to anything created in the early sixteenth century when the arts blossomed as never before. But before this could happen a great deal of work had been done by George Vanderbilt himself in selecting the site and planning the location for what he hoped would be the finest country house in America.

A student of architecture and a connoisseur of the arts, Vanderbilt was also intensely interested in arboriculture, and therefore included extensive forests in the estate which he finally created—125,000 acres of wooded hills not far from Asheville. But a château is not meant to be hidden in the woods. It is a sophisticated style of mansion, calling for a noble setting and demanding open spaces and vistas, formal gardens and ornamental water. Accordingly, a noted landscape architect, Frederick Law Olmsted, was engaged to plan the conversion of thirty-five acres of the leveled site into formal parterres, walks and pools, terraces and allées, replete with pergolas, box hedges and statuary.

Today, facing the main façade of the mansion—beyond the lawn with its great pool and fountain—is a delightful vista, a grassy slope beginning with a broad masonry *rampe douce* and ascending gradually toward the distant hilltop where tall

Biltmore has many aspects, each one of which seems to reach from the mountaintop to the sky. This one is the south façade.

The vast panorama of the Biltmore estate extending to the mountains. Beyond the mansion is the rampe douce and a half-mile vista with a terminal *pavillon* sheltering a statue of Diana the Huntress.

Hung at his North Carolina residence is this portrait of George W. Vanderbilt, painted by John Singer Sargent.

trees touch the sky. Bordered by thick woods, this long, sheltered clearing has all the fascination of a thousand-year-old Saxon parliament place. Nearer by are the walled and hedged gardens, the lily pools and terraces, watched over by marble fauns, goddesses and winged cherubs and, beyond the mansion, the outbuildings—the stables and carriage house, and the outdoor servants' quarters. In sharp contrast to all this formality, at the rear of the house the hillside, with its tree-studded lawn and bosky dell, sweeps sharply down to a meadow-ringed lake over which a breathtaking view from the house is open to the far horizon.

Though 250-room Biltmore incorporates ideas adapted from the three great French châteaux, it is like none of them in appearance or plan. It has a personality all its own with its mountainous medieval roofs of gray slate, its tall Gothic chimneys and square-domed campanile, its decorated dormers, crocketed pinnacles and metal crestings—all of which contribute to its most obvious characteristic: the utter lack of symmetry of every façade. The walls are of hand-tooled Indiana limestone, smooth and strangely free from carving. Decoration is confined to the windows and climaxed by the four-story entrance pavilion with its pierced-stone parapet, clustered pinnacles and towering finials piled upon a Gothic-arched mullioned dormer, all reinforced by twin pillars and tiny flying buttresses far more ornamental than useful.

Other pavilions close to each end of the mansion's incredible

174

OPPOSITE: The banquet hall is a 75-foot-high replica of a Norman medieval great hall with a triple fireplace at one end.

780-foot frontage are neither symmetrical nor alike in proportions or elaboration. The recesses between them and the central pavilion likewise are treated in a widely different manner. Attached to the left of the central pavilion is the stair tower said to be derived from the tall, slender one of Blois, though Chambord has two much more like it in outer appearance. In Biltmore, however, the winding stair itself is not of the newel type (affixed to a center post from top to bottom). Instead it has an open well, and is supported between floors cantilever fashion from the walls. Connecting this stair wall to the pavilion is the campanile-like tower which is actually a continuation of the windowed stair screen.

Three-centered arches also are a feature of this front, seven of them holding up the portico to the left, and one forming the main entrance. At the other side four arches—two of them the round-topped Roman style—form floor-length windows for the Palm Court.

The rear façade of Biltmore is not altogether similar in design to the front, its main architectural features being three semi-octagonal attached towers with high-peaked and crested roofs. Between two of them is an arcade of six Roman arches similar to those on the main façade. The principal difference between the two fronts lies in the 75-foot foundation wall on which the rear of the building rests because the land falls away steeply at this point.

Although the exterior of Biltmore may be imposing, dignified, and somewhat austere, the interior is alive with color and fascinating detail. After passing through the circular Palm Court with its glassed dome, hanging lanterns and central fountain, the first thing to catch the eye is the exquisite flying stair of white marble with its decorative bronze rail soaring upward in a wide sweep around the great three-tiered wrought-iron chandelier which hangs from the ceiling four floors above and lights three landings. In the daytime the stair hall and stair are flooded with light from the mullioned casement windows shaped to follow the sloping line of the stair.

Here, as in the entrance hall, the floor is of white marble, limestone arches connecting the two. Apart from the stair rail and chandelier, decorative features are limited to the few furniture pieces—lofty seventeenth-century French guéridons, or tripod stands, a sixteenth-century Spanish treasure chest, a tall-case clock by Jean Numan of Amsterdam, and chairs in Spanish leather. The only mass of color is provided by a wall-sized red velvet hanging, elaborately decorated in gold and silver, that was once the property of Cardinal Richelieu.

As might be expected, the most magnificent room in the château is the banqueting hall, a 75-foot-high replica of a Norman medieval great hall with seventeenth-century improvements such as a tremendous fireplace at one end and a gallery at the other where an organ replaces the old-time minstrels. The huge Indiana limestone fireplace (whose three fire arches recall those of Combe Abbey, Warwickshire) is deco-

This 16th-century Italian marble lion is one of a pair flanking the main entrance to Biltmore.

The statuary-dotted swimming pool which seems suspended between sky and earth.

OPPOSITE: Beyond the library fireplace is an exquisite spiral staircase in gilded bronze leading to the gallery.

The grand stairway winds around the four-story-tall chandelier.

Between the terrace steps and the swimming pool stands a charming terra-cotta statue entitled *The Dancing Lesson*.

rated with a high-relief carved panel by Karl Bitter (1867-1915), and the tapering chimney breast with the Vanderbilt armorial bearings. Fenestration is of course confined to the upper half of the stone walls, the tops of the mullioned Roman-arched windows penetrating the ribbed Gothic wooden roof, giving, from the exterior, the effect of massive dormers. Decorative stonework panels flank these windows, resting on a deep stone frieze, molded top and bottom, which divides the entire wall into upper and lower sections.

Below this heavy stringcourse, the plain side walls are almost entirely covered with tapestry hangings whose importance is accented by a pair of splendidly carved Gothic thrones. A somewhat barbaric note—popular some six centuries ago—is added by the display of mounted heads and horns along the frieze, with replicas of early state flags displayed about them, a rather incongruous combination. Other wall hangings consist of medieval armor and weapons, and flags of the world's great nations in 1492, including that of Columbus himself.

At the opposite end of the hall, normally occupied by a screen and musicians' balcony, is a splendid structure of carved wood incorporating three shell-topped alcoves with shelves displaying nineteenth-century Dutch, Spanish, and French brass and copper ware. Flanking the alcoves are four fluted attached columns topped by massive brackets that support the organ gallery, its panels enriched with carvings by Karl Bitter of scenes from Wagner's operas.

Depending from the lofty ceiling are two great, forty-light chandeliers, extra illumination being provided by concealed lights above the frieze at window level. Below the chandeliers, in the floor center, is a massive oak dining table of Italian design made in 1890, accompanied by eighteenth-century Italian high-backed chairs upholstered in red damask. Surrounding the table are four large eighteenth-century Mir Siraband Persian rugs, with a Bijar rug from Kurdistan placed between them and the wide entrance portal.

The great treasure here, of course, is the set of five tapestries around which the room was planned. These are the only known sixteenth-century Flemish tapestries woven in the Venus and Vulcan design, and may be the survivors of seven original pieces once belonging to King Henry VIII of England.

In the 90-foot-long Tapestry Gallery hang three important early sixteenth-century tapestries representing the Triumph of Virtue over Vice. Of rare beauty, they mark a transition from the Gothic to the Renaissance style of weaving, reproducing paintings with a depth and complexity never before achieved. In this room antiquarians will find of special interest the white Dresden porcelain figures representing the Twelve Apostles made by Johann Joaquim Kändler, noted Meissen sculptor, sometime between 1735 and 1741. These, together with twelve porcelain candlesticks, all bear the Austrian Imperial arms, and presumably were in some private royal chapel. Here also are chairs and sofas upholstered in late-sixteenth-century tap-

A Wedgwood fireplace, walls of Spanish leather and
red marble, and upholstery in red Genoese velvet add richness
to the dining room, whose ceiling and frieze are an
unsurpassed work of art.

Mr. Vanderbilt's bedroom contains elaborately carved Spanish and Portuguese woodwork relieved by white porcelains and rich red velvet touched with gold.

estry, and family portraits by Boldini and by Sargent, together with one of William Cecil, the great Lord Burghley (1528-1598), painted by Marc Gheeraerts in 1589. Lord Burghley's intrusion here introduces an interesting bit of Biltmore history. On George Vanderbilt's death in 1914, the estate—minus a large area of land deeded to the government—was inherited by his daughter Cornelia, who became the wife of Lord Burghley's descendant, John Francis Amherst Cecil, in 1924. Since that time the estate, diminished to 12,000 acres, has remained in the Cecil family though the house has not been used as a residence since 1930.

The Tapestry Gallery itself is interesting largely for the heavily timbered ceiling, its beams and joists lavishly decorated with painted designs, for the elaborately carved marble mantels of the twin fireplaces with their overmantel paintings, and the row of iron torchères which provide lighting.

Next to the great hall in impressiveness and importance is the library with its elaborate paneling in Circassian walnut. On the 73-foot-long ceiling is a tremendous allegorical painting on canvas (attributed to Giovanni Antonio Pellegrini, 1675-1741), once the glory of an Italian palazzo. Flanked by ceiling-high bookcases which, with their raised balcony, cover three walls is a huge fireplace in carved black Italian marble. Above it, and sandwiched between a pair of life-sized figures carved in wood, is framed a late seventeenth-century Italian tapestry covering the chimney breast.

The furniture of the Louis XVI
bedroom is upholstered in red
damask; the rug is an
Aubusson of 1850.

An entrancing feature in this exquisitely designed and furnished room is the spiral staircase to the balcony with its delicate, fluted pillars and Roman arches, its curved panels and carved details. From the library floor the gilded-bronze stair rail spirals up to a semicircular landing around which the balcony's shining balusters sweep in an uninterrupted curve. The furnishings here include Spanish settees and chairs in red damask, with velvet footstools to match the upholstery of the fender seat, a long reading table over which is draped a sixteenth-century Spanish embroidered tapis and a huge antique, double-decked book table. Interesting accents are provided by eighteenth-century white Capo-di-Monte vases and Ming porcelain goldfish bowls, one of them in the rare Mohammedan blue. The rugs are a fine Bijar in reds, blues, and greens and an eighteenth-century Persian Harati in red, light green, and dark blue. These, too, add their touch of color in a wood-lined room, but nothing could provide a more intense air of luxury than the 20,000 richly bound books themselves.

Compared with the library, the Oak Drawing Room is quite subdued yet perfectly adapted to quiet daily living. Here the walls are paneled in oak, with fluted pilasters and a deep wooden frieze and cornice, the oversized windows enframed by green velvet curtains with red and gold tapestry borders. The ceiling is enlivened with an overall strapwork pattern in plaster having pendants at the junctions. That this is definitely a man's room is indicated by the mounted hunting trophies and the

Detail of the spiral staircase
in the library.

many engravings from paintings by Sir Edwin Landseer.

Far more decorative interest attaches to the family dining room with its walls of red marble and tooled Spanish leather. Dominating one wall is a ceiling-high fireplace, its base of white marble with a mantelpiece of jasperware inlaid with panels and medallions in Wedgwood blue, all made at the Wedgwood pottery in Staffordshire. Incorporated in it are stout fluted pillars supporting an entablature on which rests a panel bearing a heraldic device modeled in *basso relievo*. A wide frieze, also patterned in relief, brings the chimney breast up the cornice, but the elaboration does not end there. The ceiling itself is heavily ornamented in a strapwork design, with four elaborate pendants in a matching pattern. At floor level the room is enriched in a different fashion. The marble of the dado is carried around the wide doorway which also has a paneled reveal and heavily molded door panels.

Turning to the bedrooms, in that of Mr. Vanderbilt the walnut paneling and carving are confined to the pillared door and fireplace surrounds and a somewhat anachronistic picture shelf. The furniture includes eighteenth and nineteenth-century Spanish, Portuguese and Italian pieces; the handsome bed is hung in red and gold. The only important rug is an eighteenth-century Bokhara from west Turkestan.

By contrast, Mrs. Vanderbilt's oval bedroom is much brighter and gayer as well as more formal. The walls are decked out in yellow silk between the white-painted, paneled dado and the deeply coved cornice. Door and window trim is white, as is the large overmantel mirror frame which is topped by ogee curves and garlands. The fireplace mantel of blue-veined marble, abundantly curved, stands between silk-covered flat pilasters. These and the twin window alcoves, with their white decorative moldings, break the curved wall into narrow vertical panels ideal for the display of attractively hung tinted prints, framed in gold, of eighteenth-century nobility and royalty. Enframed in the wall alcove openings, the draperies of yellow silk look their best with contrasting deep pelmets and wide borders of the same purple and gold Genoese velvet which adorns the Louis XIV bed.

In one of the alcoves is a fine Louis XV bombé marquetry bureau in kingwood with touches of gilt bronze. In the center of the parquet floor, on one of the two Savonnerie rugs, stands a small Louis XV glass-topped, ormolu-mounted table. In contrast, the seated furniture is white with purple and gold upholstery, but the great cheval glass and the triple mirror of the dressing table have delicate, carved and gilded frames.

This bedroom could profitably be contrasted with the other oval room known as the Louis XVI bedroom which is strikingly different. Here are the same white walls in simpler guise, the panel-shaped spaces covered in the same red damask as that used for the bed hangings and to cover the chairs and sofa and the cane-backed *lit de repos*. Apart from the Aubusson carpet with its pink border and faded gray center the contrast-

ing color is gold—gold chair and sofa and daybed frames, gold circular table, gold wall clock and sconces, candlesticks and picture frames, and even gold ormolu mounts—both *chutes* and *sabots*—on the marquetry bed.

These few examples of the interiors shed only a faint light on the overall magnificence of Biltmore with its wealth of treasures—the rare beauty of its rugs, its family portraits by world-famed artists, its exotic furniture pieces, including Napoleon's own chess table, an intricate sixteenth-century Spanish chest, an Italian ebony dresser with no surface left uncarved, Chinese bronzes of 800 B.C., and a thousand other precious works of art and ancient artifice that can never be duplicated or replaced.

Though its stones have barely begun to darken, Biltmore has the timeless authority of something that has always existed. It stands as a noble attempt to recapture the splendid architecture, the beauty and romance of the great houses of the past both as an aristocratic home and a fitting setting for these treasures of an earlier day.

Both formal and gay, Mrs. Vanderbilt's bedroom has wall panels of yellow silk, matching that of the draperies. The borders and deep pelmets are all of the same purple and gold Genoese velvet that adorns the Louis XVI bed.

New Orleans, Louisiana
THE SHORT-MORAN HOUSE

The Italian Villa with the Cornstalk Fence

The rear semi-octagonal bays of the Short-Moran House have semicircular terraces with iron galleries, of which this is one.

In 1866 building was completed on one of the most interesting houses in New Orleans—an antebellum mansion combining a fifteen-room Italian villa with Greek Revival interiors and typical Louisiana iron galleries. Designed by architect Henry Howard for Colonel Robert H. Short, the house was of brick, stuccoed and painted, and surrounded by a cast-iron fence in a pattern of cornstalks intertwined with morning glories that has been an identifying feature ever since.

As times and fashions changed, and Greek Revival gave way to eclectic mid-Victorian styles, the classic details were painted over or removed; some of the white marble fireplaces were replaced by wooden ones in walnut, and the rooms disguised under somber papers and darker paints. The exterior became a dull red-brown, its famous railings the same uninspiring color. Some structural alterations were made, including the installation of a new staircase, and an addition of a conservatory ornamented with stained glass.

In 1950 the property was acquired by Mr. and Mrs. Alfred J. Moran, who have since transformed it into a thing of beauty, both outside and in, while restoring many of its original attractive features. Today the stuccoed walls are a soft gray, with ironwork a gray-green, the blinds and doors a darker green, and the trim, including the doorways, a sparkling white. The conservatory stained glass was removed and the structure became an arcade as a section of the terrace.

Unsymmetrical in plan, the entrance, with its classic pilasters and entablature, is to one side of the main façade. Extending across the front, atop a low terrace with its intricately patterned cast-iron railing, is the two-story gallery. Up to the second-story level the gallery supports consist of four sets of twin cast-iron columns, with decorative capitals, brackets, and frieze in delicate iron tracery. Above the second floor, whose railing duplicates the one below, the supports are the usual pilasters in cast-iron filigree, topped by an iron frieze and cornice decorated with paterae in Grecian classical style.

A cornstalk and morning-glory iron fence guards the antebellum mansion named the Short-Moran House after its original and present owners.

Cast in Cincinnati, the gate, like the rest of the railing, is a masterpiece of the metalworking art.

With its stately proportions and exquisite furniture—the great table, with Regency-style pedestals, the Hepplewhite chairs, the Victorian sideboard—the dining room is as formal as it is beautiful.

Above this is the house cornice in molded stucco with heavy brackets and a parapet hiding the low-pitched roof.

From the main entrance, the hall extends through the house to a cross hall behind the twin parlors. Facing the rear parlor across the hall is a sitting room. Both of these rooms have projecting semi-octagonal bays with semicircular terraces. On the rear parlor terrace is a rounded, two-story iron gallery; on the sitting room terrace there is a similar gallery only one story high. Both contribute vastly to the beauty of the exterior.

In the cross hall is the main staircase which sweeps upward in a wide curve to the second floor. Because of the low roof the attic is unsuitable for storage. Beyond the stair hall is an immense dining room with a tall archway opening into its rounded bay. From this room a doorway gives access to the domestic quarters.

Every room on this main floor teems with interest and, with the new décor, each vies with the other in beauty. With fifteen-foot ceilings there is a general air of spaciousness that is felt immediately on entering the hall. The vista here seems endless. From the front door there is an uninterrupted view the full length of the hall and across the width of the stair hall to the far side of the dining room where the fireplace and chandelier are framed by the wide doorway with its classical Greek trim.

In the main hall itself there are three flat-arched, twelve-foot-tall doorways of the same size and style, the stiles eared,

In the dining room's semicircular bay with its fitted seat stands a custom-made hunt table in the Sheraton style.

With 15-foot-high ceilings the vista down the wide hall
entrance and across the stair hall to
the dining room fireplace seems tremendous.
Opening into it are three flat-arched 12-foot-tall double
doorways, and Corinthian pilasters support the huge oval arch
that separates it from the stair hall beyond.

Rear and front parlors are connected by a beautiful triple arch with Corinthian columns and pilasters.

the frieze and cornice topped with molded scrolls at each end and an anthemion cresting in the center. These openings can be closed by a pair of eight-panel sliding doors. At its far end, the main hall enters the stair hall through an oval arch supported by pilasters of the Corinthian order, the capitals carved in cypress. The soffit of this arch is paneled, and at its center is a carved ornament representing armorial bearings, which seems to be a later addition.

The carpet is olive-green velvet pile covering the floors of both halls, and increasing the feeling of uninterrupted space. This color contrasts interestingly with the various shades of gray used on the woodwork and plaster. The dado and cornice are lightest, the wall over the arch the darkest, and the ceiling something between the two. These varying gray tones and the white of the doorway-arch woodwork make a wonderful setting for the wallpaper with its violet-gray background half hidden by huge medallions in medium gray, violet-gray, and very pale greenish gray.

The stair, naturally, dominates the cross hall, and although this is highly decorative with its white-painted, swash-turned balusters, the fact that it is made of oak dates it at around 1900. The most beautiful features of this hall are the graceful windows on the stair landing and the antique Chinese chest. The colors here follow the pattern of the main hall, minus the wallpaper.

The rear parlor with its bay window is striking in several respects, but its most delightful and impressive feature is the triple arch with two Corinthian pilasters and two columns by which it is connected to the front parlor. The three arches —two narrow and one wide—are decorated with paterae and rope molding strongly augmented by the wide cornice above them. In addition, considerable interest centers on the bay which accommodates two tall, floor-length windows which have a carved white marble fireplace between them. Continued into the bay is the elaborate cornice with its pierced carving. Reaching up to this is an overmantel consisting of an unframed antique mirror in twelve sections. Attached to it is a pair of Louis XVI bronze and crystal sconces.

With the ceiling a light Wedgwood blue and the carpet a dark red, and the walls between them a dark Wedgwood blue, the white of the woodwork and the light colors of the painted furniture stand out boldly. These pieces consist of several Louis XVI fauteuils and one bergère, in a light blue silk, all frames being gold and white. The only Louis XV fauteuil, also gold and white, has a cane back. In the bay windows stand a pair of Empire guéridons, or tripod stands, with bronze galleries. An unusual piece, especially in a parlor, is a Louis XVI semainier in marquetry which vies for attention with an eighteenth-century English breakfront bookcase in mahogany with its original convex glass and gold teapaper lining.

The most-used room in the Moran house is undoubtedly the living room with its interesting mélange of antique and modern

furniture, all of the finest type. The color scheme here combines olive, mustard, and almond green, with accents of black and gold, and utilizing the same unobtrusive olive-green carpeting. The plastered walls are a pale green, with only the bay papered. Here is one of the carved walnut fireplaces dating back to the 1900 remodeling but with some of the design eliminated and the finish lightened to reveal the beautiful grain. The ornate bronze ten-light chandelier is also a holdover from earlier days.

In the great dining room, the semicircular bay with its built-in seat was added after the house was built and does as much for the interior as for the exterior. Today, with its stately proportions, its molded wall panels, and its Greek Revival touches in the cornice, the eared and carved doorheads, and the heavy scroll brackets in the opening to the bay, the room is as formal as it is beautiful. The tall, slender door to the kitchen area is a thing of beauty in itself, with its elongated panels and paneled overdoor, its crossettes and carving.

The white marble fireplace, too, with its solid deep carving, is ponderously dignified. On the far side of the chimney breast from the door is a massive Victorian mahogany sideboard, and in the bay stands a custom-made hunt table in the Sheraton style with slender tapering legs. The *pièce de résistance*, however, is the long mahogany dining table. The top is antique, but the pedestals, in Regency style, are far newer than they seem. In addition to the chairs, which are

The living room is an interesting mélange of antique and modern furniture, its color scheme combining olive, mustard, and almond green with accents of black and gold.

In the rear parlor bay is a white
marble mantel surmounted by an
unframed twelve-section
antique mirror reaching
up to the cornice.

Hepplewhite intersecting shield-backs with inlaid legs, there
is a pair of antique Sheraton consoles. The gilded bronze and
crystal chandelier was original with the house, and makes its
nod toward the classical Greek with its anthemion crests. Its
illumination is now fortified by four twin-light wall sconces
of bronze with crystal drops. Over this mantel is a portrait
by Vaudechamp of Mrs. Moran's great-grandmother, Clém-
ence Augustin Toby.

The predominant color in this dining room, apart from the
brick-red carpet, is gray of various intensities supplied by the
silk draperies, the wall paint, the trim, and the chair seats.
Even without the print overdraperies it is a charming and
restful room well suited to its function and quite at home with
the rest of the interiors of this delightful mansion.

Newport, Rhode Island

THE BREAKERS

An Italian Renaissance Palazzo Facing the Atlantic

At the edge of a broad promontory at Newport, Rhode Island, looking eastward over the Atlantic Ocean, stands one of the most fabulous American "country cottages" ever built—the seventy-room Italian Renaissance palazzo erected for Cornelius Vanderbilt, in 1893-95, as a seashore retreat to be used during the two-month-long summer social seasons. Today, The Breakers, as it is called, is one of the very few such Newport houses remaining as it was in its heyday, complete with its original furnishings. And to the casual visitor the wonder of it is that so much magnificence could be contrived in a mansion a mere 250 feet long and 150 feet deep whose top floor was reserved for the domestic help.

The mansion was designed in 1892 by Richard Morris Hunt, the same prominent architect who was then building another, and larger, principal residence in North Carolina for George Vanderbilt, a brother of Cornelius, and had been responsible for four other miniature palaces in Newport. For his inspiration in planning The Breakers, Hunt turned to certain North Italian villas with which he was familiar, at Genoa and Turin, though some compromises had to be made because of limitations on the area to be occupied.

Although the whole waterfront estate comprised some eleven acres, the site of the house was confined to that previously occupied by an earlier mansion which had been destroyed by fire. This necessitated the addition of an extra story to accommodate some of the staff, the increased height of the building presenting the architect with problems in developing a principal façade of impressive proportions. Despite a strong emphasis on the horizontal introduced by the second- and third-story balustrades and overhanging eaves, this was not wholly successful in increasing the apparent length to the desired degree. Nevertheless the total effect is one of impressive distinction in keeping with the superbly detailed interiors on which neither expense nor effort was spared.

The house is set well above the grounds, with its great

The Breakers—an Italian Renaissance palace in miniature.

Facing east over the Atlantic, the Vanderbilt mansion on its eleven-acre estate shares the waterfront with other famed Newport "summer cottages."

paved terrace to the east and formal gardens north and south, all encompassed by a stone balustrade, with sweeping curves at each corner, plus punctuating urns, and here and there a huge fountain and broad steps. No two fronts are alike.

The entrance front faces west, and here the curving driveway sweeps up from the distant gateway of ornamental iron and smoothly tooled limestone pillars adorned with huge bronze lanterns to the square ivy-covered porte cochere, which in turn is flanked by four great bronze candelabra of Italian design. At the south side the house's great drawing room projects in a semicircular bay continued up to second-story height and topped by a balustrade.

The whole exterior is faced with buff Indiana limestone over brick, the entire structure being reinforced with steel beams and joists in place of wood to eliminate the danger of total destruction by fire. The hipped roofs are covered with terra-cotta Spanish tiles fired to various shades of red to produce an interesting mottled effect.

To the east is the principal front overlooking the terrace and the ocean. Here two loggias, one above the other, occupy the space between the wings. The lower arcade is composed of three massive arches separated by pillars and fronted by attached Roman-Doric columns on heavy plinths, the spandrels adorned by carved figures in high relief, and the arches displaying masks for keystones, all this exquisite carving emanating from the studio of the noted sculptor Karl Bitter. The upper loggia is light and airy by contrast, each of its three sections composed of twin arches supported by a slender Ionic column in white marble. Each pair is enclosed by pillars with attached

OPPOSITE: The dining room is the most highly ornamental and colorful room in the mansion.

fluted Ionic columns in limestone in the manner of those below. Here, however, the pedestals are joined by a stone balustrade matching that which serves as a parapet above the decorated entablature.

The most elaborate and impressive of all the interiors at The Breakers is undoubtedly that of the great hall which rises forty-five feet to a richly carved and painted ceiling. The ceiling's huge center panel enframes a trompe-l'oeil painting representing a cloud-filled sky designed to make it appear to open to the heavens.

Three walls of this room are of Caen stone—a yellowish French limestone with a rippled figure—including the wide archways opening off it. Each archway spandrel is carved with swags and pendants in high relief, and inset with colorful marble panels on which are centered decorative plaques set with huge, egg-shaped polished green cabochons. The central arch of the north wall is occupied by the grand staircase, a creation of carved Caen stone with highly decorative wrought-iron and cast-bronze balustrades sweeping upward and outward in a graceful Y to the open balcony above. These arches are flanked by ceiling-high pilasters mounted on tall pediments, each shaft elaborately carved and fluted, and terminating in a composite capital with an Oriental mask in the center. Three of the walls are treated in this fashion, the fourth enframing huge windows which afford a view over the terrace to the sea.

Four giant bronze chandeliers, each with sixteen opaline globes, are suspended from the ceiling. Augmenting them are tall bronze candelabra patterned after sixteenth-century originals which incorporate exquisitely modeled figures. Much of the *giallo antico* marble floor is overlaid with handsomely patterned and colored Oriental rugs of great size.

From the hall floor the great stair soars upward in a graceful sweep to the balcony. On either side of it hangs a lovely Venetian lantern in wrought bronze crowned with tiny cupids. Under the balcony there are a number of interesting items. On the end wall a della Robbia plaque hangs over a gold-encrusted coffer with enamel-illuminated panels; massive gilt chairs flank the flying stair and, facing them, the marble fountain is set into the soffit of its springing arch, its rippling shell guarded by weirdly human-looking dolphins.

Against the balcony wall at the top of the first flight of stairs hangs a huge Flemish tapestry, 24 by 18 feet, which is over three hundred years old, having been woven by the great Emander in 1619. In the daytime its subdued colors are enhanced by the soft glow from a stained-glass skylight in the roof above it.

At its south end the great hall extends into an arcade whose groined vaulting arches over an enormous hooded fireplace of Caen stone, beautifully sculpted, and flanked by mirror-paneled sliding doors of carved mahogany. Each of the hall's eight doors is crowned with an arched pediment whose tym-

The grand staircase of carved Caen stone and bronze sweeps upward and outward from the great hall to the balcony above.

OPPOSITE TOP: Detail of the Grand Salon fireplace.

OPPOSITE BOTTOM: "Even the smallest bedroom has paneled walls."

195

The great hall rises forty-five feet to a carved and painted ceiling. Its archways are carved with swags and pendants and inset with marble panels and polished green cabochons.

Beneath the sweeping arch of the grand staircase is a marble fountain, its rippling shell guarded by dolphins in the round.

panum is filled with high-relief sculptures of classical and modern groupings depicting man's progress in the arts, in science, and in industry.

While this great hall may be the most impressive room in the mansion, the dining room is undoubtedly the most highly ornamented and colorful, with its tremendous crystal chandeliers, its procession of gilded cornices, arches, capitals, and plaques, its golden statues and life-size sculptures, its tinted and patterned walls and alabaster columns, its lush draperies in royal red damask that blend so majestically with the riot of gold, and a thousand other details culminating in the great ceiling painting entitled *Aurora at Dawn* two stories above.

The room itself is fifty-eight feet long and forty-two feet wide, with a vaulted ceiling groined where it is arched back to receive the oval, bronze-grilled sash. Twelve monolithic columns of red alabaster, with Corinthian capitals of gilded bronze, backed by pilasters of the same materials, combine to support the highly ornamented entablature whose frieze is enriched by swags and masks under a molded and modillioned cornice, all picked out in gold.

Centered in one end wall is a hooded fireplace of Cippolino marble, set into a gilded arch against a background of Renaissance design painted on silver leaf. In addition to the great chandeliers there are twelve crystal sconces, each attached to one of the alabaster columns, the whole calculated to flood

OPPOSITE: The tiny Louis XVI reception room is resplendent with carved and gilded boiserie from a Parisian house presented by Marie Antoinette to her goddaughter, Mlle. de Saint-Aulaire.

Louis XV antique paneling
in pale green and gold and a
mantel of Paonazetto marble
form an exquisite setting for
the breakfast room furniture.

the farthest recesses with a sunshine-yellow light. The room's principal furniture pieces include an extensible dining table of carved oak inlaid with lemonwood, which seats up to thirty-four in gold-mounted, high-backed chairs covered with the same red damask as the curtains.

It is interesting to compare this immense and somewhat overpowering chamber with the comparatively tiny reception room which opens off the entrance hall. This delightful interior is typically French, its wood-paneled walls painted a pale cream against which delicately carved and gilded designs of Louis XVI vintage look their lovely best. This *boiserie* was originally installed in a house in Paris which was a gift from Queen Marie Antoinette to her goddaughter, Mlle. de Saint-Aulaire.

The mantel is of white marble, its garniture consisting of a small clock (despite the large *cartel* in the adjacent wall panel), and a pair of "mermaid" candlesticks, all in gilt bronze with enamel inlay. Above this is a large, round-topped, gold-framed mirror overlaid with swags and pendants of fruit and flowers, the pendants being repeated in the tall flanking panels to which bronze doré appliqués are attached.

The painted chairs are upholstered in Beauvais tapestry, and the rug is a deep-pile Savonnerie, while the floor itself is of herringbone parquet. These complete a superb though minor interior that has all the air of a jeweled casket.

Much more in keeping with the rest of the main-floor apartments is the Grand Salon or music room (the appellation depending upon the use to which it is being put at the moment). Though this room is but a single story in height, it has one of the most elaborate ceilings in the mansion, part coffered, part coved, to create three separate zones, all finished in silver and gold.

The central, coved area extends from the fireplace into the circular bay where the musical instruments are grouped adjacent to the windows. From it are suspended two magnificent crystal chandeliers designed especially for this room. Between their points of attachment, the ceiling bears a classical painting whose allegorical figures represent Harmony, Music, Song, and Melody.

This entire room was designed by a French architect, Richard Bouwens van der Boyens, collaborating with Hunt, and every detail from floor to ceiling was made in France and later installed by French workmen. The walls are painted a pale gray and decorated in gold, as are the Ionic columns whose lower sections are encircled by gilded decorative bands and low-relief carving. These contrast wonderfully with the rich reds of the Italian cut-velvet upholstery and draperies.

The same architect designed the morning room which, thanks to its overstuffed furniture, seems far less ornate than the others, in spite of the fact that the walls and ceiling are crowded with decorative detail. The ceiling is coffered, with rosettes in the recessed centers and ornamental drops at the

corners, the coved section having its own cornice with fern-carved modillions spaced by tiny sunken panels.

In the room corners, between pilasters, are oil paintings on silver set in molded panels. These represent eight of the Nine Muses, there being, unfortunately, no space for the lovely Polyhymnia. On the panels of the sliding mahogany door are paintings in grisaille of the Four Elements, while the central ceiling panel displays the Four Seasons, both perennial subjects pleasingly interpreted. The furniture here is Italian, copied after that of the Palazzo Correr in Venice, all gilded and covered in silk damask.

One of the most important rooms designed by architect Hunt himself was the library, a gracious and comfortable interior in spite of its overpowering fireplace and sumptuous detail. The room is paneled in black walnut, stamped in gold and carved in low relief in sixteenth-century style. The upper walls are paneled in green Spanish leather with gold embossing, while the dark wood of the coffered ceiling is lightly gilded, the total effect being one of restrained elegance.

The marble fireplace is a sixteenth-century French antique from the Château d'Arnay-le-Duc yet it mates perfectly with the bookcases which are built into recesses and enclosed with glass doors. The gold-stamped bindings in many colors have no small decorative value themselves. Above the cases twin arches provide recesses for the display of figurines, both ceramic and ivory. The furniture includes Régence and Directoire seating pieces in tapestry, and Late Victorian ones in

The library is paneled in black walnut, stamped in gold and carved in low-relief 16th-century style; the upper walls are green Spanish leather, the marble fireplace 16th-century French, the setting a mixture of Victorian, Régence, and Directoire.

199

The Grand Salon interior was made in France—
the elaborate ceiling is part coved, part coffered, creating
three zones, in silver and gold, while the walls and columns
are gray and gold, contrasting with the red Italian
cut velvet of upholstery and draperies.

damask, completing a truly eclectic interior that is a delight to the eye.

The small family dining room, or breakfast room, has, as might be expected, little in common with the dining room used for state occasions, yet its decoration and furnishing leave little to be desired. It, too, has antique paneling, this time of Louis XV vintage in pale green with gilded moldings and a wide coved cornice adorned with gold filigree tracery culminating in amatory scenes over the chimney breast.

The atmosphere here is light, airy, and refreshing, the vertical accented by tall but curvaceous panels, the arched mirror, and the sweeping lines of a delicate mantelpiece of Paonazetto marble.

There is, of course, far more to The Breakers than this—the billiard room, for instance, an outstanding example of a games room of this extravagant period, with its matched slabs of gray-green Cippolino marble walls, in blind arcades of paired yellow alabaster arches, and the splendid mosaic ceiling painting of a mother and children in a Roman bath. The bedrooms are also exquisite in every detail, even the smallest enlivened with green-paneled walls as a background to its antique ivory-painted furniture. These, however, are but minor facets in a tremendous and unbelievable whole, the like of which we shall probably never see again.

An elaborately carved dark mahogany vitrine, such as this, stands on each side of the breakfast room fireplace.

The overstuffed pieces in the morning room make it seem far less ornate than the others in spite of its decorative detail.

Newport, Rhode Island
THE ELMS

A Palatial Residence with a Modest Name

The decorative detail of The Elms
main entrance includes bronze
cupids astride marble sphinxes
which flank the steps.

Newport is a place of many mansions—a city that over a period of some fifty years in the nineteenth century acquired a group of palatial residences which established it as the undisputed social capital of the United States. From the 1860's on, Newport's neat countryside character, its handsome, white-painted, old-time mansions of wood (relics of a day when local fortunes were made in shipping), its miles of sandy foreshore skirting the ocean, its cool summer climate, and the large area of farmland available for building in a township unapproachable except by bridge or boat, all combined to attract people of wealth and position in search of a place to spend their long summer social seasons.

Planters from the Carolinas and Georgia were among the first to establish summer homes here—cottages to begin with, then sumptuous villas and, finally, in some instances, mansions, châteaux, and palaces. Today, a few of these noble buildings house institutions instead of families, their treasures scattered the world over. Others have suffered the even more ignominious fate of being torn down to make way for habitations of lesser glory. Among those fortunately preserved was the splendid home that Edward J. Berwind, coal magnate, had built for himself in 1901. Berwind entrusted the design and construction of this ambitious residence to a noted Philadelphia architect, Horace Trumbauer, who turned for his inspiration to the exquisite early eighteenth-century Château d'Agnès, built by Jules Hardouin Mansart at Asnières, near Paris. The result was an architectural triumph which its owner, with unaccountable modesty, named The Elms.

Stateliness without ostentation aptly describes the exterior of this palace-in-miniature which actually seems more Louis XIV than XV, with its total absence of rococo and its classic proportions. Perched on its terraced slope, it looks out over trees and high walls that mark the boundaries of this modest estate. Small in extent yet superb in layout are the grounds that surround it, still much as they were left by the French

OPPOSITE: From twin columns of *brèche violette* marble with bases and capitals of gilded bronze spring the arches supporting the balcony of the grand staircase.

The west or garden façade of The Elms.

landscape architect, Jacques Gréber, who designed the gardens.

The mansion's west façade faces a wide lawn dotted with fine specimen trees beyond which lie the formal gardens, accented here and there with examples of topiary, with marble and bronze statuary, with fountains and gazebos. The only other buildings of size are the stable and tackroom, the carriage house and coachman's quarters, as beautiful architecturally as the house itself. The whole estate is enclosed by a high wall, relieved at intervals by tall iron grilles and the imposing, though delicately wrought, iron gates of the main entrance.

Built of Indiana limestone, now mellowed to a pearl gray, the mansion's garden façade is robbed of some of its chaste severity by well-placed sculptures, most of which seem to denote a certain preoccupation with conflict. The rather rigid line of the roof balustrade is enlivened by four life-size baroque statuary groups which accent the ends of the parapet and its junctions with the central pavilion, the face of which is adorned with applied sculpture.

The main pavilion, centered in the east façade above a short flight of marble steps, is the most elaborately decorated portion of the whole edifice. Here the principal entrance is recessed under an entablature at first-floor level which extends over massive side walls enclosing four Corinthian columns. Behind each column, against the house wall, is a pilaster, and between these are the three glazed double doors of ornamental ironwork. Decorative, semicircular iron plates seal the arches above them. Over each door is an elaborate design carved in relief. The second story also has its complement of decorative features—statuary on the roof balustrade, urns on the balcony rail, high-relief masks centered in the window lintels, and grotesques at the bases of the rusticated quoins.

The Château d'Agnès at Asnières on which the design of The Elms was based.

OPPOSITE TOP: A corner of the Louis XVI drawing room with its romping cupids and huge mirrors.

OPPOSITE BOTTOM: The state dining room's immense paintings depict the triumphs of Alexander and Scipio Africanus.

205

The ballroom has walls of painted
paneling, grisaille overdoors,
and heavy brocade draperies;
the furniture is Louis XVI
in Gobelin tapestry, standing on
a rose and ivory Savonnerie rug.

The main hall portal—a pair
of lofty twin pillars of
brèche violette marble with
gilt-bronze bases and capitals.

The entrance doors open into an expansive foyer where a tall seventeenth-century Florentine oil jar of green faïence stands in each corner. From this, short, wide marble steps ascend between a mammoth pair of bronze-trimmed granite urns on marble bases to the main hall. Here, the portal is formed by lofty twin pillars of *brèche violette* marble with bases and capitals of gilded bronze—prophetic of the exotic splendors that lie ahead. Neither the restrained beauty of the west façade nor the decorative splendor of the east façade prepare one for the sumptuous interior with its wealth of color and detail—that sheer richness of decoration and furnishings, all within the bounds of accepted good taste, characteristic of an era in America when the owners of great houses sought to recapture the splendor of an earlier day and age.

Not all, however, is as it once was.

After Mr. Berwind's sister, the last resident of the house, died in 1961, the furnishings were disposed of at auction. The building was saved from demolition and acquired through the generosity of a group of Newport citizens under the auspices of the Preservation Society of Newport County. The Society was then faced with the necessity of replacing the missing furniture with appropriate pieces of the seventeenth, eighteenth, and nineteenth centuries. Fortunately, it was able to buy in some of the original furnishings at the auction, while other pieces were acquired through gifts or on loan. Today the interior actually contains a far higher proportion of authentic antiques than formerly, when the house was principally furnished with reproductions. It can now be considered as duplicating, at least in spirit, almost any château of its architectural period that is being lived in today.

The hall, with its white marble floor, is the first interior expanse to greet the eye on entering from the foyer. Ahead is the ballroom doorway in marble with bronze trim, the space above it occupied by a sculptured marble-and-bronze panel in high relief. On either side, in huge gilt frames, are eighteenth-century paintings from the Palazzo Cornaro in Venice. Attributed to the School of Tiepolo (1696-1770), they depict episodes in the life of Caterina Cornaro, Queen of Cyprus. Beneath these huge canvases stand great Louis XIV-style console tables, elaborately carved and gilded, their tops of *brèche violette* marble. Delicately wrought lanterns of gilded bronze hang from the coved ceiling, and bronze doré five-branched sconces accent the beauty of the marble pillars which, by means of arches enriched with plaster moldings, support the balcony over the grand staircase. On the walls of the stairway hang four notable tapestries—one of them the famous Gobelin *Don Quixote*.

Lending color to the north and south alcoves of the main hall are a pair of carved and gilded tabourets with seats of crimson ciselé velvet, and armorial portieres of the same color, decorated with silver embroidery and appliqués. In each of the alcoves two large vitrines display pieces of eighteenth-century

At one end of the dining room a fountain of red marble supports a heroic-size statue of Diana the Huntress.

The deep panels of the coffered ceiling are painted cerulean blue and decorated with winged lions of St. Mark and avellan crosses in gold.

The library overmantel features an early della Robbia terra-cotta cast of the Madonna and Child.

One of the dining room paintings depicting the triumphs of Alexander and Scipio Africanus.

porcelain from the kilns of Vincennes, Chantilly, and Sèvres.

Standing on one of the hall consoles is a pair of Chinese *sang-de-boeuf* vases; on the other is a pair of flowered Chinese vases with ormolu mounts. Gilded state chairs in antique gold-embroidered crimson velvet, a large ebony and boulle cabinet, a Louis XV boulle bracket clock by Gérard Humbert (1750), a magnificent Renaissance cabinet of tortoiseshell and inlaid wood on a carved and gilded base, all add their quota of splendor to a hall which might well have been transplanted *in toto* from eighteenth-century Europe.

Four important rooms open off this great hall—the library, drawing room, ballroom, and dining room, beyond which is a small but elaborate breakfast room. It would be difficult to say which of these is the most fascinating, the most richly furnished.

Undoubtedly the lightest and gayest of all is the Early Louis XVI drawing room with its gray and white paneled walls and gold draperies, its magnificent pink-accented nineteenth-century Aubusson rug, its overdoors and semicircular upper wall panels enlivened with sprays and romping cupids in grisaille, its huge mirrors with their molded pendant husks and swags and garlands, and its ceiling painted by De Witt. Here, surfaces and textures are all in the same mood: the elegant gold tracery of a Louis XIV boulle commode; the velvety smoothness of the round lapis-lazuli table into which ormolu arrows are sunk with skillful precision; the striped silk of the carved beechwood Louis XV bergères; the Beauvais tapestry of Louis XVI chairs; and the embroidered blue silk of the Grand Dauphin's standard mounted in the fire screen where it blends so well with the blue-veined marble mantel.

In the midst of all this stands a Louis XV marquetry *bureau plat* with ormolu mounts. Against the walls are an inlaid *tricoteuse* of rare design decorated with dolphins of bronze doré, and a tambour-fronted table supporting a Sèvres group in biscuit. On the mantel, reflected in its great mirror, is a Falconet clock of Sèvres porcelain and ormolu, together with a pair of ethereal, blue and white crystal girandoles on marble bases, once the property of Catherine II, Empress of Russia.

Separated from the drawing room by the ballroom is the state dining room, rich and impressive in the Venetian manner, with its massive furniture, coffered ceiling, and immense Palazzo Cornaro paintings depicting the triumphs of Alexander and Scipio Africanus. Paneled in oak, the room has six double mahogany doors, heavy with applied moldings, and one feature overshadowing all—a room-high, elaborately pedimented mantel with massive fluted pillars enclosing the fireplace and overmantel of agate, onyx, and *verde antico* marble.

The heavily carved and bracketed ceiling, said to be copied from one at the Palazzo Cornaro, has its deep panels painted cerulean blue and decorated with winged lions of St. Mark and avellan crosses in gold. From it are suspended four bronze-and-crystal chandeliers which the wall sconces are designed

to match. In the center of the polished parquet floor, on a nineteenth-century Aubusson rug, stands a massive French dining table of carved oak with a gilded apron, its center decorated with a French eighteenth-century silver-gilt tureen and platter. Around the table are heavy carved-oak chairs upholstered in green damask. At either side of the room, beneath one of the giant Cornaro paintings, is a Renaissance-style carved and gilded buffet with a top of *verde antico* marble. At the window end of the room are cut-velvet curtains and, between them, a fountain of red marble supporting a life-sized statue of Diana the Huntress.

This statue was the subject of a somewhat amusing incident during the sale of the furnishings. When Diana was removed from her niche, the buyer discovered to his chagrin that the lady had been squared off in the rear to fit against the marble panel. The purchase was therefore promptly canceled, to the subsequent benefit of the mansion's new owners.

The breakfast room may be the smallest, but it is undoubtedly the most exquisite room on this floor. Decorated in the Chinese manner, its most striking features are four great black-and-gold lacquered panels of the K'ang Hsi period, framed in gilded oak and surmonted by shell carvings. Smaller lacquered panels serve as overdoors. The coved ceiling is decorated with a deep patterned border of gilded stucco in low relief. Three gilded, marble-topped oak buffets, carved in the Chi-

The upstairs drawing room, formerly the Berwinds' boudoir. The panels are covered in crimson damask, and the curtains are crimson brocade. A K'ang Hsi Chinese temple jar stands on the Louis XV carved and gilded wood console table with a rose marble top. The rug is a Feraghan.

The gemlike breakfast room features Chinese lacquered panels and a coved ceiling with gilded stucco filigree.

Bronze and marble statuary, a Poussin, and Flemish tapestry vie for attention in the marble-walled conservatory.

nese manner, are set against the walls. A rare Chinese blue-and-tan dragon rug dating from the Ming Dynasty (1368-1644) forms a handsome background for a painted oval French table whose apron and two circling stretchers are carved and gilded.

In the library, fine book bindings and walls covered in crimson damask form a muted but rich background for one of the art treasures of the mansion—an early terra-cotta cast of the Madonna and Child by Giovanni della Robbia, the original of which is in the church of San Jacopo di Ripoli in Florence.

In the fireplace are a patterned French cast-iron fireback and a pair of sixteenth-century Venetian bronze statuettes of Athene and Ceres. Alongside are nineteenth-century terrestrial and celestial globes with compasses in their bases. Among the other interesting pieces are a fine Kirman rug; a striking carved and gilt Venetian reading stand upholstered in green and gold damask; a pair of curious bronze candelabra, carved-oak side chairs and table dating back to Charles I of England (1625-1649); and a Dutch seventeenth-century marquetry cabinet. On the inlaid burl-walnut bookcases are blue-and-white and blue-and-gold Chinese porcelain covered jars. The pictures in this room include a portrait by Van Dyck (1599-1641), a landscape by Pynacker, and an Italian portrait of the Lombard School.

The 40-by-50-foot ballroom, centered in the west façade and extending into the pavilion, opens onto the garden. It is impressive in spite of the rather sparse furnishings common to most ballrooms. The walls are of painted paneling with grisaille overdoors in the manner of the drawing room, and the two windows and four doors are covered with heavy brocade curtains. A superb suite consisting of a Louis XVI canapé, two bergères, and four side chairs upholstered in Gobelin tapestry—made originally for the Duc de Choiseul—stands at the garden end on a pale rose and ivory Savonnerie rug.

In the conservatory, opening off the drawing room and leading to a marble terrace overlooking the garden, the focal point is a red marble fountain with a nereid and triton in bronze supported by sea horses, and its flanking basins. Other marble pieces consist of a large nineteenth-century Italian sculptured urn and a statue of white marble in each corner of the room. On the south wall is a mammoth Chinese temple urn in blue and green faïence, once the property of the famous English Field Marshal Lord Kitchener. On either side of this is a large eighteenth-century painting with classical ruins. Another striking painting is a French landscape of the school of Nicolas Poussin.

Though this necessarily brief description of the interiors may tend to obscure the fact, these are all rooms designed to be lived in, not mere showplaces—rooms in which the best of the past has been adapted to the exigencies of the present, with more than ordinary skill and éclat.

Detail of an attached
Ionic column in
the entrance hall.

Palm Beach, Florida
WHITEHALL

The Marble Halls of a Modern Midas

Enormous urns on marble steps
at Whitehall suggest the public
building rather than
the private home.

Spanish in detail and feel is the main façade of the palatial, 73-room residence that oil magnate Henry Morrison Flagler erected on a six-acre waterfront tract at Palm Beach in 1902. The entrance portico is graced by giant columns in fluted Roman Doric style with fancy necking and matching pilasters, while enormous urns punctuate the marble steps. Behind the columns are the great Roman-arched windows and doorway, the latter resplendent with a bronze grille and overdoor, and, above them, flat-topped mullioned windows with eared architraves and marble balconies with carved brackets and bronze railings. The portico ceiling is deeply coffered with carved panels, the frieze embellished with paterae, and the elaborate cornice dentiled, carved, and modillioned, and topped off with slightly projecting red-tiled eaves.

Behind the portico roof, the mansion wall rises another story to its own cornice which is interrupted by pedestals and tile-capped sections of the returned gable walls. The gables themselves are topped by twin chimneys connected by bridging parapets against which the main-roof tiles abut. At either end of the portico the façade extends the distance of a single room, the cornices level with that of the portico roof. The total effect is highly monumental, its severity softened by the tropical air of the clay pantiles and the crowding palms. This is, of course, but one aspect of the mansion which is rectangular in shape, and surrounds a large patio with formal grass plots centering on a statuary-adorned fountain. At the rear a second columned portico is flanked by wings containing the service quarters and offices, with still a third portico on the left flank of the mansion sheltering an informal entrance that Mr. Flagler preferred for his own use.

In turning over the design of Whitehall to John M. Carrère and Thomas Hastings—architects of such notable structures as the U. S. Senate Building and the New York Public Library—Flagler specified that it must be the most splendid and sumptuous of residences, as an inducement to other people

OPPOSITE: The Italian Renaissance library is notable for its exquisite carved and molded decoration and ceiling paintings.

of wealth to build in the state. The contractors were Pottier and Stymus, who also designed much of the interior embellishments and furnishings, importing craftsmen from France and Italy, and combing the continents for antiquities with which to adorn it. This ambitious project was completed in eight months. The result is a series of splendid interiors—French, Italian, English, Spanish, and Swiss—covering various periods and centuries, including Colonial American. Incorporated in these rooms are carved wood and stone, cast bronze, frescoed ceilings, brocaded walls, and marble floors.

The largest of the rooms is the marble hall, 20 feet high and measuring 110 by 40 feet, which is entered from the main portico. Its principal decorative feature is a tremendous circular fresco occupying a dished section of the ceiling, 20 feet in diameter. The artist is forgotten, but the painting is said to represent "The Crowning of Knowledge." Enframing this is some of the most elaborate gilded and painted stucco work ever executed, the frame portion consisting of a foot-thick modeled garland. Plain molding separates this from the rest of the ceiling which is divided into panels of diverse shapes, with figures in tempera and others in high relief with incredibly intricate carved backgrounds. The tempera paintings are identified as symbolizing "Prosperity" and "Happiness"; the modeled ones as cameo medallions depicting "Earth," "Sea," "Air," and "Soil."

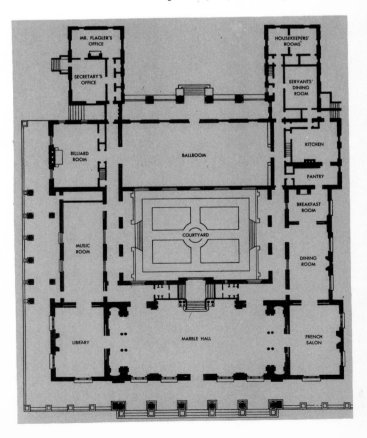

OPPOSITE: The assembly room set up for lectures and entertainment.

The west room, of stone and plaster throughout, features several stairways and a wall-high fountain. Its huge bronze and glass doors overlook Lake Worth.

The rest of the room, including the floor, is nearly all marble. There are multiple Ionic columns and pilasters with bronze caps and bases, white marble walls inlaid with black, and archways with masks for keystones, the flat-topped doorways edged with bound garlands. Distributed throughout the hall are marble urns, pedestals, and benches, and centered in one side is a wide, branching marble stairway leading to the second floor. In the hall corners are heroic-sized marble statues labeled, somewhat cryptically, "Peace," "Science," "Pensive," and "Marine."

The furniture here is scant but rich, the most prominent piece a nine-foot-tall clock of burnished bronze. Massive Louis XIV fauteuils are spaced around the floor like so many thrones, elaborately carved and upholstered in cut velvet incorporating a crown in the design. These are said to have once been used in a European monarch's palace. A similar source is indicated for two heavy pedestal tables—a three-legged one

Detail of the tapestry covering the music
room's Louis XV canapé.

In the music room twin Louis XV fauteuils
and a canapé are posed against a background of carved panels
and gold damask.

Whitehall

Decorating the dome of the marble hall is a
20-foot circular fresco depicting
The Crowning of Knowledge.

A Flemish tapestry is draped across an archway
of the great hall.

The 110-by-40-foot marble hall with its Ionic columns and
pilasters with bronze caps and bases.

Detail of the great pipe organ in the Louis XIV music room.

Boucher panels over doors and windows in the grand ballroom represent the Four Seasons.

One of the four life-size statues in the marble hall, labeled "Pensive."

with masks on the knees and the other with two pedestals incorporating winged figures and scrolls on a solid base, the aprons centered on a large cabochon smothered in foliage.

Somewhat smaller but even more opulent is the Louis XIV music room whose end wall is occupied by what was the largest residential pipe organ of its day. This great ceiling is coved, the coving itself fantastically decorated with gilded stucco designs. Here also is a central dished circle with an ethereal fresco illuminated from the circumference by concealed lights. On either side is a huge medallion decorated in relief, and from the center of this hangs a great crystal chandelier. Each window is crowned with an elaborate cornice, the architrave delicately carved with a rim of flowers and the opening draped with tasseled damask. Above a dado whose panels are outlined with narrow, carved molding, the walls are covered with gold damask as a background for a collection of fine paintings.

The ballroom, still as it was in 1902 when the first ball was given, except for the abolished minstrels' gallery, is truly an exercise in grandeur. Decorated in Louis XV style, it has its original, gold-leaf-accented white paint, hand-carved banquettes in Savonnerie tapestry along the walls, and rose du Barry silk damask draperies. The 91-foot ceiling is divided into four coved panels, above a lavishly decorated cornice. From two of the panels hang huge chandeliers, rococo in style, with decorative glass framed in gilt bronze and fringed with hand-cut crystal drops. Between the windows are mirrored panels,

Detail from one of the large Grecian urns flanking the great marble staircase.

This exquisite marble fountain depicting Susanna and the Elders stands in the courtyard.

Even the ceiling corners of the marble hall are adorned with sculpture in the round.

Between the two huge crystal chandeliers of the music room is the illuminated dome.

Grouped in a corner of the French salon are this Louis XV canapé-à-corbeille and marquise, the candelabrum, and a portrait of Flagler's granddaughter, Mrs. Roger Glenn Mook.

each with a colorful, artificial gem-decorated tree in front of it. Above the windows, decorative panels by François Boucher (1703-1770) depict the seasons, and spaced between them are gilt-bronze, five-branched sconces which help to make the room a dazzling sight after dark.

The formal dining room in which many celebrities such as Admiral Dewey, the Duke of Manchester, and Senator Elihu Root were entertained, represents the earlier period of François I (1515-1547). Finished in satinwood, the room's dominant colors are green, including the fabric-covered walls and the portieres. There is even a large green banquet cloth to match.

Scattered through the mansion are quite a few other things worthy of mention, such as the Byzantine font on the stair landing. This dates from the fifth or sixth century A.D. and is covered in mosaic and marble veneer. In the billiard room there is a finely carved Caen-stone mantelpiece and a striking oak-beamed ceiling. The French period Grand Salon, in turn, is notable for its fine collection of paintings and sculpture, and on the second floor are bedrooms with Louis XVI interiors furnished in Louis XV style.

And so it is with the rest of the apartments, all decorated and furnished with a lavish hand by a skilled decorator so that the mansion's primary function as a home, however splendid, is far overshadowed by its magnificence.

OPPOSITE: White with gold accents in Louis XV style, the ballroom has banquettes in Savonnerie tapestry and silk damask draperies.

Bratenahl, Ohio
GWINN

A Mansion Built to an Ideal

From an architectural standpoint the early twentieth-century villa called Gwinn, which looks out over the waters of Lake Erie from the Ohio shore, is an exercise in taste and proportion that defers but little to classical dogma. Together with its furnishings and setting it represents the results of one man's search for grace and refinement in his surroundings—an ideal achieved to an extraordinary degree. That man was William Gwinn Mather, an industrialist possessed of both ideals and discrimination, who was fortunate enough to enlist the aid of a like-minded architect, Charles A. Platt, and a prominent landscape artist, Warren Manning, in translating his dream into reality.

The house was built in 1907 with every possible step taken to ensure that the architecture, the interiors and the surroundings would be entirely harmonious. How perfectly the house fits into its setting is obvious from an aerial view which begins with the sweeping curve of a sea wall from which wide steps lead up to a circular terrace with its marble lily pool and fountain. From this terrace, arbored walks lead to right and left, converging toward the sea wall with a gazebo at each end where the two meet. Beyond the terrace, more steps ascend to the rounded portico with its tall Ionic columns.

The house proper is a rectangular structure, the center section of the south façade set forward slightly to form a pavilion and further extended by a loggia to balance the north portico. All exterior walls are stuccoed smooth, the windows devoid of trim except for keystoned flat arches, with louvered shutters painted the same off-white as the walls. The frieze is plain, the cornice relieved by broad dentils and supporting a heavy stone balustrade which extends around the flat roof and the north portico. The chimneys, too, are works of art with their smooth faces molded into panels, with cornices and caps. Even the service quarters, which form a low, two-story wing, have a great deal of architectural merit.

On the west façade is the main entrance, with fluted mod-

The porticoed terrace of
Gwinn overlooks Lake Erie.

OPPOSITE TOP: In the wild garden masses of
spring flowers carpet the open spaces.

OPPOSITE BOTTOM: In the formal garden
a path winds past a lily pool.

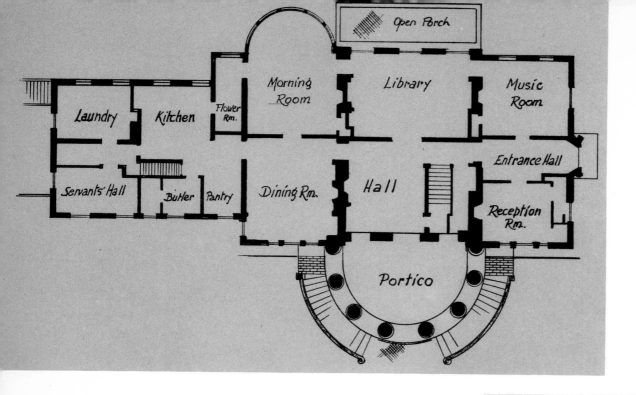

Gwinn in plan, the service quarters forming a lower wing.

The west front and garden entrance with its carriage ring.

This aerial view shows how perfectly the house fits into its setting.

Mr. Mather's bedroom (left) combines simplicity with quality from the ribbed ceiling to the rich wall hanging. Mrs. Mather's bedroom (right) has a forthright paneled and painted ceiling, a colorful della Robbia medallion on the wall, and a primitive Spanish bed.

ified Tuscan columns, and a frieze with triglyphs decorated with paterae. Leading up to this entrance is a paved carriage ring centered by a low fountain basin and flanked by huge pottery urns on plinths and shrubs in decorative tubs. The south loggia is, of course, but one story high, its front opening supported by stop-fluted Doric columns. From this point the vista extends across a wide lawn and through an allée of poplars to the distant woods. On one side of the tree-shaded lawn is a formal garden, on the other a wild one. The former begins with a pergola and ends with a loggia decorated in Pompeian style which leads to the greenhouses. In the wild garden ivy-covered elms and beeches shade rhododendron-lined paths that encircle a tall fountain.

Although the house employs certain classical architectural features, executed in concrete and usually somewhat modified, it is truly eclectic in style, with a personality all its own. This mood of polished restraint is very much in keeping with the interiors which are definitely designed to accommodate furniture of varying styles and periods, placing comfort and convenience high on the list of basic requirements.

An important feature of all main-floor rooms is that they have fine parquet flooring. For this reason rugs and carpets are little used and it is astonishing what charming interiors can be achieved without them. One of the most effective of such interiors is that of the library which is paneled in wood throughout, including the ceiling with its painted designs. All

Here and there in the bedrooms are exquisite antique carvings such as this.

A 15th-century Florentine cassone panel hangs over the morning room fireplace.

In the dining room a large Bologna chest displays 15th-century majolica platters and silverware by Paul Storr.

large areas are, however, effectively broken up by ceiling beams, wall pilasters, and the bookshelf areas where the wood is largely hidden by the rich and colorful bindings.

The large overstuffed sofa and twin armchairs, together with the cushions of two Louis XV cane-backs, are covered in the same Fortuny Venetian pattern fabric as the draperies, which unifies them in a pleasing fashion. Over the sofa recess and set into the bookshelves is a portrait by Boltraggio in a heavy architectural frame. The coffee table is modern, with a carved and gilded top on iron legs. In one of the three small-paned double French windows stands a wooden tripod planter with growing creeper. Above this is a stained-glass panel reminiscent of a seventeenth-century armorial quarry, hung in the window. The middle window is used as a door to the south loggia.

Separating the doors are large seventeenth-century Italian architectural paintings, one of them a Canaletto (1697-1768), the other by a painter of the same school. Beneath the Canaletto is a framed fragment of an early milles-fleurs tapestry, and under its companion a beautifully carved credenza. The other end of the room is dominated by a massive stone fireplace, the deep mantel carried on carved stone brackets.

In striking contrast to the library is the music room. Here the paneling is replaced by an antique French corn-ear paper in yellow and green on an off-white ground. A major architectural feature is the French mantel in white marble with simple moldings. Above it is a sixteenth-century Italian painting,

An antique French corn-ear paper in yellow and green sets off the music room's French mantel.

Near the black-lacquered grand piano is a painting by Nicolas Lancret and a series of Dewing's *Ladies*.

The library is walnut-paneled, including the ceiling which bears painted designs.

Over the library's sofa recess is a portrait by Boltraggio. Draperies and upholstery are of the same Fortuny Venetian fabric.

while the mantel garniture consists of Meissen ormolu-mounted candlesticks and clock. On each side of the hearth, on a rose-toned silk prayer rug, are Louis XV bergères and a pair of Louis XVI fauteuils. Between the two south windows is an almost ceiling-high trumeau in a rope-carved gilt frame, with a pastoral scene above the mirror. Close by hangs a smaller painting by Nicolas Lancret (1690-1743), and a series of Dewing's *Ladies*. Near the black-lacquered grand piano is a pair of small marquetry tables, and depending from the ceiling is an exquisite crystal chandelier.

In the dining room which has the same fluted pilasters and heavy wooden cornice, deep window reveals and baseboards as the library, the large paneled areas are covered with old damask in shades of yellow and brown. Wood tones therefore dominate this room also, and lend contrast to the highly decorative pewter twelve-light chandelier with its tall candles and the pewter wall sconces. The sideboard consists of a huge Bologna chest with a high, shelved back which serves to display fifteenth-century majolica platters in various colors. Also on the sideboard are silverware pieces by Paul Storr—an urn and two chafing dishes. On the wall above is a crested Louis XV gilt-

framed mirror. The dining table is a round Empire pedestal type, capable of being greatly extended, with heavily carved feet. The chairs are leather-backed and leather-seated, Cromwellian style with spiral turnings, brass-nailed and fringed.

In the adjacent hall another interesting grouping displays a fifteenth-century Italian commode against a white pilastered wall, backed by a Belgian tapestry in which red and gold predominate. This is flanked by fifteenth-century Spanish leather-backed chairs. On the commode is an early seventeenth-century French sculpture—a Madonna in white marble—and a pair of tall silver candlesticks of Spanish origin. Nearby is a painting by Tiepolo (1696-1770), and the chandelier is censer-shaped in antique bronze.

In 1957 the Gwinn estate was inherited by Mrs. Mather's son, James D. Ireland, but the house is no longer occupied as a residence. Instead, it has been preserved in its original condition as a memorial to Mr. and Mrs. Mather, and is made available to educational and cultural organizations and distinguished visitors to the city of Cleveland within whose boundaries it stands.

Separating the library's porch doors are 17th-century Italian paintings, one an original Canaletto and the other of his school.

A hall grouping displays a 15th-century Italian commode against a Belgian tapestry in red and gold.

Vizcaya's southern façade from
beyond the formal gardens.

The casino from the canal
at the rear.

Miami, Florida
VIZCAYA

An Italian Palace Sparkling in the Sun

In a thirty-acre clearing on the edge of Biscayne Bay, where dense mangrove swamps once crowded the shore, industrialist James Deering built his mansion of white coral and named it Vizcaya in honor of those Spanish adventurers who anchored their tiny caravels there almost four hundred years before. Today, this authentic-appearing Italian palazzo with Spanish overtones still sparkles in the tropical sun, sheltering under its red-tiled roof Italian and French interiors that range in period from the sixteenth to the early nineteenth centuries.

Though the mansion has no single prototype, not only is its architecture typically Renaissance in style, but incorporated in its structure are relics of half a dozen French, Venetian, Roman, and Milanese great houses—from massive doorways to painted ceilings. During the twenty-five years prior to 1914 when the building was begun, Mr. Deering had scoured Europe for examples of Italian Renaissance architectural details and art as well as now almost priceless furniture and furnishings. In those days it was still possible to export antiquities from most countries regardless of their age or rarity or historic significance. As a result, when the time came to build, Deering had a warehouse full of treasures, and he used them to good effect.

These artifacts were the guideposts that the architects, F. Burrall Hoffman, Jr., and Paul Chalfin, had to follow in designing the mansion. For example, the height of the first-floor ceiling was governed by the size of a marble-framed gateway from the Palazzo Pisani at Strá; the loggias had to accommodate the splendid doors from the Parisian palace of Eugène de Beauharnais, Napoleon's stepson; the size of the Louis XV salon was determined by the dimensions of a plaster ceiling removed from Venice's Palazzo Rossi. Other ceilings and walls had to provide space for paintings on canvas from a princely residence in Milan, and huge fireplaces made to look as though they had not been disturbed in four hundred years. And so it was for almost every room.

View of the courtyard from the east loggia.

233

Vizcaya

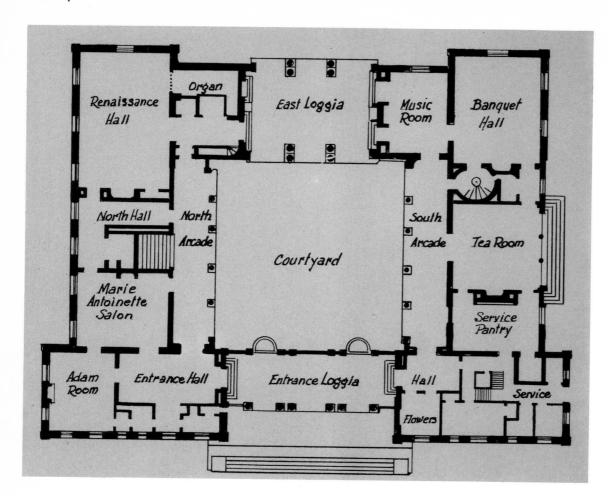

Renaissance Hall

Organ

East Loggia

Music Room

Banquet Hall

North Hall

North Arcade

South Arcade

Tea Room

Marie Antoinette Salon

Courtyard

Service Pantry

Adam Room

Entrance Hall

Entrance Loggia

Hall

Service

Flowers

The palazzo in its tropical setting is as enchanting from the air as on the ground.

To provide stone for the building, Deering bought a nearby coral quarry, and in order to secure properly weathered, hand-made red tile he stripped the roofs of old Cuban houses, re-covering them with modern roofing to everyone's satisfaction. Also imported were all the necessary foreign craftsmen—stonecutters and sculptors, plasterers, woodworkers, and painters—to supplement the local talent. Even so it took two years to complete the structure, and an additional five years to lay out the ten acres of formal Italian garden.

Simple in design and moderate in scale, Vizcaya is vastly interesting both for its exterior and interior architecture and for its decoration and furnishing. Almost square in plan, it centers on a flagged cortile, or courtyard, so that through ventilation is available for every room. Onto the cortile open two entrance loggias and two Roman-arched arcades with sturdy Tuscan columns. Above each arcade is a gallery with slender Ionic columns supporting the overhanging roof. The loggias are barrel-vaulted, with deep-cut panels in the soffits of the coral groins and arches, together with plaster decorative designs, and plain panels with egg-and-dart moldings in the vaultings. On each façade the coral walls are stuccoed smooth with the exception of the quoins and the incipient brackets decorating the frieze. The exotic-appearing chimney tops are bracketed out and tile-covered, as is the round top of the circular stairway well which is carried above the main roof.

Hung with Robert Browning's tapestries, the Renaissance banquet hall boasts a 15th-century Italian sideboard and 16th-century chairs.

At the ocean landing a statue-bedecked stone barge constitutes a breakwater.

235

The casino from
the formal gardens.

Flying cupids, medieval musicians, and Roman
deities fill the casino's trompe-l'oeil ceiling
with light and life.

OPPOSITE: Much of the reception room's interior structure,
including elaborate ceiling and boiserie, came from
Italian palazzos.

The formal living quarters of the main house are on the first floor and the family rooms are on the second floor, the west entrance loggia having nothing but a service passage over it. The narrower eastern loggia supports a bathroom, together with stairs up to a gallery extending around three sides of the cortile. Here are the kitchen, breakfast room, two salons, and five guest rooms, as well as the owner's bedroom and offices and the indoor servants' quarters. The two towers accommodate four other guest rooms. Main stairs are provided at both ends of the building.

Mounted on a high terrace with lawns, the house is surrounded by a stone balustrade with obelisks and statuary on the pedestals. Four sets of wide stone steps descend to a lower level—on the east to the sea-wall promenade, on the south to the formal gardens, on the west to the entrance driveway, and on the north to the swimming pool. Directly in front of the east façade is an elaborate boat-shaped breakwater known as the Stone Barge, with its carved coral mermaids and sea monsters, its free-standing statues, its obelisks, terraces, plantings, and stone bulwarks.

At the south end of the curving promenade is a lattice-roofed tea house, and beyond the gardens (in which everything growing provides a native approximation of Italian foliage) is an elaborate casino or pleasure house. This stands at the foot of a water stairway down which a fountain pool empties in a cascade. The gardens themselves are reminiscent of those of the Villa Albani in Rome and the Villa d'Este at Tivoli. Other authentic Italian touches are supplied, in the forecourt, by a sixteenth-century entrance gateway of pink marble and Istrian stone from the Palazzo Bevilacqua Lamassa at Verona, by huge Venetian vases and, in the entrance loggia, by an ancient Roman sarcophagus of yellow marble serving as a fountain basin and reflecting in its waters a seventeenth-century Italian Bacchus. In the gardens there is also a seventeenth-century travertine marble fountain from Bassano di Sutri near Rome, and a second-century marble altar and eleventh-century Romanesque columns. Such is the lavish setting, and the house interiors are in keeping with it.

A review of the rooms in Vizcaya is a study in period interiors. One of the earliest of these rooms is the banquet hall where the floor is of marble slabs, the walls of white plaster which handsomely sets off the fifteenth-century Italian fireplace mantel of Florentine sandstone. Below the wide frieze and decorated cornice hangs a seventeenth-century appliquéd velvet valance. Displayed on these walls are tapestries from Robert Browning's villa at Asolo, and close by stand tall Corinthian columns of *verde antico* marble, surmounted by vases which form bases for the candelabra. Most massive of the furniture pieces is a huge panel-backed fifteenth-century Italian sacristy cupboard which now serves as a sideboard. The heavily carved dining chairs were made in Florence in the early sixteenth century, but sometime in the eighteenth century

In the Adamesque library is this Directoire bookcase with an elaborate gold-leaf design.

Pride of the classic tea room are these 18th-century gates from the
Palazzo Pisani.

This most beautiful of guest rooms is named Espagnolette after its Spanish casement fastenings.

they were taken to England by Lord Craven for use in his residence, Combe Abbey, Warwickshire. The massive banquet table, which is both carved and inlaid, is of approximately the same date.

Also of this period is the Renaissance hall with its huge French Renaissance chimney piece, part of which is said to have come from the château of Catherine de Médicis, wife of King Henri II of France, and part from the ruined Château Regnéville. The room has a heavily bracketed cornice of wood which supports a decorated beamed ceiling, some of whose timbers were once part of a Venetian palace. The door and door frames are enriched with gold and black, their broken pediments adorned with white marble busts in place of finials. The furnishings are dominated by an expansive Italian tapestry woven in 1550 for Duke Ercole II of Ferrara. Here, too, is a splendidly carved table, its pedestals augmented by winged unicorns in the round, badge of the noted Farnese family.

In the Louis XV reception room there are several items of note. The mid-eighteenth-century plaster ceiling, exquisitely modeled and painted in a design which reveals a strong French influence, was removed from the Palazzo Rossi in Venice. This room at Vizcaya was proportioned to accommodate it as well as the paneling and woodwork from a palace in Palermo. The walls are covered with eighteenth-century silk, woven in a palm-tree design so that the vertical lines of the trunks emphasize the room height.

OPPOSITE: The ceiling of the Italian rococo music room is ornamented in plaster, while the wall panels bear cornice-high sculptured paintings

Because of this mantel with its relief decorations, the library is known as the Adam Room.

Over the delicately carved limestone mantel is a trumeau with a carved Venetian, rococo-style frame, gilt on black, with molded and painted decorations, and sconces on either side the mirror. The doors, French windows, and intervening spaces are treated in the same manner. Under one of the wall mirrors is an elaborate gilded Louis XV console on which stands a carved and gilt urn serving as a four-branched candelabrum. The armchairs in this room are carved and painted Louis XV cane-backs, and from the ceiling hangs a complicated gilded wood and crystal Venetian chandelier.

The music room is decorated in an Italian rococo style which seems even more ornate in some respects. The paneled ceiling of canvas on wood is decorated in relief with plaster ornaments which are carried down into the frieze. The elaborate bow-topped doors have scenic panels above them, and the walls bear ceiling-high sculptural paintings on canvas from a palace in Milan.

The chairs intermingle Italian adaptations of Louis XV painted, open-backed styles with Italian rococo armchairs in striped silk, both of which look perfectly at home with a spinet of 1645 by Horatius Albana.

The library is called the Adam Room for a logical reason; it contains an Adam fireplace and carved overmantel flanked by vertical panels, all decorated in relief in the Adam manner. The central horizontal panel of the mantel is notable for the high-relief carving of *The Dying Gaul* with a wall of the Colosseum as background. The overmantel is equally important because of the Roman-style mosaic panel let into it. The seated furniture in this room is of the early French Empire style, the chairs having once been the property of Napoleon's sister,

The loggias accommodate doors like this from a Parisian palace.

OPPOSITE: The rococo-style bedroom displays its gay chinoiserie.

243

The upstairs sitting room, an entrancing mixture of Directoire,
Adam, and Louis XVI.

Pauline, wife of Prince Camillo Borghese of Rome.

The so-called Tea Room is as lavish as any in this remarkable mansion. For one thing it opens onto the south arcade through eighteenth-century wrought-iron gates, formerly of the Palazzo Pisani, which determined the height of these main-floor rooms. Above the marble frame of these gates is the frieze with its blue-tinted metopes decorated in relief, plus a deep cornice and coffered ceiling decorated with designs in stucco. The walls are enlivened with painted panels, pilasters, borders, and architectural scenes, and a great African marble fireplace set against a marble mantel. Venetian pole-lanterns are spaced around the walls, their light supplemented, when necessary, by antique oil lamps hanging from the ceiling. The floor is patterned in varicolored marble, and two large marble consoles are set against a wall. The furniture consists of eighteenth-century Italian wooden versions of bronze Roman chairs.

Somewhat similar, at first glance, is Mr. Deering's sitting room, although this is a mélange of designs with its French Directoire painted and gilt stucco decoration on white, the Adam fireplace, the bronze-mounted tables, the Louis XVI armchairs, and a pair of Directoire wood columns. There are many other details of interest in Vizcaya, such as the 1814 hand-blocked Dufour *Galerie Mythologique* wallpapers in grisaille; the huge bronze-mounted cedar doors in their marble frames from an ancient palace owned by the Torlonia family in Rome. On the second floor are French murals in the manner of Claude-Joseph Vernet, painter to Louis XV, and an early eighteenth-century English chinoiserie lacquer mantel with its display of Chinese *objets d'art*. Even in the casino there is a painted ceiling with a border from the studio of Tiepolo and a panel restored by Paul Thevenaz—a satisfying indication that even such dependencies were required to meet the high standard of decoration set by the mansion itself.

The tentlike bathroom is a Grecian poem in marble.

This exquisite paneling and boiserie of the Louis XV reception room originated in a palace at Palermo. The chairs are Louis XV cane-backs.

San Simeon, California

LA CASA GRANDE

Mudejar on an Enchanted Hill

The bell tower of La Casa Grande—Spanish Renaissance campaniles faced with blue and yellow Moorish ceramic tiles.

Few private residences built in this century can exceed in exotic architecture, interior elegance, or overall cost, the so-called "castle" of the late William Randolph Hearst at San Simeon, California. This palatial mansion was first occupied in 1925, after three years of construction, but was still incomplete on the owner's death in 1951. Presumably it will now never be finished.

Built from the inside out, its design altered as often as the demands of newly acquired treasures for exterior modification or interior enlargement imposed themselves, the 146-room structure defies any neat architectural analysis. The main façade, facing west, consists of what seems to be a Roman basilica flanked by a pair of Spanish Renaissance campaniles whose blue and yellow Moorish ceramic facings vie with copper domes, a sculptured stone balustrade, the marble lacework of the tower windows, the iron tracery of balcony rails, and the elaborate carving of a massive doorway adorned with life-size statuary and fifteenth-century bronze gates from a Spanish convent, all crowned with a red-tiled roof over a carved teakwood gable from an Indian temple.

The bells are two bronze carillons from Belgium, the tower weather vanes cruciform Early Venetian, but much of the basic structure is plain concrete and steel. The nominal architect was Julia Morgan of San Francisco, working under extraordinary handicaps, involving the tearing down of what she had built whenever the client changed his mind, or adding another floor to an already completed building because the owner belatedly discovered he enjoyed the view. Nevertheless, she succeeded splendidly in unifying many disparate elements and imposing order on chaos.

From this central block of the main house, four- and five-story wings flank a rear courtyard, the walls pierced by flat-topped and Gothic windows, with arcaded two-story balconies, stair towers, Tuscan roofs and decked pavilions, many at unrelated levels. Fewer compromises, fortunately, are evident

The principal façade features a sculptured balustrade, an elaborately carved massive doorway, life-sized statuary, and 15th-century bronze gates.

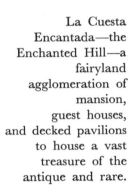

La Cuesta Encantada—the Enchanted Hill—a fairyland agglomeration of mansion, guest houses, and decked pavilions to house a vast treasure of the antique and rare.

The library passageway illustrates the extremes to which decoration is carried through the use of priceless relics of ancient buildings—walls, floor, ceiling and furniture.

in the elaborate setting of the mansion—the three large guest houses, the marble terraces and pools, the gardens and lawns, ornamented with Roman, Greek, and Egyptian statuary, sarcophagi, and a complete Greco-Roman temple from the Tiber, surrounded by marble terraces and dotted with tall, conical cypresses that contribute a somewhat funerary air. But it is the interiors that tell the story of La Casa Grande on its "enchanted hill," now a California state monument.

The furnishing of "The Big House" represents the fruits of many years of collecting treasures from almost every corner of the earth. One is first reminded of this on stepping through the main entrance doors onto the tesselated pavement of the vestibule—a complete floor unearthed at Pompeii where it had lain buried under volcanic ash since A.D. 79. To one side is a sculptured group, *Pygmalion and Galatea* by Jean Léon Gérôme (1824-1904), against a background of rare tapestries. And here is a wide portal in carved alabaster that leads to the incredible treasures within.

One of the most palatial of these interiors is that of the vast assembly room, a hundred feet long, forty-two feet wide, and twenty-two feet from floor to ceiling. Centered in one long wall is a huge sixteenth-century fireplace, the mantel supported by two pairs of atlantes. In the overmantel these are replaced by caryatids, with a central panel in high relief, all carved by some French Renaissance sculptor. In each end wall are set two great marble medallions, weighing a ton apiece, carved in

In another hallway the ceiling coffering incorporates exquisite bracketed paneling displaying masterpieces of 16th-century Italian art.

The north Doge's Room with its baroque carving makes concession to modern living in the lighting and the rug.

An enchanting aspect of the Neptune swimming pool is afforded by the ancient Greco-Roman temple with its exquisite carving of Neptune and the Nereids in the pediment.

Denmark by Albert Bertel Thorvaldsen (1774-1884). The deeply coffered ceiling is carved and painted, just as it came from a demolished Italian palazzo, and the antiqued-ivory walls are lined with centuries-old high-backed choir stalls which form both seats and elaborately carved wainscoting. Above them hang seventeenth-century Flemish tapestries which once belonged to the Spanish royal family, depicting the adventures of the Roman general Scipio Africanus.

Among the more important architectural features of this room are the giant gilded doorway frames, baroque in style, with pedestals, pillars, and massive carved entablatures having scroll pediments which center on descriptive panels in the manner of ancient triumphal arches.

Within this setting are huge, antique Italian tables and benches, marble statuary, candelabra, gold-framed diptychs, oversize antique Oriental rugs, and a hundred items of virtu usually found only in museums.

Just as impressive, though slightly smaller, is the refectory, the great dining room, medieval in splendor and concept, which can accommodate more than a hundred persons in "Dante" chairs with stamped leather backs at the carved pedestal tables. Its wooden ceiling, which once graced a sixteenth-century Italian monastery, contains a life-sized carving of a saint in each of its deep panels. At one end of the room is a Gothic arched musicians' gallery, at the other a great French Gothic mantel from a château which played an im-

A fine Gobelin tapestry of the Gothic period hangs in the billiard room.

Even the smaller, comfortably furnished morning room has its share of antique treasures.

OPPOSITE: Above the assembly room's ancient choir stalls hang 17th-century Flemish tapestries.

The indoor Roman pool with its golden mosaic balcony.

The della Robbia bedroom gets its name from a colorful plaque over the mantel.

portant part in the French Revolution. Here, too, are tall carved choir stalls, almost black with age, from a cathedral in Catalonia. Equally rare are the Gothic tapestries portraying the story of the Biblical Daniel in mellow tones of red, green, blue, and brown. From the walls alongside the clerestory windows hang the banners of knighthood bearing the crests of noble families of Siena.

In the Gothic study on the third floor quite a different atmosphere prevails, its vaulted ceiling upheld by a procession of Spanish Gothic arches, every inch covered with carved and painted figures and scenes. Iron-grilled bookcases line the walls over carved storage chests and below stone-arched and cusped clerestory windows set with rare stained glass.

The Doge's Room is different again with its massive ceiling of gold-encrusted panels, the central circular one incorporating gilt masks in its deeply molded frame. The walls are hung with antique fabrics, and even the doors have sunken, decorated panels, richly gilded. Over them are elaborately carved and painted crestings. Here, as in so many of these rooms, are art objects of every description—statues, paintings, furniture, pottery, icons—and a tremendous hooded Italian fireplace above whose mantel is a giant carved floral wreath enclosing a *basso relievo* sculpture of Madonna and Child.

Of the many sleeping apartments, the most unusual probably is one with a sitting room and offices at one level, the bed on a balcony above. The carving, decorating, and gilding

OPPOSITE: Medieval in splendor is the refectory whose ceiling once graced a 16th-century Italian monastery.

In the master bedroom family
photographs vie for attention
with parchment lampshades
bearing Gregorian chants.

Cardinal Richelieu's
bed—reserved for favored guests.

The main library with its figurines of gold and the largest rug in the castle.

Two sections of a triptych and other religious art distinguish the north bedroom.

A Spanish Renaissance four-poster
in the guest cottage
La Casa del Monte.

The fifty-seat movie theatre
with walls of red Italian brocade.

The gilded bedroom of the Celestial Suite in one of the twin towers.

of the twisted pillars and woodwork, the gold-stamped velvet hangings, the elaborately decorated stair risers, and the rich antique furnishings contrast amazingly with the almost Spartan simplicity and hygienic modernity of the tile, porcelain and marble of the bathroom when the door is open.

Much more normal in this incredible residence is the della Robbia bedroom whose ancient Spanish beds have thick carved posts topped by decorative urns, and intricately carved crestings with central masks, the heads arcaded and insulated from the plaster wall by a ceiling-high, multicolored tapestry whose wide border displays busts of early French monarchs. In vivid contrast to all this obvious antiquity is the room-sized Chinese rug dotted with flower sprays, birds, butterflies, and temples on a field of rich, dark, velvety blue. The chamber gets its name from a magnificent della Robbia group on the mantelpiece.

There is much more, of course: the great indoor pool, all tiles and Roman statuary and alabaster lamps; the Celestial Suite in the tower top where its owner enjoyed distant views of mountains to the east and out over the Pacific Ocean with its awe-inspiring golden sunsets to the west. But this should be sufficient to give some idea of the extravaganza in stone known as La Casa Grande, the largest and most expensive private residence in America—the centerpiece of what was reputedly conceived as a shrine to beauty atop a California hill, La Cuesta Encantada. It is a fabulous mansion fabulously furnished without regard to cost, built from the remnants of old-time castles, châteaux, palazzos, and temples, and fitted out with antiquities ranging in age from 2000 B.C. to A.D. 1800 alongside examples of twentieth-century craftsmanship on which physical comfort so much depends.

A private suite—bed on balcony, sitting room and bath below.

257

Kohler, Wisconsin
RIVERBEND

English Tudor on the Sheboygan

Riverbend from
the sunken garden.

Few early styles of architecture lend themselves so well to the modern home as English Tudor of the early sixteenth century. And, in the United States, few adaptations of that style can have been so successful as that represented by Riverbend. This great house not only is wholly suited to the rolling, tree-clad countryside of Wisconsin, but it also meets the basic requirements of its original owner: a maximum of interior comfort and accommodation combined with an exterior grace and an utter lack of pretentiousness—an effect so hard to achieve when utter formality prevails.

Here, then, is a rambling fifty-room mansion that follows no rigid plan, a splendid residence with many angles and varied aspects, composed of a multiplicity of interesting architectural units that form a fascinating whole. It presents a medley of surfaces and textures, of odd-shaped gables, dormers, roof hips, and turrets, and chimneys with pale yellow pots like so many dyed beaver hats. Here are romantic leaded casements in stone-mullioned windows with antique carved labels, flat-topped voids combined with Tudor four-centered arches, the lights and shades of unexpected recesses and projections, the varying reflectance and changing hues of smooth pale stucco and rustic brick, stone corbels and gargoyles, and the ragged lines of thick slates in lavender and blue—all held together by the long backbone of the main roof, gently undulating to simulate the ancient ridge of irregular hand-hewn timbers.

This was the choice for his own home that Walter Jodok Kohler made on his visits to Europe and Great Britain in company with his wife, Charlotte Schroeder Kohler, and on occasion his architect, Richard Philipp, for answers to problems in designing the world-famed Kohler Village. In 1923 his house was built and the laying out of the gardens begun by Olmsted Brothers, the noted landscape architects of Boston. Rustic stone walls were erected; rock gardens, sunken lawns, an allée of evergreens, formal beds, and a

A fifty-room Tudor mansion, a medley of weathered surfaces and textures that endow it with a timeless air.

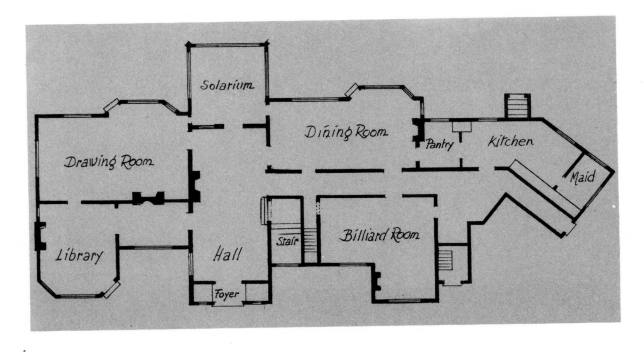

The main-floor plan gives no hint of the many large rooms the roof shelters.

The great entrance hall with its Vermont granite floor gives direct access to all family rooms. The runners are Kurdistan rugs.

Facing the hall fireplace is the main stair. Twelve bronze torchères light the entrances to the rooms.

bowling green were arranged to complement the natural surroundings of woods and willow-bordered stream.

The architectural features of the rooms are every bit as interesting as those of the exterior, although no attempt is made to reproduce an authentic Tudor atmosphere. The basis of their appeal lies rather in the judicious use of stone and plaster, the decorated arches, timbered ceilings, the stone and tiled floors, carved fireplaces, and decorative detail, including stained-glass medallions in the windows.

In the twenties the interiors, in the fashion of the time, emphasized ample draperies and wall hangings, handsome but heavy; the walls were dark and the upholstery somber-toned velvets and tapestries. The furniture was also in dark woods—principally Jacobean oak and William and Mary walnut so that against these backgrounds their innate beauty was not immediately apparent. But time races on, and tastes change. In 1928 Walter Kohler became Governor of Wisconsin; in 1940 he died, and seven years later his wife, too, passed on. In 1947 the property was acquired by one of their sons, John Michael Kohler, and his wife, Julilly H. Kohler, who took up residence there with their four young children.

Among the new owners' immediate problems was that of bringing more light and life into the interiors, both to make the most of the existing fine craftsmanship and to display the timeless furniture pieces and art treasures to their best advantage. Today the windows admit more sunlight; the first-floor walls and ceilings are mostly white, the bedrooms in pastel colors or papered; eighteenth-century mahogany mingles with other pieces; heavy draperies have been removed, and brighter fabrics and colors substituted wherever possible. The results are obvious the moment one steps beyond the leaded-glass doors of the foyer into the great hall.

The floor of this huge room (20 by 42 feet) is paved with granite slabs, heavily waxed and gleaming. The wooden ceiling is supported by cased oak beams on corbels; the stucco walls are a dead white between the arched doorways and windows. Its principal feature is a fireplace in honey-colored Madison sandstone, with tapering octagonal columns under the projecting mantelpiece, Italian style. Let into the chimney breast are stone slabs carved in high relief. On either side are high-backed William and Mary chairs with twisted legs and carved stretchers, the cushions and backs in antique crimson cut velvet. On the floor, two antique Kurdistan runners in pale rose and beige add their quota of color. Opposite is a mahogany tall clock with brass finials, dated 1800, and, nearby, a Jacobean court cupboard in oak, its doors bearing carved masks in bas-relief.

From the hall a wide, flat archway opens into the drawing room. Here also the ceiling is white, with a decorative stucco border. The light sandstone fireplace is flanked by pilasters, the overhanging mantel supported by scrolled brackets, the shelf by mutules, and under each rounded end is carved, in

A charmingly designed circular stair leads up from the second floor to the third.

The dining and breakfast rooms, like the tables, extend as one to seat thirty for dinner. The floor is of reddish Moravian tiles.

In the master bedroom the ceiling is coved and decorated, the walls are pink, and the rug is a white Moroccan.

Antique Kentucky furniture of cherry graces the eldest daughter's bedroom; the dresser is Empire, the draperies and bedspread are pale pink chintz in a shell pattern.

high relief, some small animal of the ferret tribe. Probably the most interesting feature, however, is the turned oak grille on either side of the mantel, each set into an opening in the wall. These grilles were originally intended to disguise the pipes of an organ. That organ never having been installed, the grilles were lined with white fabric to hide humidifier ducts substituted for them. Actually, the grilles are highly decorative, and somewhat Oriental, panels that naturally pique one's curiosity.

The draperies are of antique crimson brocade—a tone repeated in a pair of black lacquer and gilt banquettes in antique crimson velvet and, to some degree, by the red velvet of a carved walnut chair. Sufficiently close to afford a contrast are two couches in oyster-white mohair, plus an armchair and a small barrel chair in a raw-silk print in gray, white, and rose. In the bay window is an inlaid Sheraton game table and two 1780 armchairs with carved stretchers. The latter are upholstered in antique Flemish tapestry in muted greens and blues. Beside one of them stands a delicate wine table of 1780 with a galleried top. Also deserving of special mention are two pieces bought in England by Walter Kohler. One is a rare Queen Anne bureau-bookcase (c. 1719) in burl-walnut veneer, the other a Chippendale bachelor chest of 1780.

The dining room and breakfast room are divided merely by a curtain of heavy cream twill with wide borders of crewel-work. Both rooms have vaulted ceilings with molded plaster

Off the master bedroom is this small study, its dark green walls and fireplace decorated with tile and Japanese prints from the collection of Frank Lloyd Wright.

The drawing room acquires its rich atmosphere from its dark oak floor and red-on-beige Sarouk rugs.

Flanking the highly architectural pilastered fireplace are Oriental-looking wooden grilles concealing nonexistent organ pipes.

OPPOSITE: The library passage is enlivened with an antique Ferraghan runner and displays of antique glass, English porcelain and Italian pottery. The three-foot bronze of Abraham Lincoln is by Daniel Chester French.

265

The library is tiled in reddish brown and the chimney breast in green-tinted unglazed tiles enclosing a ceramic sculpture to illustrate the mantel quotation.

A carved medallion ornaments a balustrade beneath the stair arch which frames a 16th-century Flemish tapestry on the landing wall.

decorations in Tudor designs, and from their centers depend six-branched bronze chandeliers of a Jacobean pattern. The floors are of Moravian tiles of a reddish hue set in a pattern of circles.

These two rooms share a shelfless fireplace, the opening lined with unglazed Moravian tiles of a slightly darker hue than the sandstone. The chairs and the two refectory tables were made especially for this room. The tables, when put together and extended, accommodate thirty persons.

The principal entrance to the library is from the hall, along the library passage whose granite floor, an extension of that of the hall, is covered with an antique Feraghan runner. The walls are lined with shelves of books and display collections of antique glass, English porcelain, and Italian pottery. Among the latter are some fine Caltagirone (Sicilian) vases. Here also, set into a niche, is a three-foot bronze of Abraham Lincoln by Daniel Chester French (1850-1931). The library itself has a vaulted ceiling ornamented by a scattering of single flowers in stucco.

Around the carved stone fireplace a panel of unglazed tile rises to the ceiling in a frame of green-tinted smaller tiles. Set into this tile over the mantel is a *basso relievo* ceramic sculpture by Charlotte Schroeder Kohler, showing a stream winding through tall pines. This is intended to be symbolic of "our haunt from public life," which the quotation from *As You Like It* carved below the mantel continues with "Tongues in Trees, Books in the Running Brooks"—a room set aside for study and contemplation, revealing more of the spirit and the intellect behind the creation of this great house than any description of its structure and contents.

Sarasota, Florida
CA' D' ZAN

Venetian Splendor on Sarasota Bay

A colorful Venetian-style mansion, reminiscent of the Doge's Gothic Venetian palazzo on which it was modeled, nestles on the water's edge at Sarasota Bay. It reflects the same bright westering suns from pale pink stucco, rose-tinted carved stonework, and multicolored decorative panels, medallions and moldings of glazed terra-cotta, pierced stone balconies and bracketed cornices that adorn its principal façade. Above this gay and glittering front are red-tiled roofs—the barrel tiles hauled from distant Barcelona by the shipload—and one long, decorated parapet over traceried ogival windows, all dominated by a dwarfed square tower, once intended as a soaring campanile, which also is faced in terra-cotta tiles of buff and reddish brown set in diamond pattern.

To the tower face clings a semicircular stone-balustered stair, reaching up to the balcony whose pierced-stone parapet surrounds an elaborately carved and decorated stone kiosk. Across the base of the projecting central section are five wide, Gothic-arched French windows, with two more in the ends, all spaced between heavy marble columns, and set in massive figured bronze frames brought from Europe. Ornamented with various forms of marine life, these rest on continuous steps of purplish German formosa marble leading down to a 200-foot-long terrace laid in blocks of varicolored marbles patterned in chevron stripes and extending to the sea wall. From this point thirteen more steps in English veined marble lead down to the boat landing stage.

All the house windows are of handmade Venetian glass in tones of rose, amethyst, purple, green, and straw, their wavy surfaces adding to the air of antiquity that permeates the whole. This colorful mansion gains emphasis by being set against a fabulous semitropical background of palm trees, banyans, live oaks, hibiscus and oleanders, through which meander walks and driveways lined with scores of Italian statuary figures, grotesques, urns and terra-cotta oil jars, and

The square tower of Ca' d' Zan from the garden.

From Sarasota Bay, the Ringling residence looks like a Venetian palazzo in pink stucco with its carved stonework and panels of glazed terra-cotta.

Some of the seventy statues topping the art museum's balustrades.

beguiling cupids, as well as fragments of ornamental carvings from the ruins of ancient Italian buildings.

This spectacular pile of masonry was the home of John Ringling of circus fame and his wife Mable, from the time they conjured it into reality in 1925-26 until her death in 1929 and his in 1936. Today it is one of the showplaces of Florida's west coast, together with a remarkable art museum which John Ringling built essentially as a private gallery in 1929-30 to house the five hundred or more huge paintings he had acquired in four short years.

It was Mable Ringling, however, who was the moving spirit behind the mansion, commissioning a Sarasota architect, Thomas R. Martin, to do the preliminary planning. Her idea, apparently, was to build a miniature palace with a principal façade featuring details adapted from the Venetian palazzo, plus an imposing tower. The latter feature was considerably modified when the project was turned over by Ringling himself to the noted New York architect, Dwight James Baum.

Somewhat belying the impressive exterior, none of the twenty-six principal rooms of this luxurious residence is particularly large with the exception of the great hall and its foyer.

The principal entrance is on the east or garden side of the house, its massive doors of carved walnut set behind screens of decorative ironwork adorned with copper details. These open into the spacious foyer which in turn leads through wide

OPPOSITE: Ca' d' Zan's great hall is notable for its Renaissance coffered ceiling and massive marble balcony.

The museum itself consists of an Italian garden enclosed on three sides by arched loggias. At the open end is a giant bronze copy of Michelangelo's *David*.

pillared archways to the great hall—a vast two-and-a-half-story interior court serving as the main living room.

This room has a remarkable coffered ceiling in Renaissance style, the timbers of pecky cypress framing inner skylights of colored glass. From it hangs a glittering but somewhat ethereal crystal chandelier. At second-story level is a massive marble balcony occupying three sides of the great hall with its delicate stone balustrades and slender pillars and its painted ceiling. At one end massive marble columns support the Gothic arches spanning the entrance from the foyer. Above these the main balcony ceiling with its pillars and carved entablature are returned at right angles to the east wall, leaving between their ends a wide gap to accommodate a window topped by a handsome bombé-style balcony rail of wrought iron which gives on to a third-floor passageway.

On the walls of the main balcony, between each pair of chamber doors, hangs a notable seventeenth-century tapestry, either French or English. These tapestries serve a double purpose since they conceal the pipes of an organ which is another feature of the room. The floor of the great hall is laid with squares of black and white marble in checkered pattern, placed diagonally to increase the feeling of spaciousness. To one side is a beautifully carved and bracketed fireplace of *verde antico* in the Italian Renaissance style, whose effect is somewhat diminished by the splendor of the balcony's

OPPOSITE TOP: A huge canvas of oxen plowing by Rosa Bonheur dominates the breakfast room.

OPPOSITE BOTTOM: In the state dining room stands a huge gilded console table with a top of black marble.

271

Paintings of dances of the world by Willy Pogany cover
the ballroom's coffered ceiling. The large canvas
by Alfred Stevens portrays famous turn-of-the-century Parisians.

carved frieze and cornice above it. The tapered chimney breast is adorned with a fifteenth-century carved and polychromed head of a saint. Four more of these are centered in the spandrels of the window arches.

The furniture here is French, a mixture of Louis XIV, XV, and XVI. Some of the thronelike chairs have long, oval footstools to match, and these, together with the other gilt pieces, are upholstered in red cut velvet.

More lavishly furnished is the state dining room which has a tremendous late-nineteenth-century gilded console table with a top of black marble occupying most of one wall. Over this hangs a huge painting by Giovanni Granieri entitled *The Crowded Market Place*, its rococo gilt frame standing out brilliantly against the dark walnut of the wall panels. The massive carved dining table and its accompanying chairs are of walnut in the Italian Renaissance style, the chairs in red velvet embroidered in silver and gold, and heavily fringed and tasseled. The fireplace is a carved stone copy of the same period with blue marble inlays, the overmantel decorated with a green and white glazed terra-cotta *tondo* in the della Robbia manner. The ceiling, however, is the real *pièce de résistance*, its intricate coffering enameled in gold, red, and bright blue. On the black and white marble floor is a plain rug in deep red, matching in color the damask draperies.

Entered through elegantly wrought double iron gates is the breakfast room, which was also the informal dining room. Its principal feature is a large oil painting of oxen plowing by Rosa Bonheur (1822-1899). This contrasts wryly with a grim scene from the Franco-Prussian War by Édouard Detaille (1848-1925). The furniture consists of a long table with heavy carved oak pedestals, and a dozen equally elaborate tall-backed chairs which are quite sturdy and painted green to match their leather seats and backs. Under each chair is a green leather cushion to be used at breakfast to keep slippered feet off the chilly marble floor.

Opening off the opposite side of the great hall, beyond the gilded churrigueresque columns, is the teak-floored ballroom, a blaze of gold with its walls of rich yellow brocade, its coffered ceiling a coppery gilt honeycomb of octagonal recesses filled with paintings by Willy Pogany depicting dances of the world. Light is furnished by tall gilded torchères, and music by a German Steinway piano in a rosewood and ormolu case signed by Mellier. One large painting by Alfred Stevens (1828-1906) portrays a group of famous Parisians of both sexes, with the "Divine Sarah" Bernhardt in the foreground.

Off the state dining room is a small and intimate bar-lounge which has wall panels of leaded glass and a massive bar, a relic of a famous restaurant in St. Louis which Ringling patronized. From the coved ceiling hangs a German *Lusterweibchen*, a chandelier composed of a polychrome mermaid balanced on a pair of antlers. She holds a shield bearing an unidentified coat of arms and the date 1665.

John Ringling's marble bathroom with its fixtures of gold.

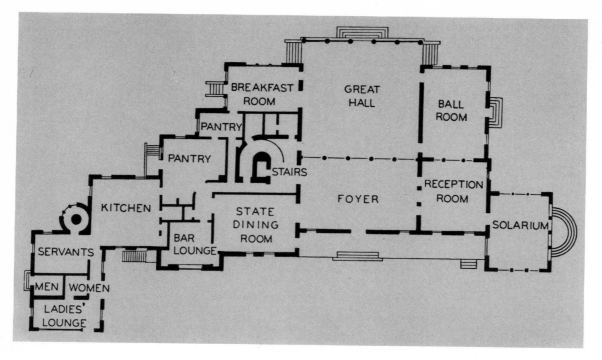

The first floor of the Ringling residence.

Mable Ringling's rose garden has its quota of limestone statuary.

John Ringling's bedroom is furnished in French Empire style,
with carved and gilded door and window trim,
and an oval ceiling painting of a mythological subject.

A section of the art museum's Rubens Collection. Those showing are part of *The Triumph of the Eucharist* series of which several copies were made.

On the second floor the most imposing apartment is the master bedroom with its Napoleon III style furniture, resplendent with gilded bronze putti, angels, dancing figures, and female busts; even the door and window frames are carved and gilded. The floor is of white-veined black marble, and on the ceiling is a huge oval painting of some cloud-enveloped mythological subject in a gold frame. Between the two beds hangs a small framed portrait of Jacopo di Lusignan, a fifteenth-century king of Cyprus.

A doorway in one corner of this room leads to John Ringling's bathroom whose pride is a tub carved from a block of yellow Siena marble. The walls are faced with this same marble and the lavatory top made of it. The floor, however, is of the same black and white marble slabs used elsewhere throughout the mansion. Less harmonious is the modern barber chair which, surprisingly enough, once stood in that elegant bedroom!

Mable Ringling's bedroom is furnished in sandalwood with tortoiseshell inlay and ormolu mounts in the Louis XV style as interpreted in the later nineteenth century when the curvilinear rococo forms were once again revived. Though highly ornamental the décor of the room is totally devoid of the representations of the female anatomy that embellish the master bedroom and is in other respects comparatively modest.

Separated from this by a small bath-dressing room enriched with delicate painted decoration, is the bedroom used by the second Mrs. Ringling, which is totally different in character. The furniture is of gray lacquered wood, elaborately typical of the turn-of-the-century period. A pair of gilt cupids on the wall over the bed along with two four-branched gold sconces are characteristic of the times.

At least equally as spectacular as the house is the art museum which Mr. Ringling planned for a year before the mansion was completed. This was designed to house what he hoped would be the finest collection of baroque paintings of the sixteenth to eighteenth centuries, a period he admired for its great vitality. Within the next few years he acquired more than five hundred paintings and provided the magnificent building in which they were to be displayed. These paintings included the country's most extensive collection of masterpieces by the great seventeenth-century Flemish painter, Peter Paul Rubens.

The museum itself was styled after a fifteenth-century Florentine villa by the architect, John H. Phillips. It consists of an Italian garden enclosed on three sides by arched loggias. At the open end is an elevated terrace in the center of which stands a giant bronze reproduction of Michelangelo's *David* which was cast in Italy. In the garden also are two large fountains, and many copies of classical sculptures. In the loggias are some hundreds of archaeological artifacts from the Cesnola collection of Cypriote antiquities, plus several East Indian sculptures. Topping the roof balustrade are seventy limestone statues. One of the building's great beauties is that it appears as though it had been built over a period of centuries, which doubtless was its designer's aim.

The residence and museum, together with their contents, were left to the State of Florida, which has added a delightful and historic little theatre from Asolo, Italy, whose interior dates back to 1798. This was purchased in Venice in 1949, and re-erected in a special building adjoining the museum in 1957. Today it is the only original eighteenth-century Italian theatre in America and a major attraction to almost everyone who visits Ca' d' Zan—the House of John.

The Ringling bar from Cicardi's Winter Palace Restaurant in St. Louis.

Mable Ringling's bedroom, furnished in sandalwood with tortoiseshell inlay and ormolu mounts in the French manner.

Theodore, Alabama
BELLINGRATH

A Modern Mansion Dedicated to Beauty

The patio at Bellingrath with its wall fountains and flower bed.

Inspired by a garden, the Bellingrath mansion is a house beautiful enough in itself to serve as a focal point for all the natural splendor around it. Mansion and garden—the jewel and its setting—are complementary to such a degree that it would be almost impossible to visualize one without the other.

The gardens which adorn this Ile-aux-Oies River estate near Mobile flood the landscape with beauty the year round with their flowering plants and shrubs and moss-draped forest giants. They surround the house of mellow brick and wrought-iron tracery with a flood of color whose tide laps the foundations, spilling over into the patio and splashing the sunny walls with a filigree of green, while towering trees shelter it from the burning summer suns and turn it into a faëry palace in the moonlight. And the story behind this happy marriage of landscape and mansion is as romantic as the setting.

Almost a half century ago Walter D. Bellingrath's wife began to beautify their fishing camp on the Ile-aux-Oies by planting azaleas in the woods surrounding the lodge. So spectacular were the results, thanks to a semitropical climate, that during the next fifteen years the camp became subsidiary in importance to the gardens around it. In 1925 the architect George B. Rogers, who had laid out the sixty-five acres set aside for planting on this eight-hundred-acre estate, designed and built a house close by the original camp lodge as a permanent home for the owners. This is the house that today not only seems a part of its natural surroundings but constitutes a storehouse of treasures on its own.

For many years Bessie Morse Bellingrath was a discriminating collector of things beautiful—silver, china, glassware, and furniture—with which the house is filled today. Here these exquisite and often rare relics of earlier days can be seen in their natural setting, in rooms that not only form a perfect background for their contents but are, in themselves, interesting examples of architectural design and detail.

278

OPPOSITE: The dining room sparkles with crystal, silver, mirrors, and chinaware.

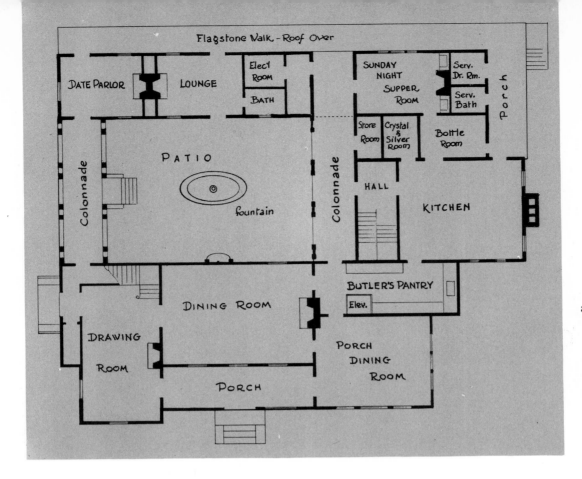

Flagstone Walk - Roof Over

DATE PARLOR | LOUNGE
Elec'l Room
BATH
SUNDAY NIGHT SUPPER ROOM
Serv. Dr. Rm.
Serv. Bath
Porch

PATIO
fountain
Colonnade
Colonnade
Store Room | Crystal & Silver Room
Bottle Room
HALL
KITCHEN

DINING ROOM
BUTLER'S PANTRY
Elev.
DRAWING ROOM
PORCH DINING ROOM
PORCH

The plan reveals a house designed for a subtropical climate.

The front of the house from which steps descend to the Isle-aux-Oies River.

Apart from all of this, the two-story mansion represents a satisfying architectural achievement in itself—a successful intermingling of French, English, and Mediterranean influences, with emphasis on the romantic. Antique lacy ironwork is combined with old handmade brick under weathered red-tiled roofs, incorporating porches, colonnades, and covered flagstone walks arranged around a flagged patio complete with pool and fountain.

The Bellingrath residence, then, is no ordinary house; everything about it is not only splendidly decorative but unusual in its layout and room arrangement. The main entrance, with its steps and terrace sweeping around a rocky pool, opens into a porch which, in turn, offers entry to any of three rooms—the drawing room, the main dining room, and the dining porch. A side entrance, also with steps and platform, gives access to a miniature foyer and, through that, to the drawing room. From the latter an open staircase ascends to the second floor.

At the inner end of the patio is a colonnade off which opens a stair hall with a door to the kitchen. Other external doors give access to a small room called the Date Parlor and into an equally small lounge (with attached bath) neither of which is connected to any other room. The large and small dining rooms have doors to the butler's pantry and to the inner colonnade which leads to what the owners called the "Sunday-night Supper Room."

From the dining porch an elevator ascends to the second floor. Upstairs, as might be expected, are the bedrooms—two for the Bellingraths and two for guests, each with its own bath. Between the guest rooms is the morning room which

OPPOSITE: The drawing room's Belter pieces combine charmingly with French antiques, including a Baccarat chandelier and Louis XVI overmantel mirror.

281

The grotto is always ablaze
with seasonal flowers.

Examples from the china collection are
displayed in every corner.

opens onto an outside porch. Another porch looks over the patio, and off the stair hall is one of those iron-railed outside balconies that add such a romantic touch to any façade. Each bedroom, with the exception of Mrs. Bellingrath's, has its own fireplace, as has the morning room. Beside the elevator is a large closet designed to accommodate Mrs. Bellingrath's collection of dolls.

On the main floor French windows abound; upstairs they give access to balcony and porch, so that no plan could be more open to the outdoors. On the second floor the open porch lined with ceramic plant-pots on pedestals in file like so many soldiers, the balconies, the large casement windows, and even the airy iron tracery, all add to the feeling of intimate contact with nature at its most voluptuous. Indoors, where the furnishings are so rich and the art objects so rare, one gets the impression that these rooms were expressly designed to show them both to the best advantage. That such should have been made possible while preserving all the amenities of a private and comfortable home suggests that those responsible were possessed of both talent and discrimination. Certainly Mrs. Bellingrath, with all her years of experience in collecting beauty, knew what she wanted and, obviously, George B. Rogers was able to supply it, just as her husband was happy to provide the means.

Probably the most striking of this assembly of individual apartments is the drawing room. Here the stage is set by a delicately proportioned staircase across the end wall where the ceiling sweeps around the stair well to meet the cornice in a graceful curve. Below, the descending handrail turns with an elegant jog to encircle the clustered balusters on the curtail step. The dark mahogany rail matches in color the ends of the steps and risers, silhouetting the carved and molded stringer, and setting off the delicately turned triple balusters, all of which are painted dead white.

Other architectural highlights are the paneled door reveals and dado, the round-topped French windows and entry archway, and the Adam mantel with black marble facings around the opening. Augmenting this background is a French Baccarat ten-branched crystal chandelier, lush antique brocaded satin draperies with green and pink muted designs, a huge Louis XVI overmantel mirror in its delicate gold-leaf frame, and a rich velvet carpet in light tan against which the dark woods of the furniture stand out in high relief. Most of this is French of a mid-nineteenth-century vintage, formerly owned by the Baroness Micaela Pontalba of New Orleans.

In one window is a handsome Meissen urn (c. 1800) on a gray-marble-topped ormolu tripod stand, while the mantel garniture consists of French blue and gold porcelain vases and a clock made by Jacob Petit. Other fine porcelain pieces are Capo-di-Monte and Louis XV urns serving as lamp bases and, on the same platform, a tall Sèvres porcelain urn (c. 1786) in rose Pompadour with ormolu mountings. On each side of the sofa are Chinese Chippendale galleried tables, and below the Bellingrath portraits are Empire card tables. Of especial interest here is the particularly beautiful eighteenth-century fireplace fender, made by Robert Adam and used in his Adelphi Terrace residence in London.

While the drawing room is elegant in a Late Victorian manner, the dining room has a splendor all its own, sparkling with crystal and silver, mirrors and chinaware, especially when the lacy napery is spread and the Chippendale chairs with their bright-patterned seats are drawn up for a banquet. The ceiling is cream over a heavy decorative cornice of the same tint with shading of a darker hue. In the delicately paneled walls a deep and wide recess enframes a pair of windows flanking an immense mahogany sideboard over which a twenty-eight-piece mirror is secured to the wall. In the flanks of the recess, at right angles to the windows, are shell-topped open cupboards displaying china made by William Ellis Tucker of Philadelphia in the early 1800's. This china has quite a romantic history, the set of over 100 pieces having been brought to Mobile by a young bride from Philadelphia. It was still intact when Mrs. Bellingrath bought it from descendants of the original owner.

The windows here, as well as the French windows opening onto the patio, are draped in crimson silk damask, with Meissen-and-ormolu tiebacks, and topped by lambrequins under gilded pelmets. These draperies tone in delightfully with the maroon ground of a 200-year-old gold-patterned

Over the dining room's Adam mantel is a fine oval Adam mirror in gilt filigree.

A corner of the upstairs morning room.

The twin beds of the upstairs guest room are Sheraton pieces, as is the high chest. The slipper sofas are Empire style.

The upstairs hall is furnished with parlor pieces from the home of Baroness Micaela Pontalba of New Orleans.

In the small dining room each wall displays its own group of china plates.

Aubusson rug. From a molded plaster medallion in the ceiling's center depends a particularly fine ten-branched French Baccarat crystal chandelier.

At the fireplace end of the room, over an Adam mantel, is an equally delicate Adam oval mirror in gilt filigree between solid bands molded in gesso and covered with gold leaf. The filigree forms intertwined garlands of laurel leaves, with a cresting of roses leading up to an urn finial. This is an exquisite piece of work and apparently far less fragile than it appears. Perfectly centered in it is a reflection of the crystal chandelier. On the mantel, below the mirror, stand a pair of late-eighteenth-century white porcelain Meissen covered urns, fourteen inches high, of the Marcoloni period (1774-1814), decorated with amorini and garlands.

The mahogany dining table, with its beautifully nulled edge, and eight matching chairs are English Chippendale from the home of Sir Thomas Lipton. Other Chippendale chairs ranged against the wall have curled ears, rope moldings, and shell crests, with lattice backs that betray the Chinese influence. Two wing chairs in red silk damask that flank the fireplace are also English Chippendale, but the two large serving tables at the drawing room door are an Irish version of that style. By the French doors, on a three-tier mahogany "telescope" table, is an interesting collection of biscuitware figurines. Other antiques of note in this room include an unusual table centerpiece of Meissen ware dating from about 1800. Its design is said to have been inspired by the balustrade of Versailles. It is of white porcelain lined in gold, and on each of the fourteen pedestals stands a gaily colored figurine. The whole is mounted on a French mirror with an elaborate ormolu base having eight decorative bronze feet. Here also is a pair of elaborate Waterford crystal six-branched candelabra with prisms and teardrops, dating back to 1783.

In the informal dining porch, which opens off this room, the mosaic-tiled floor is partially covered by a rich Chinese carpet in gold with a blue border. Needlepoint and petit-point pictures of early American statesmen hang on the bare brick walls, and seem quite at home with the Late American Empire furniture which includes a Baltimore pillar-and-claw card table, a Swiss music box, and an antique melodeon. The same lighthearted informality characterizes the "Sunday-night Supper Room" which is furnished with a surprisingly harmonious collection of antique pieces originating in Russia, China, France, England and the United States.

These two rooms, light, bright, and cheerful, set a pattern for the rest, beginning with the upstairs hall and the long corridor extending from it. These areas, with nothing but a decorative arch to divide them, are as carefully planned as any room. Here, too, are fine porcelains, mirrors and ancestral portraits against a background of cream-colored walls and paneled dado, with gold hangings at the windows, and more pieces of the Pontalba furniture—sofa and chairs in predom-

One of the prize pieces in the Purple Room is the nine-foot Empire secretary.

The tiny Bottle Room is full of Venetian, Waterford, and other fine glass, and Royal Doulton plates portraying Dickens' characters.

Needlework portraits of
Generals Washington, Lee,
and Jackson hang in the porch
dining room.

In the porch stands a fabulous hand-carved
table of mahogany and Chinese blackwood.

inantly blue brocaded satin. Louis XVI marquetry cabinets, in satinwood with ormolu mountings and glass doors, display miniature Dresden and Crown Derby porcelains. Elsewhere, on cabinets and tables, are 1771 Sèvres porcelain *compotiers* with ormolu mounts, brilliantly colored porcelain vases with a clock to match, French porcelain urns converted to lamps, and shelves full of nineteenth-century ornaments.

Off this corridor is Mr. Bellingrath's bedroom, carpeted in reddish-brown velvet, with white walls and ceiling, all thoroughly masculine in spite of the delicate Adam mantel. Colors here are browns and yellows, with touches of leather and cane. The Jacobean desk and high-backed chair have that no-nonsense air that the ivory and mother-of-pearl inlays do nothing to dispel. Well suited to the solidly built oak desk are a heavy pair of astral lamps on stepped marble bases, with fluted brass columns, long pendant prisms, and cut and frosted shades. The sturdiest pieces, however, are the elaborately carved Late Victorian four-poster bed in mahogany, innocent of tester, with pineapple finials and, at its foot, a Belter sofa table with a pair of side chairs to keep it company.

The tan-leather accent is provided by a high-backed armchair with a carved apron and roll feet, and a pair of footstools to match. Additional elegance is added by the pierced-brass fireplace fender and fan-shaped screen of 1800 vintage and the accompanying decorative brass coal scuttle. But the *pièces de résistance* are the colorful Victorian vases and clock that adorn the mantel, mostly in cobalt blue with gold tracery and varicolored flowers.

Of the three remaining bedrooms, Mrs. Bellingrath's is not only the largest but also the most attractive in a definitely feminine manner with its soft pink fabrics accented by the blue of the chinaware. The bed is a massive creation, hand-carved by Mallard of Louisiana in 1838, and at its foot is an equally imposing daybed.

In the largest guest room is an 1829 tall-post bed in carved mahogany, with a trundle bed underneath it, and steps alongside as an aid in retiring. Against the bottom rail is an early Phyfe mahogany sofa, accompanied by an ottoman, both covered in striped satin.

All of this is in sharp contrast with the other guest room which has twin Sheraton beds with testers and reeded posts, each backed up by an Empire slipper sofa. The carpet is velvet of a deep rose color, while the window and bed draperies are of cream faille dotted with pink flowers.

All three rooms have their quota of additional pieces—Belter chairs, Empire secretary, Sheraton highboy, Chippendale desk, Victorian chaise longue, French mirrors, and so on, together with antique china, lamps, and small accessories of wood, such as one might expect to find in the home of a collector of things old and charming but useful. To list them all would be purposeless, for this a true collector's home where special rooms are devoted to the storage of bottles, dolls, crystal and silverware, so that the living quarters remain uncluttered and nothing of the normal, lived-in look is lost. Among the china treasures available for use on very special occasions are such fabulous things as four different sets of 22-carat overlay service plates (one of them signed by Angelica Kauffmann) plus eight complete, rare dinner services—truly an antiquarian's paradise, housed in a mansion designed to bring together the beauties of nature, craftsmanship and the arts, not the least of which is architecture, the friend of them all.

The pride of Mr. Bellingrath's bedroom—a Jacobean oak desk inlaid with ivory and mother-of-pearl.

The hand-carved bed in Mrs. Bellingrath's bedroom was made by Mallard of Louisiana about 1838.

GLOSSARY

ACANTHUS MOLDING

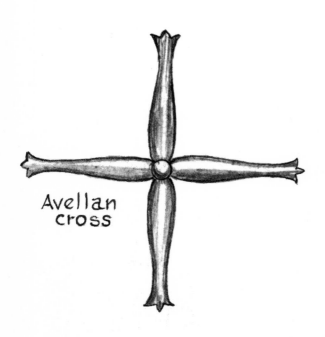

Avellan
cross

ABACUS: The flat topmost member of a capital (See: ORDER)

ACANTHUS: Ornament portraying leaves of acanthus plant

ALCOVE: Recess in a wall, especially one to contain a bed

ALTO RELIEVO: Carving in high relief

ANCHOR IRON: Bar or ring terminating bolt holding masonry tight to wood beam

ANTA: A pilaster at end of a side wall; its base and capital not conforming to those of the building's columns

ANTHEMION: Decorative design based on the honeysuckle plant

ARABESQUE: Arabian-style surface decoration of a complex geometrical pattern

ARCADE: A series of arches together with their supporting columns or pillars

ARCHITRAVE: The lowest member of an entablature; also the frame around a door or window (See: ORDER)

ASHLAR: Carefully squared and surfaced blocks of stone

ATLANTES: Carved male figures used as columns to support an entablature (See: CARYATID)

ATRIUM: A rectangular hall, usable as a room, from which other rooms open

AVELLAN CROSS: A cross in the form of four unhusked filbert nuts

BARGEBOARD: A board covering the end rafters of a gable (verge board)

BAROQUE: An extravagantly decorated architectural form common in Europe between the early sixteenth and eighteenth centuries

BARREL VAULT: A roof or ceiling in the form of continuous rounded arches

BERGÈRE: A closed-arm chair

BOISERIE: Interior paneling and woodwork, such as wainscoting, ceiling panels, etc.

BOLECTION MOLDING: A molding covering a joint between surfaces at two different levels

BOMBÉ: A bulbous or kettle base to furniture, etc.

BOUILLOTTE LAMP: A candelabrum with an adjustable shade, used in playing the card game "bouillotte."

BOULLE (BUHL): Furniture inlay developed by A. C. Boulle (1642-1732), using tortoiseshell and metals

BRONZE DORÉ: Gilt bronze

BUREAU PLAT: A flat-topped table-desk

CABOCHON: Originally an uncut jewel, or oval convex ornament, now also applied to decorative inserts of other shapes

CANAPÉ: A sofa

CAPITAL: The molded or carved head of a column (See: ORDER)

CARTEL: A wall clock

CARTOUCHE: A scroll-like ornamental tablet

CARYATID: A draped female figure in place of a column supporting an entablature (Male figures are atlantes)

CHINOISERIE: Chinese-style art decoration

CHURRIGUERESQUE: Early Spanish baroque characterized by profuse ornamental detail, named after José de Churriguera, its chief exponent

CINQUEFOIL: Ornament of five cusps used for windows, panels, etc.

CISELÉ VELVET: Velvet in which the pattern is formed by cutting some of the loops

CLERESTORY (CLEARSTORY): Windows in the upper part of a wall

COFFER: A sunken panel, usually in a ceiling, as a decorative feature

COLUMN: A round pillar of classical form comprising a base, shaft, and capital (See: ORDER)

CONSOLE: A scroll-shaped bracket projecting from a wall, or a table supported wholly or in part by a wall

CORBEL: A block projecting from a wall to support a beam, etc.

CORNICE: The upper projecting portion of an entablature; a molding in the angle between wall and ceiling, or between roof overhang and wall, that following the roof slope being termed a raking cornice (See: ORDER)

CROCKET: Foliated decorative roof ornament

CROSSETTE: Decorative offset at corner of door, window, and panel frames

CUPOLA: A lookout or similar small structure atop a roof

CUSP: A point terminating foils in Gothic tracery (See: CINQUEFOIL)

DADO: Wall space below a chair rail

DIAPER: A pattern consisting of the constant repetition of one or more units of design

DIRECTOIRE: The French period 1795-99; the transitional furniture period between the Greek style of late Louis XVI and the Egyptian style of Empire

DENTILS: Toothlike blocks in series used as ornaments below a cornice and on furniture

ECHINUS: The curved molding supporting the uppermost section in a Greek Doric capital

EGG AND DART: A molding showing eggs and arrowheads alternately

EN RESSAUT: Projecting

ENTABLATURE: The upper section of a classical order from the column capitals to the roofing; architrave, frieze and cornice (See: ORDER)

ENTASIS: The amount of swelling given to a column to make its sides appear parallel

EXTRADOS: The outer surface of an arch

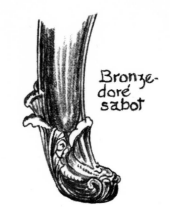

Bronze-doré sabot

cusp

Cinquefoil

Diaper

Fauteuil (Régence)

Finial

EYEBROW WINDOW: A low sash below the eaves admitting light at almost floor level in an Early American attic

FAMILLE-ROSE: A rosy pink variety of glassware or of porcelain decoration

FAUTEUIL: Armchair with open arms

FAUX BOIS: Any surface painted to imitate a wood grain

FAUX MARBRE: Any surface painted to imitate marble

FENESTRATION: Placement of windows

FIELDING: A raised flat surface as of a panel

FILLET: A band separating two moldings

FINIAL: A vertical decorative ornament terminating pinnacles, roof ridges, etc.

FLUTING: Shallow round-bottomed grooves on columns or furniture

FOILS: The lobes formed by cusps in Gothic tracery — trefoil (a group of 3), quatrefoil (4), and cinquefoil (5) (See: CINQUEFOIL)

FRESCO: Painted wall decoration on plaster

FRIEZE: A decorative band at the top of a wall; the decorated space between architrave and cornice of a classical entablature

GABLE: The triangular space formed by a ridge roof along the end wall of a building

GADROONING: Fluting or reeding of a rounded edge

GARGOYLE: A projecting spout draining a gutter behind a roof parapet

GENRE PAINTINGS: Depiction of realistic scenes from everyday life

GUÉRIDON: A round table, originally for supporting a candlestick, now applied to any circular table with or without shelves

GIALLO ANTICO: Antique yellow marble

GOTHIC: An architectural style of the Middle Ages (twelfth to sixteenth century) characterized by the pointed arch

GOUGEWORK: Early decoration by carving with a carpenter's gouge, often combined with chisel and punch work

GREEK FRET: Decorative bands or borders in geometrical figures formed by straight vertical and horizontal lines

GUILLOTINE WINDOW: Vertical sliding twin sash

GRISAILLE: Decorative painting in gray monochrome

GROTESQUE: Fanciful decoration having flowery tendrils combined with fabulous creatures, often half-human

HALF-TIMBER: A method of house construction, using heavy vertical and horizontal timbers, the exterior ones left exposed with their spaces filled

HERMA: A pedestal surmounted by a human bust (originally that of Hermes) used to support a cornice or entablature

HAMMERBEAM: A Gothic form of roof in which rafters rest on a horizontal projecting beam which combines with a vertical brace to form a bracket for an upper collar brace

IMPOST: A block atop a post on which one end of an arch rests

INTRADOS: The inner curved face of an arch

JERKIN HEAD: A clipped or truncated gable, hipped for only part of its height

K'ANG HSI PERIOD: Part of China's Ch'ing dynasty, A.D. 1662-1723

LABEL: A projecting molding over an opening serving as a dripstone, which is the commoner name

LANTERN: A small windowed turret on a roof to admit light

LAPIS LAZULI: A stone of a rich azure blue, also its color

LIERNE: A short intermediate rib in Gothic vaulting, crossing the panels from one main rib to another

LOGGIA: A gallery behind an open arcade

LUNETTE: A curved opening in a vaulted roof to admit light

MANSARD ROOF: Has two slopes, the lower one steeper, and probably curved inward, continued around four sides of a building

MASK: A carved face as decoration on walls and furniture

MEDALLION: Circular decorative tablet with scene or figure in relief

METOPE: Space between two triglyphs in a Doric frieze, latterly decorated by carving (See: ORDER)

MODILLION: Bracket supporting upper members of a cornice of Corinthian and Composite orders; also called a console

MUDEJAR: A Spanish style incorporating Gothic and Moorish figures, plus intricate ornamental detail

MULLION: Heavy stone or wood separator between individual grouped windows

MUNTIN: A glazing bar, holding the separate sheets of glass in a window. Also the middle vertical member of a paneled door

MUTULE: A block on the inner side of a Doric cornice above a triglyph (See: ORDER)

NAILHEAD: Small pyramids carved in relief, usually forming decorative bands

NEREID: A sea nymph, usually represented as riding a sea horse

NICHE: A wall recess, often arched, as a setting for statuary, etc.

OGIVAL: Having the form of an ogive, or pointed arch

ORDER (CLASSICAL): A column of classical proportions, with base (if any) and capital surmounted by an entablature. The Greek orders were: Doric, Ionic, Corinthian. These were modified by the Romans, who added Tuscan and Composite (See p. 293)

ORIEL: A bay window projecting from an upper story, usually supported by corbels or brackets

ORMOLU: Gilded metal, usually brass or bronze

PALLADIAN WINDOW: A group of three sashes, the center one being taller with a rounded top; formerly called a Venetian window

PARQUET: Flooring composed of wood blocks or strips of a fixed length

PATERA: A flat, circular ornament, often representing acanthus leaves

PAVILION: A projecting section of a façade with a separate roof, or a small, free-standing ornamental building

PEDIMENT: A triangular wall area enclosed by one horizontal and two sloping cornices above the entablature over a portico. The slanting members may be bowed or ogee (swan-necked) in form, or open at the peak forming a "broken" pediment. Small pediments are often used over doors and windows (See: ORDER)

PENT ROOF: A small roof attached to a wall at second-story level or across gables to the eaves

PIANO NOBILE: The principal story, usually referring to the raised main floor of a Southern mansion

PILASTER: A rectangular column projecting slightly from a wall and designed to simulate a square column with capital, shaft, and base

Lunette

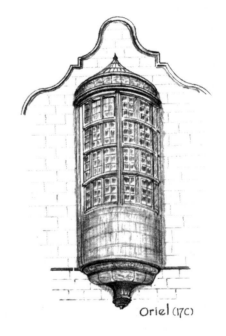

Oriel (17C)

PATERA

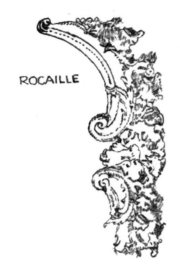

ROCAILLE

SWASH
TURNING

PILASTERED CHIMNEY: A chimney to which additional exterior flues have been added giving the effect of pilasters

PLATERESQUE: A richly ornamental Spanish silversmith's style corresponding to Late Gothic and Early Renaissance elsewhere

POLYHYMNIA: The Muse of the sacred lyric

PUTTI: Figures of nude cupid-like children (not winged). Singular: putto

QUOIN: Heavy blocks of dressed stone, or wood cut to simulate stone, used at building corners to reinforce masonry walls, or in wood as a decorative feature

REEDING: A small convex molding, the reverse of fluting

RELIEVING ARCH: An arch built into a wall above a lintel or arched opening to divert some of the pressure to the flanking wall

RÉGENCE: The French period, 1715-1723, between the reigns of Louis XIV and Louis XV

RENAISSANCE: The style originating in fifteenth-century Italy marking the reintroduction of the forms and principles of classical architecture of Roman antiquity

REPOUSSÉ: A pattern formed in relief by pressure or impact on the reverse side

REVEAL: The inner surfaces of an opening in a wall

ROCAILLE: Asymmetrical shell and rocklike ornamentation of the rococo style

ROCOCO: A later phase of the baroque style popular in mid-eighteenth century

ROMANESQUE: The architectural style prevalent in the eleventh and twelfth centuries, preceding the Gothic

RUSTICATION: The tooling of masonry walls in a rough or irregular pattern; also the chamfering and recessing of the joints

SANG-DE-BOEUF: Oxblood, a color found in ancient Chinese porcelains

SCAGLIOLA: Imitation marble composed of cement, gypsum, glue, marble dust providing the pattern

SCROLLED STEPS: Stair steps ornamented with carved or cut-out end brackets

SPANDREL: The wall space between two arches, or one arch and a wall

STRINGCOURSE: A horizontal band projecting from a house wall at upper floor level, marking division between the stories. Sometimes called a belt course

SWASH TURNING: A corkscrew turning often used for balusters

TERRAZZO: Flooring of chips of marble set in cement and polished

TONDO: A circular painting or sculptured medallion

TRIGLYPH: Upright blocks spaced along a Doric frieze, decorated with two vertical grooves on the face and one at each angle (See: ORDER)

TRIPLE WINDOW: A window of three equal sections; not to be confused with a Palladian window

TROMPE-L'OEIL: An eye-deceiver; painted decoration giving a three-dimensional effect

TROPHY: Sculptured or modeled group of arms and armor used as decorative feature of Renaissance times

TRUMEAU: Looking glass incorporating a painting or carving

TURKEY WORK: A textile imported from the Orient

CLASSICAL ORDERS

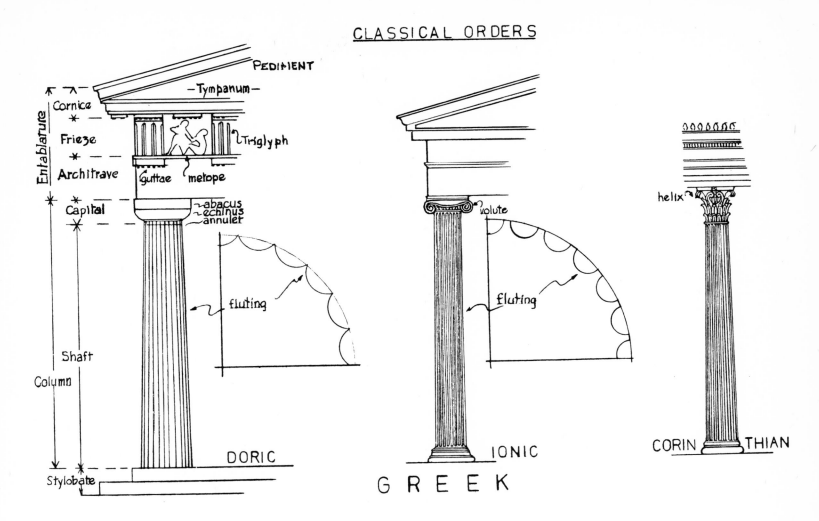

G R E E K

TYMPANUM: The space enclosed by a pediment (See: ORDER)

VENEER: A thin sheet of material (wood, brass, tortoiseshell, etc.) applied to another surface

VERDE ANTICO: Antique green marble

VERMEIL: Silver-gilt

VOUSSOIR: A wedge-shaped stone used in arches

WATER LEAF: A peculiar form of Greek leaf ornament, probably representing an ivy leaf

WATER TABLE: A horizontal stone or brick setback on an exterior wall at or close to foundation level

ACKNOWLEDGMENTS

Our sincerest appreciation and grateful
thanks are expressed to numerous individuals,
curators, foundation officials, and
historical societies for their unstinting patience,
courtesy, and assistance to us when
gathering material for this book.
Also to: Mr. and Mrs. Thomas H. Berry,
Helen Duprey Bullock, Mr. George H. V. Cecil,
Mr. James D. Ireland, Mr. and Mrs. Washington
Irving,
Mr. and Mrs. John M. Kohler,
Captain and Mrs. Hugh P. Le Clair,
Mr. Louis C. Madeira, Mr. and Mrs. Alfred
J. Moran,
Mr. John C. Pearce, Mr. Richard W. E. Perrin,
F.A.I.A., Mr. H. Rodney Sharp,
Mr. and Mrs. Allan Shivers, Mr. Holbert T.
Smales,
Mr. Jack Stark,
Mr. John A. H. Sweeney, Mr. Harold R. Talbot,
and Mr. William J. Wagner, A.I.A.

Farmington: Courtesy The Historic Homes Foundations Inc., photos by James N. Keen (*Louisville Courier-Journal*), 112-21; H. Harold Davis, 112.

The Owens-Thomas House: Frederick C. Baldwin, 122 top, 125-28; Mrs. Malcom Bell, Jr., 122 bottom; Walter H. Miller, 129; *House & Garden*, © 1963 by The Condé Nast Publications Inc., 123, 124.

Lyndhurst: Courtesy The National Trust for Historic Preservation; photos by Louis Reens, 130, 132 top, 133, 134, 135, 136 top, 137, 138, 139; Sleepy Hollow Studio, 136 bottom; Metropolitan Museum of Art, Dick Fund, 131, 132 bottom.

The Campbell-Whittlesey House: Courtesy The Society for the Preservation of Landmarks in Western New York; photos by *Good Housekeeping*, © 1960, 140; Len Rosenberg Studio, 141, 142 top, 144 bottom, 148 top, 149; Lodder Photo Service, 142 bottom, 144 top; Richard Quataert, 143 bottom, 145; Earl Kage, 146, 147 bottom.

Shadows-on-the-Teche: Courtesy The National Trust for Historic Preservation; photos by Gleason Photography, 150; James K. Mellow, 151, Edmund Barrett, 152, 154; *House & Garden*, © 1962 by The Condé Nast Publications Inc., 152 bottom, 153, 155, 156 bottom, 157.

Woodlawn: Bill Malone, 158-65.

The Beehive House: Courtesy Church Information Service of The Church of Jesus Christ of Latter-Day Saints; photos by Maynard L. Parker, 168, 169.

Biltmore: Courtesy The Biltmore Co.; photos by Putnam Photography, 179, 181, 183; Joseph Hall, 182.

The Short-Moran House: Clarence J. Loughlin, 185 top; Richard Koch, 185 bottom, 188; Industrial Photography, Inc., 186, 187, 189, 190.

The Breakers: Courtesy The Preservation Society of Newport County; photos by Joseph Hopf, 191, 192.

The Elms: Courtesy The Preservation Society of Newport County; photos by Joseph Hopf, 202, 205 top, 206, 207, 208, 211.

Whitehall: Courtesy The Henry Morrison Flagler Museum; photos Florida State News Bureau, 212, 215-22; The Florida Development Commission, 213, 214, 223.

Gwinn: Walter P. Bruning, 225, 226 center, 229 top, 230 bottom, 231 top; Rebman Photo Service, 226 bottom, Martin Linsey, 224, 227, 228, 231 bottom; Cleveland Museum of Art, 229 bottom, 230 top.

Vizcaya: Courtesy Park and Recreation Department, Metropolitan Dade County, Florida; photos by Rada, 233, 242; Dave Millspaugh, 241; City of Miami News Bureau, 240; Richard B. Hoit, 245 top.

La Casa Grande: Lee Blaisdell, 246, 247, 249-53, 256, 257 bottom; Tom Myers, 248, 254, 255, 257 top.

Riverbend: Richard W. E. Perrin, F.A.I.A., 258, 259, 261 bottom; Big Cedar Studio, 260, 261 top, 262-66.

Ca' d' Zan: The Florida Development Commission, 267, 268 bottom, 271; Joseph J. Steinmetz, 268 top, 269, 270, 272-77.

Bellingrath: Courtesy The Bellingrath-Morse Foundation; photos by Fred W. Holder, 279, 280.